The
KINGS & QUEENS *of*
SCOTLAND

TIMOTHY VENNING

AMBERLEY

First published 2013
This edition first published 2015

Amberley Publishing
The Hill, Stroud
Gloucestershire, GL5 4EP

www.amberley-books.com

ISBN 978 1 4456 4819 4 (paperback)
ISBN 978 1 4456 1324 6 (ebook)

British Library Cataloguing in Publication Data.
A catalogue record for this book is available from the British Library.

Typesetting and Origination by Amberley Publishing.
Printed in Great Britain.

Contents

Introduction

The creation of the kingdom of Scotland, as of its English neighbour, was a complex and lengthy process and was by no means as historically inevitable as it appears at first glance. It first emerged as the peoples of the northern part of the British mainland faced the threat of conquest by far-voyaging Scandinavian incomers in the ninth century, as did those of the southern part, and the first 'King of Scots' is generally held to be Cinaed mac Alpin (Kenneth mac Alpin) who was two generations older than the royal English hero Alfred 'the Great' of Wessex. The kingdoms of the 'Picts' and 'Scots' traditionally united around 840; England was unified by Alfred's son Edward in the 910s, thus giving Scotland the priority in a similar but less well-known process. In fact the traditional medieval account of irreversible Picto-Scottish unification is too simplistic, as there had been one king ruling both kingdoms before and the title of 'King of the Picts' was still in use by Cinaed's sons. There may just have been a 'union of crowns' rather than a merger of states at first. Indeed, the creation of 'Scotland' incorporated not only the northern British realm of the Picts in central-eastern Scotland but also that of the descendants of Irish immigrants in 'Dal Riada', centred on Argyll, with modern DNA confirming that the Picts were ethnically connected to the southern British 'Celts' and that there was much Irish immigration to Dal Riada. The kingdom of 'Alt Clud' or Strathclyde in south-western

Scotland – part of the 'Celtic' states of the 'Old North' of Britain – also merged with that of Cinaed's descendants in the tenth and eleventh centuries, by a somewhat slower political process. Meanwhile the lands of Lothian, originally British but settled and ruled by Germanic Angles as part of Northumbria in the seventh century, were regained by the Scots kingdom during the later tenth and eleventh centuries, with the 'Border' remaining flexible as late as the 1150s and Scots kings ruling in Cumbria and Northumberland well after the Norman Conquest. The new kingdom thus had four separate political constituents, plus eventual annexation of Scandinavian-settled lands in the Inner and Outer Hebrides, and did not achieve its full extent as modern Scotland until the Orkneys and Shetlands were acquired from Denmark-Norway in 1469. The complex politico-cultural picture was symbolised by the variety of languages that were originally spoken there – Northern Brittonic ('Pictish'), Gaelic, Old English in Lothian and Norse in the Hebrides.

The creation of Scotland was thus a gradual merger of widely disparate cultures and states, the original three (Picts, Dal Riada and Strathclyde) brought together under the impact of Scandinavian settlement and peripheries added later. This turbulent creation was reflected in the picture of endemic political violence and a high royal mortality rate reflected in the chronicles – though the latter give a somewhat distorted picture as only crises were recorded and much political life at a lower level was probably more settled. Indeed, little is recorded of the early period and much is owed to later poetic myths and heroic sagas, and the subsequent period between around 1100 and the cataclysmic failure of the royal line in 1286/90 was mostly an era of peace, prosperity, competent rulers, and cultural progress. The age of bitter invasions of each other's territory by the English and Scottish monarchs, Border feuding, and 'tit-for-tat' low-level cattle-rustling did not commence until the aftermath of the failed Edwardian attempt to conquer Scotland; the great abbeys of the region bear witness to a much more settled and prosperous society before then. When compared with their English counterparts the pre-1286 Scots kings were usually remarkably capable and consensual rulers facing far fewer revolts from their elite, and the struggle for independence against a vastly superior war-machine in 1296–1327 witnessed the triumph of one of medieval Europe's outstanding rulers and generals – Robert Bruce. After his death and a little-known second war of independence (1332–41), the traditional historical view is that Scotland fell into near anarchy with a series of weak rulers unable to control their 'over-mighty' nobles, great dynasties whose ambitions and feuds shook the throne, such as the Douglases. Certainly, some of the early Stuarts were unimpressive as statesmen, though arguably they faced a task beyond their resources, disastrous luck and crucial destabilising threats from their own kin. But despite poor resources and the sporadic English threat, four of the first five King Jameses were talented and commanding figures, and the abilities of the Stuart dynasty as a whole have been marginalised. Even the equally lionised and reviled Mary Stuart, a staple of the romantic novel and tourist industries, was as much let down by her allies as she was by her seemingly rash judgements and incompetence at politics. With the exception of Mary the medieval and Renaissance Scots monarchs have attracted little media attention compared to their English counterparts – though most have been covered by the Scottish historical novels of Nigel Tranter, my own inspiration in writing this book. But their story is no less interesting and a better verdict on their achievements is overdue.

1

The Constituent Kingdoms

Kings of the Picts

The name and identification of the Picts is somewhat
problematic, the name meaning 'Painted Men' and probably
being a nickname given by themselves or their enemies.
Logically it refers to their use of woad or tattoos to decorate
themselves. The name is first recorded around AD 300, in
the Roman historian Eumenius's account of the reconquest
of the province of Britain from a rebel regime by 'Caesar'
(deputy emperor) Constantius 'Chlorus' ('the Pale'), father
of Constantine 'the Great'. Having defeated and killed rebel
emperor Allectus and regained London and the South in
296, Constantius proceeded to restore the Northern frontier
– Hadrian's Wall – by a war with the 'Picti' who had been
attacking across it, suggesting that they were the people
directly to its north in the Southern Uplands of Scotland as well
as further north. The main question faced by earlier modern
historians was whether the Picts were to be considered as a
branch of the 'mainstream' peoples who inhabited the island of
Britain before the Romans, known subsequently as the 'Celts'
and by themselves as the 'Britanni', or a separate race. Was
there any difference in culture or ethnicity between the peoples
of what is now England and those of Scotland – and if so where
was the 'dividing line'? There was no clue in British literary
tradition, as the pre-Roman peoples had not left any literature

and the earliest post-Roman 'Celtic' – Welsh – reference to the peoples of Scotland was in the largely fabulous work of the 1130s 'historian' Geoffrey of Monmouth, populariser of the King Arthur legend. His mythical account of Britain had the kings of Scotland descended from Albanactus, a legendary figure of around 1000–900 BC who was supposed to be a son of the founding British king Brutus – an exiled prince of the royal Trojan dynasty, living in Italy and connected to the ancestors of Romulus, founder of Rome. Quite apart from the name of this king clearly being invented to create a connection to the ancient name of Scotland, 'Alba' (as Wales, or 'Cambria', was first ruled over by his brother 'Camber'), the story was evidently a literary fabrication devised to give a prestigious British royal link to the Ancient Roman story of its Trojan founders, Vergil's *Aeneid*. The Scottish sources were later and were no more trustworthy than Geoffrey of Monmouth, but at least they spoke of a distinct 'Pictish' kingdom of supposedly ancient lineage with a long line of monarchs. These men might be a dim literary memory – via centuries of oral record? – of the kings who had led the Caledonians and Picts against Rome. But had there ever been one ancient kingdom? And did stories of one Scottish kingdom reflect an anachronistic desire to create a 'back story' for the early medieval kingdom into the centuries of Roman rule and back beyond the time of Christ?

In the hillier areas of south-central England and the North, 'Celtic' culture was distinguished in archaeological remains by a greater difference between social 'classes' than in Neolithic Britain, with a Neolithic civilisation of farmers living in small 'farms' or villages eclipsed by concentrations of people in larger settlements and in defensible hill forts (which became larger and more elaborate from *c.* 500 BC to *c.* 100 BC). This culture extended into what became Southern Scotland, with tribes such as the Votadini in Lothian, the Damnonii in the Clyde valley and the Novantae and Selgovae in Galloway who were culturally, and thus presumably ethnically, kin to their

Southern neighbours. Great hill forts in Southern Scotland, such as Traprain Law in Lothian, were thus part of 'Iron Age' British culture, but although 'tribal' names, with normal Brittonic wording, were recorded north of the Firth of Forth by the second-century AD Roman geographer Ptolemy (e.g. the Epidaii in Argyll and the Taexaci, probably in Buchan) there were fewer hill forts in this region. In Roman times the use of hill forts indeed declined even in the South, being replaced by smaller, but still fortified, farmsteads. North of the Great Glen they were virtually non-existent, and society appeared to be atomised into smaller local communities. Was this a sign of a different culture from the 'Iron Age British' culture of the South – or even of an entirely different ethnic civilisation? Was this a different kingdom – or leaderless? Or was it just due to poorer resources in a less fertile area that could not support large farming communities?

The unusual nature of the transmission of the 'Pictish' kingship, which did not pass once from father to son from its known origin in around the early fifth century until the 780s in the preserved 'king-lists', suggested a divergence from normal patrilineal 'Celtic' practice. The early Irish legends (confirmed by the Tyneside historian Bede in around 730, so known to the Angles of Northumbria by that date) alleged that there was matrilineal descent, though Bede only says that it was allowed – presumably when there were no sons or brothers – not that it was the norm. This could therefore be a survival from an earlier culture that practised such rules of inheritance, a logical possibility for such a remote kingdom. This was duly linked by anthropologists to the supposed existence of a matriarchal cult of the 'Great Goddess' in pre-'Iron Age' Britain, as in pre-Classical Greece, with the supreme Goddess being usurped by male gods some time before Roman rule.

Furthermore, the archaeological evidence of the 'broch' culture in Northern Scotland and the Orkneys in the years from *c.* 200 BC to AD 200 indicated divergent building practices from the Celtic 'norm' to the South. This could be linked to the Picts either representing this un-Celtic culture or at least being influenced by it. On the basis of linguistic evidence, however, Kenneth Jackson concluded in 1955 that the Picts were a mainly Celtic people, speaking the 'P-Celtic' branch of the Celtic tongues of mainland Britain (e.g. Wales) and Brittany rather than the 'Q-Celtic' of the Goedelic/Irish branch, but with strong influence from a pre-Celtic language. By inference, the latter influence had come from the pre-Celtic 'broch' culture. However, later analysis has argued that there was a much stronger Celtic element to names in the 'Pictish zone' in Ptolemy's map of Britain of *c.* AD 120 than Jackson allowed, and that the survival of the use of earlier names did not necessarily mean that the peoples using such words were non-Celtic. It would appear that most of the tribes inhabiting the area by *c.* 120 were 'Celts' even if they used some pre-Celtic place names. Also, there is no hint in Tacitus's account of the Caledonians in his biography of Agricola, the governor of Roman Britain (fl. AD 78–84), that they were not 'ordinary' Celtic tribes.

Kings and Kingship in the Early Centuries

By the time of Eumenius in the 290s, the Picts were the raiding enemies of the Roman province of Britain on its northern frontier. Ammianus Marcellinus in the 370s refers to the Picts as consisting of two tribal divisions – the 'Dicalydones', evidently the Caledonians, and the 'Verturiones', apparently the men of the area between Tay and Forth that came to be known as 'Fortriu'. These would seem to be the Northern and Southern kingdoms of the 'Picts' respectively. The later Irish king-lists of the Picts are a dubious source for early history, but seem to rely on legend and to be hazy about dates and details of rulers until the first half of the fifth century – suggesting that not much was remembered about the earlier period of the Pictish 'kingdom' if it existed as an identifiable unit at this period.

Apparently there were two distinct provinces in the Pictish kingdom, Moray and the Fortrenn area being the centres of these territories. Some of the Pictish kings are referred to as being rulers of 'Fortriu' rather than of the Picts as such, and D. P. Kirby initiated the resultant conclusion that there were therefore two separate sub-kingdoms divided by the 'Mounth' whose rulers alternated the 'High Kingship' between them. That would account for the absence of father-son descent of the kingship – the elites of the two kingdoms insisted on a rota and no ruler was powerful enough to break this tradition. Marjorie Anderson preferred to maintain that there was one royal dynasty with matrilineal descent, whether or not this represented an ancient survival. It is also notable that a number of non-Pictish rulers came to the throne of the Pictish kingdom, at a time when the kingdom was militarily strong and so did not have a foreign ruler imposed by conquest. The choice of princes from foreign dynasties as Pictish 'High Kings' seemed to indicate that nobody from the 'native' line was eligible or acceptable to a majority of the lords – or that the newcomers were imposed by their own non-Pictish families on a weak Pictish polity?

It has been suggested that the clue to this problem should lie in there being a custom that any descendant of a former ruler was eligible as a contender for the kingship. This would include the sons of Pictish princesses who had married foreign rulers – hence the two Brideis (one possibly Welsh, one from Strathclyde), Gartnait and Talorcan mc Eanfrith (Northumbria). Possibly the multiplicity of claimants, none of them willing to give up their claim in favour of another part of the dynasty having a monopoly, and the potential of 'native-born' contenders fighting over the kingship at each vacancy was such that the kingship *had* to alternate among all potential lines claiming it. Alternating the kingship among rival families, and bringing in outsiders, was a way of avoiding civil war as any one line of princes trying to monopolise the kingship would face endless plots from their frustrated rivals. The alternation of succession among eligible lines of descent may well only refer to the 'High Kingship' of the Picts, the over-kingship that claimed the allegiance of various sub-kingdoms. There is no reason to assume that the kingship of the sub-kingdoms did not descend from father to son in the normal manner.

Cruithne and his sons, dated to a century or two before the era of Christ, are cited as the first rulers of the Pictish kingdom by one tradition, having come over from Ireland. The name of 'Cruithne' is in fact that given by ancient scholars to the Pictish people as a whole, and probably originates from the 'Q-Celtic' word for 'Britons'. He was seen as being Irish-speaking and/or of Irish descent, as stated in the early legends which had him being the son of an exiled Irish king, Gub. The traditional length of the supposed reigns of his descendants would put his arrival in Scotland at around 100 BC, with the 'caveat' that it was a common mistake of early recorders of dynastic lists to line up all the names in their possession as a neat father-son descent whereas it was probably more complicated. Some kings may have ruled concurrently. The seven sub-principalities of the kingdom – later ruled by the seven 'Mormaers' and, in the twelfth century, by the Normanised seven 'Earls' – were supposedly traceable to Cruithne's sons, as the sub-principalities of Gwynedd in North Wales were traceable to the sons of fifth-century founder, Cunedda. These mini-states were listed in 'De Situ Albanie', a document in its surviving form part of the early thirteenth-century 'Poppleton Manuscript' in the Bibliothèque Nationale, Paris. The first of its two lists gives Angus/Mearns ('Enegus cum Moerne'), Atholl/Gowrie ('Adthole et Gouerin'), Menteith/Strathearn ('Sradeern cum Meneted'), Fife/Fortriu, Mar/Buchan, Moray ('Muref')/Ross and Caithness. The second list is more difficult to interpret, being geographical in dividing the seven states up by their 'boundary' features (rivers and mountains) one of which ('Hilef') is unknown, but includes Argyll. The line of the

Pictish 'High Kings' in Pictish and Irish sources was descended from the eponymous Cat, ruler of Caithness – which suggests a political tradition, used by later genealogists, that Caithness was the most powerful sub-kingdom. An alternative first ruler was Cathluan, son of the exiled Irish Pict king, Gub.

The first definitively historical king recorded in non-Pictish evidence was Drust mac Erp, whose death is placed at AD 449 by the Irish 'Annals of Clonmacnoise' (possibly a few years out). He reigned for allegedly twenty-nine years (100 years according to the Pictish Chronicle), and St Patrick's mission to Ireland in around 435 is supposed to have been in his nineteenth year as king. Logically the end of Roman rule in Britain in 410 led to some, if not all, of the garrisons of Hadrian's Wall leaving, possibly in the army of the rebel emperor Constantine III to fight in Gaul in 407 – though archaeology shows settlement by farmer-soldiers on this frontier continuing into the mid-fifth century. Someone – seaborne Picts? – burnt down the Roman signal-stations on the Yorkshire coast around 400, and there was a fifth-century Germanic settlement on the lower Humber which may have been founded by the mercenaries whom British/Welsh legend says the British King Vortigern employed. But little apart from approximate regnal dates is known even of the longest and/or most successful Pictish rulers of the fifth and early sixth centuries, assumed to include Drust and his brother, the mid-fifth-century Nechtan 'Morbet' ('of the Speckled Sea'). Nechtan was apparently exiled to Ireland by his brother, who was succeeded by an obscure king called Talorcan, but returned to take the throne for twenty-four years. His sobriquet might refer to his coming from overseas to rule. According to legend he founded a Christian monastery at Abernethy to give thanks for his safe return. He was succeeded by an equally obscure king called Drest, who ruled for around thirty years, then by Galam/Galan (fl. 500) who ruled for fifteen years, then by co-rulers Drest mac Drust (or mac Uudrost) and Drust mac Girom. Then came Gartnait for six or seven years, his brother Cailtram for one or six years, Talorcan mac Muircholach for eleven, Drest mac Munait for one year and Galam for two or four years.

The choice of an outsider, Bridei/Brude mac Maelchon, around 557 suggests an inability to find a suitable local candidate. Given that his predecessor Galam reigned with him for at least a year and may have died as late as 580, it is possible that discontented nobles staged a revolt in Bridei's favour and forced Galam to accept him as co-ruler and later to step down – or that Galam was seen as an inadequate ruler for wars with the Irish settlers of Dal Riada. Maelchon is an unusual name and has been claimed to be King Maelgwyn of Gwynedd in North Wales, notably by John Morris in the 1970s, though this remains unproven. There is no tradition of Maelgwyn – the strongest ruler in Wales – using an army to force the choice of his son on this distant kingdom, so if he was Maelchon he presumably married a Pictish princess and the Pictish nobles called on his son as a 'neutral' candidate. Or did Bridei bring useful Gwynedd troops to a kingdom under threat from the recent Irish settlements in Argyll? But some historians still do not accept the identification of Maelchon with Maelgwyn. Bridei/Brude was recorded by the Irish 'Annals of Ulster' as routing the Dal Riadans early in his reign, in 558 or 560, so he may have brought new military vigour or reorganised the Pictish army.

Bridei/Brude mc Maelchon was succeeded by another presumed son of a Pictish princess and a foreign ruler, Gartnait, son of Aedan of Dal Riada. The Life of St Columba makes it clear that when the saint went to Bridei's court around 565 he was reigning over a pagan Druid-led establishment based at a hill fort on a rock near Inverness, probably Craig Padraig near the Beauly Firth. A prince of the ruling Irish 'High Kings' dynasty of the Ui Niall in Midhe, the formidable Columba/Columbcille, founding abbot of Derry ('The Oaks') in Ulster, had organised a coalition of mutinous princes to rebel against centralising King Diarmait Ui Cerbhaill in the 550s and bore a heavy responsibility for the resulting bloodshed. His 'side' won the resulting battle, but the rest of the ecclesiastical hierarchy were antagonistic to the ambitious Columba and he was exiled as a troublemaker. Allegedly vowing to make up for the bloodshed he had caused by winning new peoples to Christ, he settled in the Inner Hebrides on the island of Iona and started to convert the neighbouring Irish-descended Dal Riadans. His mission duly extended to their Pictish neighbours too; did his lack of a warm welcome (or many converts at first) result from him being seen as a Dal Riadan ally? King Bridei shut the gates of his main residence near Inverness as Columba arrived, but they miraculously flew open to admit the saint. After assorted trials of miraculous powers between Columba and the Druids, the king was duly impressed and he and his followers are supposed to have been baptised en masse in Loch Ness (and the saint put flight to the 'Monster' on its first recorded appearance). A sixth-century monastic community has recently been discovered near Portmahomack in Easter Ross, not far from Bridei's 'capital', so this may be a monastery placed there by Columba to help convert the court and nobility.

Gartnait mac Domelch, Bridei's successor, may have been the Gartnait who was son of the Picts' neighbour, King Aedan of Dal Riada. If so his choice implies a radical change in inter-state relations to alliance with the former foe, logically against a mutual enemy – the southern Pictish (sub-) state of the 'Maetae' in Fortrenn who are recorded as fighting Aedan around 590? Did Aedan's ally, Columba, promote this Pictish-Dal Riadan alliance? Gartnait died around 599 according to the Irish 'Annals of Tigernach'. Another Nechtan (mac Erp), this time with no definite foreign connection, then succeeded and reigned for twenty or twenty-one years; one theory has it that he was also ruler of the neighbouring kingdom of Strathclyde and so had a British father but this is only a guess. He was definitely a Christian and promoted the religion in his dominions; Bridei mac Maelchon may have eventually converted but if so was not known as a Christian enthusiast. Nechtan gave sanctuary to Eanfrith, son of his predatory neighbour Aethelfrith of Northumbria, after the latter was killed by his challenger Edwin near Doncaster in 617. Northumbria now controlled Lothian and the Firth of Forth region, formerly the Kingdom of Din Eidyn (Edinburgh). Thus its kings were a threat to the Picts as well as to their surviving British neighbours in Strathclyde, and it was logical for the Picts to take in a useful pretender with a 'rightful' claim on its throne.

Eanfrith's son Talorcan succeeded Talorc mac Gwid, possibly his uncle and thus Nechtan's brother-in-law, to the Pictish throne around 653. It is not known if this represented an alliance between Talorcan's uncle, Oswy of Northumbria, and the Picts. Oswy was threatened by the Angles of Mercia under Penda, ruler from around 626 to 655, who had killed Oswald in 642, and their Welsh allies to his south and needed allies. Talorcan's chief claim to fame was killing the King of Dal Riada, Dunnchad, in battle at Strath Ethairt in 654. Gartnait mac Donuel (Domnall?), who succeeded Talorcan around 657 and reigned for six or six-and-a-half years, may also have been a Northumbrian vassal or nominee. Again, his father's Irish name gives cause for speculation, as Domnall 'Brecc', 'the Freckled' (killed 642), had been King of Dal Riada in the 630s; was Gartnait's selection a sign of an alliance to Dal Riada? His brother Drust succeeded him in approximately 663, a rare example of the throne staying in the same family and possibly enforced by Oswy; Dal Riada was currently pushing northwards to overrun the Inner Hebrides so the Pictish kingdom may have been under serious military strain and needed Northumbrian help. Oswy's death in 670 led to a Pictish revolt which may have unseated Drust (671). The Picts suffered a severe reverse and massacre by Oswy's son and successor Ecgfrith in around 672, but their loss of Skye was reversed around 680 by a new king, Bridei/ Brude mac Beli. His mother was probably a daughter of

Eanfrith and his father was son of the Strathclyde ruler Beli mac Nechtan, so his selection probably indicates an alliance with Strathclyde against Northumbria (Bede refers to him as Ecgfrith's maternal cousin). He is said to have defeated the Scots heavily and besieged their principal fortress, Dunadd in Lorne, then to have attacked Dunottar in Angus (held by Ecgfrith?).

The Pictish lands north of the Firth of Forth came under severe threat of conquest by Northumbria from the 670s; Northumbria even imposed its own bishop in Fife. This was reversed after King Brude defeated and killed Ecgfrith in February 685 at Nechtansmere in the Mearns. The siting of the battle suggests a large-scale Northumbrian offensive up the east coast of Scotland, north of the Tay, possibly the most ambitious war by a ruler of Northern England since Roman times; the unusual date in winter suggests a surprise attack by one party on the other. The aggressive Ecgfrith presumably hoped to crush the Picts decisively; instead he lost his life and crippled Northumbria's northern expansionism. A Pictish military revival followed, logically incorporating the manpower of reconquered Fife and the Firth of Forth region. Brude died in 693 and was the first Pictish king to be buried on the holy island of Iona with the Christian kings of Dal Riada, by Abbot Adamnan (St Columba's biographer) who was clearly a personal and political ally. His successor Taran was deposed within four years by a rival, Brude mac Derile, who resumed the state's military success. The next but one king, Nechtan mac Derile (who succeeded his brother Brude in 706), was converted to Christianity by Curetan, a missionary bishop despatched from Iona. Nechtan had been in Ireland for an important synod at Birr in 697 with Abbot Adamnan of Iona, and evidently saw the advantage of aligning his kingdom with the Church. Now there was a new wave of conversions under the eighth-century religious movement of the 'Celi De' (Culdees), the 'Friends of God', who were to set up monasteries in Pictish lands such as that at Dunkeld.

Pictish power suffered from some sort of internal strife in the 720s, when Nechtan retired or was deposed. Possibly the fact that he had succeeded his own brother gave rise to resentment that his family was monopolising the throne. Nechtan's successor (in 724), Drust, faced revolt from him in 726, defeated and imprisoned him, but was then driven out by Alpin mac Eochaid, a Dal Riadan prince (great-grandson of Domnall Brecc) but son of a Pictish princess. Order was restored by King Angus (ruled 729–61), who defeated Drust in three battles, drove out Alpin, and resumed a period of Pictish military predominance. Around 736 he became king of the Dal Riadans too – the first union of 'Scotland' north of the Forth. Details are so obscure that we cannot tell if this by was by consent or by conquest, but it was clearly the Picts who were the senior partner in the alliance. The union apparently ended after Angus's brother Talorcan was defeated by the army of Strathclyde under King Teudeber at Mugdock in 750, weakening his power and emboldening a Dal Riadan revolt led by Aed 'Find' ('the Fair'). Angus held onto the Pictish kingdom until 761, and was succeeded by his brother Brude. Then in around 763 the throne passed to Ciniod mac Feredach of Loarn (Lorne), from a different branch of the dynasty that had been fighting Angus. He suffered a decisive defeat by Aed 'Find' in 768. Around 775 Ciniod was succeeded by Alpin mac Feret, who was replaced in turn by Talorcan mac Drust (possibly 'Dubthalorc', 'Black Talorc', king of the Southern Picts, who died in 781). The next king – Talorcan mac Angus, ruled *c.* 782–85 – may have been the son of the great mid-century King Angus. In 789 the Dal Riada Prince Constantine, presumably with a Pictish mother, drove out King Conall mac Tadhg and probably seized the Pictish throne; sources disagree on the length of his reign (over thirty years?). He was to ascend the Dal Riadan throne too in 811, and was clearly the most powerful and secure Pictish ruler for a generation. He built a new fortress at Forteviot in western Fife and a church at Dunkeld, and was probably driven to relocate Pictish power to the east of Scotland by heavy Scandinavian settlement in the north-west. Constantine's brother Angus II succeeded him in both kingdoms in 820–34, possibly aided by the need for them to act together against the Viking threat; the union was unlikely to have lasted if they had not faced such a foe and had to pool their resources. But Cinaed (Kenneth) Mac Alpin, who succeeded to the Pictish throne after their army was destroyed by the Vikings at Forteviot in 839, was the first to make such a union last. This was no doubt due to loss of Pictish manpower during Viking ravages, which was most apparent after the defeat and death of King Eoganan and his nobles in battle in 839. The later patriotic Scots assumption that Cinaed/Kenneth conquered the Picts by force (and a legend that he murdered their last, disputed king, Drust, by treachery) are now thought to be less likely than an agreement by the latter to merge their realms to combat the Vikings. Notably, the title of 'King of the Picts' continued to be used for Kenneth and his brother Donald and son Constantine I; the latter was later reckoned in the Pictish royal chronicle to be their seventieth and last ruler. This would seem to indicate a 'personal', not institutional, union of the kingdoms. Thus the Picts did not see Kenneth as 'first King of Scots' but as a normal 'King of the Picts'.

Name	Date of accession	Date of death/dep.	Years ruled
'Argentocoxus' fl. 210 (Roman records, leader of 'Maetae')			
Feradach	mid-C4th?		
Gartnait	*c*. 360/70?		
Talorc (predecessor of Drust)	*c*. 400/410??	*c*. 424	
Drust mc Erp	*c*. 424	*c*. 453	*c*. 29
Talorc mc Aniel	*c*. 453?	*c*. 457?	*c*. 4?
Nechtan mc Erp	*c*. 457	*c*. 481	*c*. 24

Drust	*c.* 468	*c.* 498	*c.* 30
Galan	*c.* 498	*c.* 513	*c.* 15
Drest mc Girom	*c.* 513	*c.* 528	*c.* 15
Drest mc Drust/			
mc Uudrost	*c.* 513	*c.* 528	*c.* 15
Gartnait mc Girom	*c.* 528	*c.* 535	*c.* 7
Cailtrom mc Girom	*c.* 535	*c.* 541	*c.* 7
Talorc mc Mordeleg	*c.* 541	*c.* 552	*c.* 11
Drest mc Munait	*c.* 552	*c.* 553	*c.* 1
Galam II	*c.* 553/4	*c.* 557/8 (d. *c.* 580)	*c.* 4
Brude/Bridei mc Maelchon (son of Maelgwyn of Gwynedd)	557?	584	27?
Gartnait mc Domech	584	599?	15?
Nechtan II	599	620?	21?
Cinioch	620?	630/1	10
Gartnait mc Guid	630/1	635	4
Brude mc Guid	635	641	6
Talorc mc Guid	641	653	12
Talorcan mc Eanfrith (son of Eanfrith of Bernicia)	653	657	4
Gartnait mc Donuel	657	663	6
Drust mc Donuel	663	672	9
Brude mc Beli (son of Beli of Strathclyde)	672	693	21
Taran mc Enfitach	693	697	4
Brude mc Derile	697	706	9
Nechtan III (i) mc Derile	706	724	18
Drust	724	726	2
Nechtan III (ii)	726	729	3 (Total: 21)
Alpin	726	728	2
Angus/Oengus			

Mc Fergus	729 (also Dal Riada from 739)	761	32
Brude mc Fergus	761	763	2
Ciniod mc Feredach	763	775	12
Alpin mc Feredach	775	779	4
Talorcan mc Drust	779	781	2
Drust mc Talorcan	781	782	1
Talorcan mc Angus	782	785	3
Conall mc Tadhg	785	789	4
Constantine mc Fergus	789 (also Dal Riada from 811)	820	31
Angus mc Fergus	820 (also Dal Riada)	834	14
Drust mc Constantine	834	837	3
Talorc mc Uuthal	834	837	3
Eoganan	837?	839	2?

Kings of Dal Riada

Ruled by an Irish dynasty from the similarly named kingdom of 'Dal Riata' ('Riata's share') in north-east Ulster, some of whose inhabitants had apparently been moving sporadically across the North Channel into Kintyre and Argyll since the third century AD. The ruling dynasty of the Irish kingdom claimed descent from Cairbre 'Riata', son of High King Conaire mac Moglama of Ireland, who allegedly moved from Munster to Ulster to escape a famine in the early third century and may have gone on later to rule over the settlements established in Argyll too. The Irish kingly genealogies formalised in the medieval period presented Conaire as the uncle of High King Cormac mac Art (r. *c.* 220–60), from whom the later High Kings were descended (though the genealogy of the rulers before Niall in the early fifth century is dubious), and thus the royal house of Dal Riata/Dal Riada claimed kinship to the Irish rulers to the eleventh century. It is unclear precisely how 'Hibernicised' the peoples living in Dal Riada were in these early centuries, and to what extent an immigration from Ulster supplanted the Celtic tribes of the area named by Ptolemy (*c.* AD 120) such as the Epidaii. The extent of cultural and racial difference between the earlier 'native' Brittonic peoples and the Irish 'immigrants' may also have been exaggerated by the legends of the ruling dynasty's foreign origins, though it seems that the language spoken in Ulster ('Q-Celtic') was different from that of the early Highlands ('P-Celtic'). By the sixth century interpreters were needed for dealings between the two peoples, according to the later seventh-century 'Life of St Columba'. Modern DNA evidence backs up the theory of substantial Irish immigration to Argyll, though it cannot pinpoint the date.

The dynasty only definitively settled in Kintyre in around 500 under Fergus 'Mor' ('The Great'), whom the Irish annals recorded as dying within a year or so. Fergus ('Man of Force') was the son of Erp, allegedly arriving from Ireland to rule over the settlers who had been established in Argyll for several hundred years. He was descended from centuries of the kings of the dynasty's original homeland, Dal Riata in eastern Ulster; their founder was supposed to be Cairbre 'Riata', a third-century King of County Antrim. Cairbre and his followers had migrated north to Antrim from Munster in a famine, and he also made a journey to Argyll to secure recognition of his rule from the Irish settlers there. The founder of the latter was supposed to be another Fergus ('Feradach') who had lived in around 330 BC, from whom Cairbre was descended, but his existence must be doubtful

since the first source to mention him is the Scottish historian
Hector Boece around 1520.

The kingdom set up by Fergus mac Erp around AD 500
was known as that of the 'Scots' as well as 'Dal Riada', but
in fact the term 'Scots' was a general one for the Irish which
Late Roman writers used to denote raiders of Britain from
Ireland (e.g. in the Irish-Pictish-Saxon attack of 367). It was
traditionally regarded as having three main political divisions,
which were attributed to the rulers being the descendants of
Fergus, ruling in Kintyre, and his younger brothers Loarn
(founder of the line of Lorn) and Angus of Islay. Fergus
allegedly brought the 'coronation stone' later used by the
kings of Dal Riada, the 'Lia Fail', from Ireland; by the later
sixth century it was set up at Dunadd for the king to sit on
at his Coronation and it was later claimed to be the Irish
'High King's' coronation stone from Tara. The kings of Dal
Riada from the early sixth century were regarded as the
descendants of two rival lines established by brothers, the sons
of Fergus's son Domangert – the 'Cenel Comgall' descended
from Comgall (*c.* 507–38) and the 'Cenel Gabhran' descended
from Gabhran who succeeded him (d. *c.* 558). The Irish annals
record Fergus's father Erp as dying in 474. Fergus's death was
recorded as occurring in 501, the year after his arrival, and
his son Domangert – evidently already adult – succeeded him
and died as 'King of Cenn Tire' (Kintyre) in 507 according
to the Irish 'Annals of Innisfallen'. This suggests that Fergus
was probably born in the 450s/460s, with a son at least in his
late teens by 500; Domangert had at least one son (Comgall)
able to succeed and hold onto his kingdom by 507. A new
kingdom hard-pressed by its Pictish neighbours would have
been likely to break up if it did not have an adult ruler in the
crucial period of the 500s and 510s.

Any strict alternation of the kingship between rival lines
was tempered by the realities of political power. Comgall
mac Domangert (r. 507–38?) was succeeded by his brother
Gabhran. Gabhran was succeeded by Comgall's son Conall

(558), then his own son Aedan (574); Aedan's son Eochaid retained the throne for his line but was succeeded (April 608) by Conall's son Conadd after whom followed Eochaid's son Domnhall 'Brecc' (629) and then Conadd's son Ferchar (637). Gabhran apparently married a princess of the royal family of the Gododdin in Lothian, suggesting a Dal Riadan-British alliance against the Picts. But the Irish annals record that the Scots fled from the resurgent Picts under the latter's new king, Bridei/Brude mac Maelchon, in 558 or 560. This coincided with or followed Gabhran's death but it is not known if he was killed in battle. His nephew Conall mac Comgall succeeded him (558), and was succeeded in 574 by Gabhran's son Aedan; possibly there was a formal agreement between the two sub-dynasties to alternate the throne and so prevent civil wars. Alternatively, Aedan was too young to succeed in 558 and a more seasoned battle-leader was needed.

Aedan, who appears to have initiated a period of success against the Scots' Pictish neighbours, also benefited from the support of the new Irish missionary church established at Iona in his dominions by St Columba (a prince of the Ui Niall 'High Kings' family) in 563 – Columba supposedly acted as 'kingmaker' or arbiter in selecting Aedan as king in 574 with angelic assistance. The story in Adomnan's biography of Columba's selection of Aedan clearly shows the influence of the Old Testament story of the prophet Samuel's selection of Saul as the first King of Israel; Columba was thus seen as a new Samuel and his protégé as divinely supported. Aedan and Columba thus began the long association of the Scottish kingly line with the Church, to the benefit of both parties and initially to the detriment of the still-pagan Pictish kingdom. Aedan probably had enough military power to force his superiority on the northern Picts in the 580s, though his two elder sons, one of them called Artuir (one candidate to be an 'original' for the legendary ruler 'King Arthur'), were killed in battle near the Firth of Forth by the local 'Maetae' tribe around 590. He had a fleet and was able to attack the Isles of Orkney in *c.* 580 and the Isle of Man in 582, regaining the latter from his Irish foes of Dal N Araide. But he was less successful in extending his martial ambitions southwards against the expanding Anglian power of Bernicia. He was defeated by King Aethelfrith at 'Degsastan', probably Dawston in Liddesdale, around 603, and thus lost the chance to hold Lothian after the British kingdom there collapsed.

In Aedan's time the question of the power of Dal Riada over their Irish cousins in 'Dal Riata' was temporarily resolved with Columba's aid at the 'Convention of Druim Ceat' (575), which agreed that the latter might be vassals of Aedan's kingdom in Scotland but still owed military assistance to the Irish 'High Kings'. The current 'High King' was Columba's cousin Ainmere, so the saint was probably the principal agent of this alliance. This apparently followed a military reverse which Aedan had suffered at the start of his reign from the 'Dal N Araide' ruler Baetan mac Cairill (ruled *c.* 572–81), current 'High King' of Ulster, who is supposed to have forced Aedan to become his vassal for his Scottish lands as well as in Ireland itself.

Aedan was succeeded by his youngest and only surviving son Eochaid 'Buide' in April 608, two older sons having been killed in battle; according to St Columba's biographer, Abbot Adamnan, the saint had predicted that Eochaid would be the next king when was he brought to see him as a small boy. Eochaid ruled for the final year or two of his reign (627–29?) with the obscure Conadd 'Cerr' ('the Left-Handed'), either a son of his or a son of Comgall. Conadd, also interested in Ulster politics and possibly chosen as co-ruler (and intended successor?) as younger and more dynamic than Eochaid, defeated King Fiachnae mac Demnain of the 'Ulaid' in Ulster, but was killed in 629 at Fid Eoin by the army of 'Dal N Araide'. Eochaid outlived him, briefly; Domnhall 'Brecc' ('the Freckled'), his son, succeeded within a year. He was restlessly, and arguably recklessly, ambitious, and was the last ruler to play a major role in Irish affairs. He miscalculated by abandoning his father's alliance with Columba's kin, the 'Cenel Conaill' branch of the Ui Niall dynasty of Irish 'High Kings', in favour of their enemies, the Ulster kings of 'Dal N Araide'. Fighting with them against the Ui Niall 'High Kings', he shared in their disastrous defeat at Mag Rath in 637 and was twice defeated by the Picts too. In what appears to be a classic case of a ruler's ambition outstripping his realm's resources, Domnhall's kingdom in Scotland then suffered from his Irish defeat as the latter emboldened his local rivals and neighbours to revolt. He was killed in battle by the British of Strathclyde at Strathcarron in 642, which led to an eclipse of the Scots' kingdom for another century and a revival of Pictish power.

Domnhall's cousin and co-ruler Ferchar, son of Conadd 'Cerr', succeeded briefly to a united Scots kingdom. The 'Dun Albanach' manuscript gives his reign as sixteen years, so he was probably co-ruler (and intended successor?) from the early–mid-630s. The Kingdom of Dal Riada was divided on Ferchar's death in 650 between Conall (II) 'Crandomna' and a mysterious Dunchad (mac Coniang) whose position in the genealogy is unclear. Dunchad was killed in 654 by Talorcan, the Pictish king. From 660 Domnhall's son Domangert ruled as sole king and appears to have restored the realm's position to some extent, but the major military powers of the era were firstly Northumbria (which ruled Fife to 685) and, after its defeat at Nechtansmere, its Pictish defeater. Domangert was killed in 673 according to the 'Annals of Ulster', and the succession is uncertain, which probably indicates rule by several contending dynasts. In 695 the Scots kingship even passed out of the hands of the direct line of Fergus 'Mor' for the first time that can be ascertained, into the control of Ferchar 'the Tall' of the line of Loarn. His rule lasted for twenty-one years according to the 'Dun Albanach', but it is unclear if this means his rule of Loarn or his rule of all Dal Riada. Domnhall 'Donn', who apparently ruled for thirteen years and died in 696, and his brother Mael Duin (died 688) appear to have been two of the contenders. There were several violent struggles for the throne over the next few years, probably a 'stand-off' between the rival dynasties of the 'Cenel Gabhran' (Gabhran's descendants) and the kings of Loarn. Eochaid (possibly nicknamed 'Riannamail', 'Crook-Nose'), son of King Domangert, was killed in 697 according to the 'Annals of Ulster'; his replacement was Ainbcellach mac Ferchar of Loarn. Within a year Ainbcellach was deposed and exiled to Ireland by his own brother Selbach, but it is unclear if the usurper secured only Loarn not all Dal Riada at this point. Certainly another claimant existed for the kingship of Dal Riada, Fiannamail ua Dunchado, who was killed in 700; the 'Annals of Tigernach' record him as King of the 'Dal N Araide' in Ireland too but an account of the synod of Birr (which he attended) in 697 names another king as their sovereign, namely Fiachrae Cosalach. This synod issued the famous 'Law of Adamnan', called after its initiator the Abbot of Iona, banning attacks on non-combatants (priests, women, and children) during warfare and was a pioneering attempt to 'civilise' the endemic warfare in Irish society. Fiannamail was clearly prepared to back this in person. He was, however, soon removed by Selbach, who ruled for over twenty years.

Selbach, as head of the Loarn dynasty, faced challenges from both his exiled brother Ainbcellach (who returned from Ireland to attack him in September 719 but was killed in battle in 'Finnglen') and his neighbours. His relatively successful reign saw him destroying Dun Olaigh (Dunolly near Oban, later chief stronghold of the Mac Dougalls) in 701, being defeated by unknown enemies in 'Glen Lemnae' in 704, defeating the Britons of Strathclyde at 'Lough Eclet' in 711 and at 'the rock of Minuirc' in 717, and besieging Dunavert in Kintyre in 712. Within a month of his killing Ainbcellach in September 719 he had to fight a sea-battle against his rival, Dunchad 'Becc' of the 'Cenel Gabhran', off 'Ard Nesbi'. He abdicated in 723 and became a monk, being succeeded by his son Dungal; Ainbcellach's son Muiredach appears to have become sub-king of Loarn sometime in the 720s and another of his sons, Ruadri, was ancestor of the kings of Moray and may have migrated there himself. Dungal was deposed or killed by Eochaid mac Echdach, of uncertain origin, in 726; Selbach took up arms to attempt to remove the usurper in 727 but failed and died in 730. Muiredach then succeeded Eochaid in 733, but was defeated and probably driven out of his kingdom by Talorcan the Pict at the battle of 'Croc Cairpre' around 736. He died in exile as late as 771/76 according to the Irish 'Annals of Four Masters', which suggests that he was only in his twenties or thirties at the time.

In the eighth and early ninth centuries several Dal Riada kings also ruled the Picts, reflecting on the inter-marriage between the two royal families. Firstly Alpin, brother of Eochaid (III) mac Echdach who ruled Dal Riada in 726–33 and grandson of Domangert (ruled 660–73), briefly occupied the Pictish throne in 726. He was expelled within two years and went on to succeed to Dal Riada, possibly on Muiredach's expulsion. It is probable that he had a Pictish mother to be eligible for their throne. Then one Angus, apparently a Pictish prince with a claim on both thrones, secured the Pictish kingdom and took Dal Riada too in a civil war; he was probably driven to intervene lest Alpin use Dal Riadan resources to regain the Pictish throne. He ruled a united realm as the first secure 'King of Picts and Scots' until his defeat by Strathclyde in 750 emboldened Eochaid III's son Aed 'Find' ('the Fair') to lead a successful revolt in Dal Riada. In 768 Aed 'Find' scored a decisive victory over King Conall mac Tadhg of the Picts in Fortriu, confirming Dal Riadan revival. If anything, the events of the 730s–50s indicate that the Picts had the militarily stronger kingdom at this point – at least if an energetic ruler was in charge – as it was their realm that provided Angus with the main force for his 'empire'. The constant coups and the multiplicity of royal contenders with uncertain genealogies in Dal Riada through the eighth century indicate that the latter was a more fractured and unstable polity – but it managed to throw off Pictish rule after 750.

Aed 'Find' was succeeded around 778 by his brother Fergus, but for some reason (youth?) Constantine, usually regarded as Fergus's son (though this is not certain), was unable to secure the succession in 781. Instead he went on to take over the Pictish kingdom in 789, implying that he probably had a Pictish mother and useful allies in that land; the two kingdoms' affairs were now becoming heavily entangled. An obscure Domnall, identified by some as Constantine's son, ruled Dal Riada from 781, possibly at first with the even more obscure Donncorci (d. 791), to 805. Conall mac Tadhg, ex-King of the Picts, and Conall mac Aedan then fought for the throne, before Constantine finally secured it in 811; he and his brother Angus ruled to 834. At this point both kingdoms seem to have been weakened by the threat posed by the Vikings who settled on the isles of the western seaboard and threatened what remained of the Kingdom of Dal Riada and their Pictish rivals. It is likely that Scandinavian settlement throughout the Hebrides was accompanied by killings and forced evictions; the local DNA and place names are mainly Scandinavian. The monastery on Iona, centre of Christianity in Dal Riada, was repeatedly raided and was eventually evacuated, most of the monks fleeing to Kells in Ireland. It is clear that the incessant raiding and settlements were one reason why the kingdoms united under one ruler in the early ninth century with less apparent strife than had been the case when Alpin and Angus attempted it in the eighth century; survival required uniting of their resources, and cultural similarities (and inter-marriage?) were increasing. Logically many of the Dal Riadan kingdom's rival princely dynasts were probably killed or lost much of their landed/manpower resources, especially in the west.

A brief return to separate realms from Angus's death in 834 was ended in approximately 837 when Eoganan, Angus II's son, secured the joint throne, but he was killed in 839 in a massive Viking invasion. Most of the Pictish aristocracy seem to have fallen in the battle, and this laid the leaderless kingdom open to the claim of a minor prince of Dal Riada, Cinaed/Kenneth mac Alpin, to secure both realms against the imminent threat of total Viking conquest. This time the union proved permanent. But it is testimony to the unsettling effect of the warfare that Kenneth's dynastic links to earlier kings are unclear; he was evidently a 'new man', reliant on his military competence, not the heir of a long line of senior Dal Riadan princes used to taking on 'national' power.

The centre of the kingdom was at Dunadd in Lorn until the Viking raids made that area too exposed and Dal Riada lost control of the seaways; Kenneth mc Alpin relocated the centre of his new, combined Kingdom of the Picts and Scots inland to Dunkeld. The 'coronation stone', the 'Lia Faill' – supposedly an ancestral Irish heirloom removed from Tara, or else St Columba's portable altar – was symbolically removed with the 'capital' to Dunkeld and was later placed at Scone. But where possible the kings of Scotland continued to be buried with their Dal Riadan ancestors on Iona.

Name	Date of accession	Date of death/dep.	Years ruled
Fergus 'the Great'	*c.* 500?	*c.* 501/2?	1 or 2?
Domangert	*c.* 502?	*c.* 507?	*c.* 5?
Comgall	*c.* 507?	late 530s?	trad. 31
Gabhran	late 530s?	*c.* 558?	trad. 16
Conall Mc Comgall	*c.* 558?	574	16?
Aedan mc Gabhran	574	April 608	34
Eochaid 'Buide' ('Yellow-Haired')	April 608	629	21
Conadd 'Cerr'	627?	629	2?
Domnhall 'Brecc' ('the Freckled')	629	642	13
Ferchar	634?	650	16
Conall II	650	660	10
Dunchad	650	654	4

Domangert	660	673	13
Maelduin	673	688	15
Domnhall 'Donn' ('Brown-Haired')	683?	696	13?
Ferchar 'the Tall'	695 (Loarn; since 676?)	697	2
Eochaid 'Crooked Nose'	695?	697	2?
Ainbcellach mac Ferchar	697	698	1
Fiannamail ua Dunchado	698	700	2
Selbach mac Ferchar	700	723 (abd.) d. 730	23
Dungal mac Selbach	723	726	3
Eochaid mac Echdach	726	733	7
Muiredach mac Ainbcellach	733	736? (d. 771/6)	3?
Alpin	733 (previously Picts)	736	3
Eogan	736	739	3
Angus/Oengus (King of Picts)	739	750	11
Aed 'the Fair'	750	778	28
Fergus	778	781	3
Domnhall mc Constantine	*c.* 781	805	*c.* 24
Donncorci	*c.* 781	*c.* 791	*c.* 10
Eochaid 'the Poisonous'	*c.* 781 (Kintyre)	?	

Conall mc Tadhg	805 (previously Picts)	807	2
Conall mc Aedan	807	811	4
Constantine mc Fergus	811 (also Picts)	820	9
Angus mc Fergus	820 (also Picts)	834	14
Alpin of Galloway	*c.* 834	*c.* 840?	*c.* 6?
Eoganan	836?	839	3?

Kings of Strathclyde

Also known as 'Alt Claith/Clud' from the alternative name of its main royal residence, Dumbarton Rock, in the Brittonic tongue; 'Strathclyde' was its Gaelic name.

A British kingdom, the former tribal territory of the Damnonii and Selgovae. It was the western counterpart of the post-Roman kingdom of the Votadini (Gododdin) to its east, and had its 'capital' or principal royal fortress at Are Cluta (Dumbarton, 'fortress of the Britons'). The first definitely recorded ruler, Ceretic, is dateable by a letter of complaint about his raiding by St Patrick in around 459; his grandfather Cinhil may be the Roman name 'Quintilius' and his great-grandfather Cluim the Roman 'Clemens'. John Morris assumed from the likely timescale of the genealogy that Clemens was a 370s Roman client-king, though this is not definite. Ceretic was known to medieval Welsh genealogists by the title of 'Gwledic', an archaic term for an overlord of other kings such as the fifth-century Ambrosius (post-Roman ruler of southern Britain) and Cunedda (founder of Gwynedd). He was thus evidently a powerful ruler, probably of all the lands from the Clyde valley and the Antonine Wall south to the Carlisle area. Ceretic's grandsons Dumnagual or Dyfnwal 'Hen' ('the Old') and Tutagual ruled around 500, with the former the senior ruler. Presumably Dyfnwal was noted for his long rule. He was succeeded by his son Clydno ruling the west (Galloway), possibly another son called Gwyddno, and a nephew called Cinbelin (the pre-Roman kingly name 'Cunobelinus'). A second Tutugual, nephew of Clydno and grandson of Dyfnwal, came under severe pressure from the new power of Bryniach to the east, whose king, Morcant, seems to have occupied much of the kingdom in around 550. He or another Tutugaul was remembered as a tyrant. Rhydderch 'Hael', Tutugual's son (according to the medieval Welsh dynastic genealogy and the biography of his contemporary St Columba) and presumed successor, was baptised in Ireland. He succeeded to the kingdom in around 575, possibly expelling Morcant's invaders. He was a contemporary and patron of St Kentigern in the mid-sixth century, allowing that pioneering North British evangelist (son of a daughter of a ruler of Lothian) to found a see and monastery at Glasgow; the twelfth-century hagiography of Kentigern has a struggle between pagan Druids and Kentigern's missionaries in the kingdom in the later sixth century.

Rhydderch was one of the most powerful of the Northern British kings of the era, joining Urien of Rheged's coalition against Bernicia around 589 according to the ninth-century 'Historia Brittonum' by the Gwynedd bishop Nennius. Nicknamed 'the Generous' and so presumably able to attract an effective body of warriors and client-kings, he was also able to fend off the new power of Dal Riada to his north under Aedan, whose bishop Columba was on good terms with him. He was apparently followed in around 612 by a new dynasty (or distant relative) with a Pictish name, Nechtan/Neithon ap Gwipno, from whom the later kings claimed descent. Nechtan was supposed to be Rhydderch's cousin, a grandson of Dumnugual 'Hen', according to the Welsh royal genealogies. The latter are indeed our sole source for the names of many of its kings in the seventh to ninth centuries, of whom little is known.

The eclipse of the British kingdoms of the North in the 600s left Strathclyde exposed to the power of Northumbria to its south-east and that of the Dal Riada Scots to the north-west, and it thereafter frequently became a vassal of the more powerful of these two neighbours. It was either unable or unwilling to save the other kingdoms of the Northern Britons from vassalage to Aethelfrith and Edwin of Northumbria in around 604–33, and may have been a Northumbrian ally or vassal too as it was apparently not attacked by these two great warlords. Its only, brief return to military glory came after King Owen/Eugenius map Beli defeated and killed King Domnhall 'Brecc' of Dal Riada in the Battle of Strathcarron in 642. Very little is known of the kingdom's history in the eighth and ninth centuries. The Irish 'Annals of Ulster' name a King Guret as dying in 658, having usurped the throne after Owen's death; was Owen's son underage? Then comes Elfin or Alpin, possibly the 'Alpin mac Nechtan' who died in 693 according to the 'Annals of Ulster'. King Dumnagual mac 'Aun' (Owen?) died in 694 according to the 'Annals of Ulster'; by the early eighth century the ruler was probably Elfin's son Beli. In 750 King Teudebur, son of Beli, achieved a rare victory over the Picts under their great ruler Angus, whose brother Talorcan was killed at 'Mocetauc' (probably Mugdock), but otherwise the kingdom seems to have been a minor power. Northumbria appears to have been overlord of Strathclyde at this point. Teudebur died in 752 according to the 'Annals of Tigernach'; his successor Rhodri, not in the genealogies so possibly a usurper, died in 754 according to the Welsh 'Annales Cambriae'. Presumably Teudebur's son Dumnugual, who died in 760, then succeeded. In 756 his 'capital', Dumbarton Rock, was attacked by both King Eadberht of Northumbria and King Aengus the Pict, and it was stormed and looted; it is not clear if they were acting in a coalition.

Dumnagual's son in the genealogies, Eugenius or Owen, presumably succeeded him; his son was Rhydderch and the latter's son was another Dumnagual. In his son Artgal's reign the Vikings, who had overrun southern Northumbria (867) and created a new kingdom at York, led by Ivarr 'the Boneless' stormed Dumbarton after a four-month siege as the rock's well ran dry. This was presumably part of the attempt by Ivarr and his brother Halfdan Ragnarrson, the rulers of York, to link up their new kingdom of York with the Danish settlements in Ireland. Artgal was taken prisoner and presumably became a Viking vassal; his son Rhun had married a daughter of King Kenneth Mac Alpin of the Picts and Scots, ruler of all lands north of the Firth of Forth, and in 872 Kenneth's son King Constantine acquiesced in Artgal's murder. Was Artgal seen as a Viking lackey or as an obstacle to Constantine imposing his brother-in-law Rhun as his own vassal? Rhun died around 878, when his son Eochaid succeeded. Strathclyde's final native ruler, Eochaid, linked its fortunes closely to his ally Giric, King of Scots, Constantine's cousin, as its new patron in the 880s and one source ('Chronicle of the Kings of Alba') names him as co-ruler of Scotland with Giric who was apparently his foster father. Was this a formal alliance of the two kingdoms against the Viking threat? Strathclyde was evidently unable to resist the 'Norsemen' on its own. Apparently the two kings were both driven out of their lands, probably by Giric's supplanter in Scotland/'Alba' (his cousin Donald), in 889.

Strathclyde as a Scots Dynastic Dependency

Following the removal of the royal house in 889, the kingdom was taken under the protection of the new Kingdom of Scots. Its ruler thence was a junior prince of the ruling dynasty, sometimes the heir to the throne, with King Constantine II installing his heir Donald/Domnhall mac Aed as its ruler in around 908. He was replaced by Constantine with Owen mac Donald, a cousin, in 925 – possibly as a conciliatory gesture to the new overlord of York, the Wessex-led Kingdom of England, as Constantine was not yet ready to challenge King Athelstan. Both Constantine and Donald came to meet (and do homage to?) Athelstan at Eamont Bridge in 927 as he annexed York, but in 934 Athelstan attacked Scotland and in 937 the two Northern 'Celtic' kings and their Viking allies fought him unsuccessfully at 'Brunanburh'. Owen was killed and was succeeded by another Donald, son of Donald mac Aed, who lost his family's southern territories in Cumbria to Athelstan's brother Edmund in 945 after the Battle of 'Dunmail's Rise' near Thirlmere. Possibly he was the 'Dunmail' commemorated by that name. The subsequent Anglo-Scots treaty gave Strathclyde to Scots King Malcolm I's cousin and heir, Indulf, who succeeded to Scotland in 954 and passed Strathclyde on to his heir Dubh. In 962 Dubh, now King of Scots, terminated the arrangement of giving Strathclyde to the heir by passing over his own heir Cuilean (Colin) in favour of the son of the late ruler Owen, Donald. The latter faced attack by the 'cheated' Cuilean in 966, but his son Rhydderch defeated the invader and he survived to do homage (?) to King Edgar of England at Chester in 973. He then abdicated and his son Malcolm (r. 973–97) retained Strathclyde without any succession to Scotland, probably having become vassal of King Edgar to secure English support for his position.

The later King Malcolm II of Scotland gained control of Strathclyde after Malcolm Mc Donald in 997, but when he became King of Scots in 1005 the latter's brother, Owen 'the Bald', secured the kingdom. Owen assisted Malcolm with an invasion of Northumbria in 1006 when they besieged Durham, and may have been killed at the Battle of Carham in a Scottish defeat in 1018 (though this is unclear). Malcolm took Strathclyde over at some point and gave it to his grandson Duncan. From Duncan's succession to the Kingdom of Scotland in 1040 the kingdoms were formally combined. It seems that in 1054–57 Duncan's son Malcolm III was installed in Strathclyde (and Lothian) by Edward of England's general Siward before conquering the rest of Scotland – though some maintain the 'Mael Coluim mac Donnchad' who Siward installed was another man. In 1094 King William II of England installed his own candidate to rule

Scotland, Malcolm III's third son Edmund, in Strathclyde (and Cumbria?) as a move to undermine their mutual foe, Malcolm's brother King Donald 'Ban'; after Edmund annoyed William by supporting a baronial revolt in Northumberland in 1095 he was replaced by his next brother Edgar (who took the Scots throne in 1097). The two territories were again practically independent of the rest of Scotland under David, youngest brother of kings Edgar and Alexander, in 1107–24, as nominee of both the Scots king and King Henry I of England.

Name	Date of accession	Date of death/dep.	Years ruled
Cluim?	Later fourth century?		
Ceretic	Early to mid-fifth century		
Dumnagual 'Hen' ('the Old')	*c.* 500?		
Cynbelin, Clydno and Gwyddno	Second quarter of sixth century?		
Morcant of Bryniach (usurper)	550s?	*c.* 575?	
Rhydderch 'Hael' ('the Generous')	*c.* 575	*c.* 612	*c.* 35/40?
Nechtan	*c.* 612	*c.* 629?	*c.* 17?
Beli mc Nechtan	*c.* 621	*c.* 633	*c.* 12
Owen mc Beli	*c.* 633	*c.* 645	*c.* 12
Gwriad/Guret	*c.* 645?	658	*c.* 13?
Elfin/Alpin	658?	693	35?
Dumnagual	?	694	
Beli mc Elphin	694	722?	28?
Teudubur	722?	752	30?
Rhodri	752	754	2
Dumnagual	754	760	6
Owen/Eugenius	?		
Rhydderch	Later eighth century		
Dumnagual	?		

Artgal	?	872	
(Viking conquest)			
Rhun	872	878?	6?
Eochaid	*c.* 878	889	*c.* 11
(Union with Scots kingdom)			
Donald mc Aed (Prince of Scots; brother of King Donald II)	908	*c.* 925	*c.* 17
Owen Mc Donald (Prince of Scots)	925	*c.* 937	*c.* 12
Donald mc Donald	*c.* 938	945	*c.* 7
Indulf	945 (King of Scots 962)	954 abd. (d. 962)	9
Dubh	954 (King of Scots 962)	962 abd. (d. 966)	8
Donald mc Owen	962	973	11
Malcolm mc Donald	973	997	24
Malcolm mc Kenneth (later King of Scots)	<997?	1005 abd. (d. 1034)	
Owen 'the Bald' Mc Donald	?	*c.* 1018	
Duncan (grandson and heir of Malcolm II)	*c.* 1018	1040	*c.* 22

(Union with Scotland 1034)

2

Kings of Scots from AD 843 to 1057

Kenneth (Gaelic 'Cinaed') McAlpin claimed descent from the royal house of Dal Riada, but even his most ambitious genealogists could not link him directly to the main line. The 'official' genealogy, preserved in the Bodleian Library (Rawlinson Mss. B 502), makes his father Alpin son of 'Eochaid', son of King Aed Find of Dal Riada, son of King Domangert, son of King Domnhall 'Brecc'. It is most acceptably proposed that Alpin was a ruler of Galloway and was descended from Eochaid 'the Poisonous' of Kintyre (fl. 781) and thence from Eochaid 'Crooked Nose' (fl. 695); the link to Aed Find is uncertain. Historians have debated fiercely over whether the link was invented to make Kenneth a more plausible claimant to be heir of the prestigious royal line of Dal Riada from Fergus 'the Great' to Aed Find rather than a parvenu. It is likely that he had some genuine connection to the main line, as otherwise he would not have been accepted by the fiercely clannish Dal Riadans, but was no close relation.

Possibly the Galloway sub-dynasty of the Dal Riadan royal family, unlike Inner Hebridean rivals, had been able to fight off the Vikings – there were far fewer settlements in their region – and thus built up a successful war-band to contend for power. Thus Kenneth, like Alfred of Wessex a generation later, benefited from the Viking extinction of his rivals for 'national' kingship. He was known by the eleventh century as 'An-Ferbasach', 'the Conqueror', but it is now thought less likely that he actually conquered the Picts rather than being accepted by most as their leader to fight off the Vikings. The lurid story in the 'Prophecy of Berchan' of him treacherously inviting Pictish king Drust and his nobles to a banquet and then killing them (by causing the table to collapse and plunge them into a pit of stakes) is now thought to be myth, though the late twelfth-century Welsh historian Giraldus Cambrensis believed it.

Whatever the accuracy of his claims, his real power relied on military achievement and the kingdom was lucky to survive the peril of a Viking occupation force in its southern regions between Forth and Clyde (a route from York to Dublin) in the 860s. His alliances extended to Strathclyde, where a daughter married King Artgal's son and heir, Rhun, and to Ireland where another daughter (Mael Muire) married two 'High Kings' in succession – firstly Aed Finlaith, King of the 'Cenel Eogain' branch of the Ui Niall dynasty (died 879), and then his cousin and successor Flann Sinna of 'Clan Colman'. He died at 'Cinnbelachair' in February 858 according to the Irish sources, and was succeeded by his younger brother Donald in whose reign the (religious?) 'Laws of Aed Find' were promulgated at the new royal residence of Forteviot (western Fife). Kenneth's elder son Constantine I then succeeded; there is some dispute over whether an inscription on the 'Cross of Dupplin' near Perth referring to 'king Constantine of the Picts' means him or the early ninth-century King Constantine but at this date the kings were still known as rulers of the 'Picts' rather than of 'Alba'. This may suggest that a full union of the two realms was a gradual process. Possibly the name 'Alba' was adopted as a neutral one which did not refer to its holder as king either of the Picts or of the Scots/Dal Riada.

Constantine, alternately an ally and opponent of the Dublin warlord Olaf 'the White', who held much of the south of his kingdom in the 860s, and then of the sons of Ragnar Lothbrok, faced major Viking invasions from the time that the

Viking 'Great Army' landed in England in 865/6 and overran York in 867. The Scandinavians settled in Yorkshire under the sons of the pirate leader Ragnar 'Lothbrok' ('Leather Breeches') – Halfdan, Ivarr 'the Boneless' and Ubbe. The trio had ambitions across the British Isles and in Ireland too, and it seems that Halfdan and Ivarr followed up their invasion of Mercia (868), conquest of East Anglia (869–70) and unsuccessful attack on Wessex (winter 870–71) with an expedition to Dublin. Around 873 Ivar became King of Dublin, and there appears to have been a Viking 'corridor' of mobile raiding armies in Southern Scotland protecting the route between Viking Yorkshire and the Irish Sea coasts. Probably the Lowlands around the Firth of Forth passed under Viking control for a time. Already in 866 another Viking army under Amlaith, probably a Dane (the name is the original of 'Hamlet'), had attacked Fortriu and secured loot and prisoners, and in 870 a Viking force from York linked up with him to besiege and sack the principal fortress of Strathclyde, Dumbarton Rock. King Artgal was captured and taken off with a multitude of prisoners, and seems to have been restored later as a Viking vassal-king. In 872 Constantine was involved in his murder, plausibly to secure the throne of Strathclyde for a more reliable candidate – his own sister's husband, Artgal's son Rhun.

Constantine's Pictish realm suffered another large-scale invasion by the Vikings in 875, in which the locals were defeated at Dollar. He was killed, probably by Halfdan's forces, in another attack in 877 – at Inverdovat near Newport-on-Tay according to the 'Chronicle of the Kings of Alba' or at the 'Black Cave' (Chronicle of Melrose)/'Black Den' (John of Fordun). He was probably in his forties. His brother Aed, 'The White-Footed' or 'Wing-Footed', succeeded briefly but was assassinated in an ambush at a pass near the 'civitas of Nrurim' (Chronicle of the Kings of Alba) a year later; this may be near Inverurie. Andrew of Wyntoun says he was killed in Strathallan by his cousin Giric, Donald's son, who succeeded him. The latter, who may have ruled with his sister's son (and his foster son) Eochaid (son of Rhun) of Strathclyde, reigned for eleven years and was probably more militarily successful than his cousins. He was nicknamed 'Mac Rath' ('Son of Fortune') in the early medieval 'Prophecy of Berchan' and in later centuries he was known as 'Gregory the Great', alleged conqueror in England and Ireland. Northumbria to his south had been broken in two by the Vikings, and the remaining Anglo-Saxon mini-state of Bernicia (based at Bamburgh) would have been militarily inferior to his realm so a useful target. He may also have helped his cousin Mael Muir's second husband, Irish 'High King' Flann Sinna, against the Vikings or local dynasts in Ireland. In 889 he was followed by Constantine's son Donald (II), later known to the eleventh-century 'Prophecy of Berchan' as 'the Mad' (in the sense of having a tendency to berserk violent outbursts). Donald was killed at either Dunnottar or Forres, probably by Vikings, in 900.

The kingship originally alternated between different lines of the family, as with contemporary Irish provincial kingships where a ruler would usually be succeeded by a brother or cousin rather than directly by his son. It is possible that there was a regular alternation between two equally 'throne-worthy' lines in deliberate emulation of the alternation of the Irish 'High Kingship' between the two lines of the Ui Niall dynasty. Thus Kenneth, with two sons, was succeeded by his brother Donald, then by these men (Constantine I and Aed). Then came Donald's son Giric, 878; Constantine's son Donald II, 889; Aed's son Constantine II, 900; Donald II's son Malcolm I, 954; Constantine II's son Indulf, 962; Malcolm I's son Dubh, 966; Indulf's son Cuilean (Colin), 971; Dubh's brother Kenneth II, 992; Cuilean's son Constantine III, 995; Dubh's son Kenneth III, with his son Giric, 997.

It is possible that Aed's name was the origin of the mysterious 'Mace Heth' or 'Mac Aed' dynasty who were to claim the Scottish throne from Malcolm III's line in the twelfth century; they appear to have had a link to the royal line of Ross and Moray, though the latter were apparently (also?) descended from late seventh-century kings of Dal Riada.

Lothian was ceded by England as part of a diplomatic agreement between Indulf and King Edgar in the 960s, regularising the fact that the Wessex-based new English kingdom found it difficult to enforce its rule of the restive north-east unlike the York-based kingdom of Northumbria had done. Constantine II, who had the longest reign of his dynasty, initially kept out of warfare apart from a possible Viking raid on Dunkeld around 903 but had to face a rapidly changing situation in Northern England in the late 910s as first the Vikings (by dint of extra Norse settlement in Cumbria) and then Wessex threatened him. He first intervened to assist Ealdred, independent Anglian ruler of Bamburgh, against the Vikings of York in 918 and fought an inconclusive battle with them, probably at Corbridge on the Tyne. He then organised a military alliance with the Scots' old foes, the Vikings of Dublin and York, to oppose the northwards advance of the new English kingdom, whose rulers Edward and Athelstan had enforced vassalage on the Vikings of York (920 and 927). He faced the first English invasion of his realm (by Athelstan) in 934, probably by sea as well as land, and was probably forced to admit to vassalage to England as he was at the English court at Buckingham to witness a charter (the usual role of sub-kings) in September 934. He was evidently chafing at being treated on a par with the weaker rulers of Wales and turned back to his old Viking allies for aid. In 937 the Celtic-Viking alliance masterminded by Constantine – including the Norse of Dublin under Olaf Guthfrithson – was heavily defeated at 'Brunanburh', an epic battle in Northern England, and English power was confirmed. The Anglo-Saxon victory poem in their official 'Chronicle' noted the prominent part in the battle played by the 'hoary-headed warrior' Constantine, 'old crafty one', and exulted in his defeat and the loss of his son (Cellach) and assorted other kinsmen in the battle.

The death of Athelstan and the subsequent revolts of York and the 'Five Boroughs' against Edmund in 939–40 saved the Scots from further pressure, but in 942/3 Constantine was apparently forced to abdicate by his impatient cousin and heir, Malcolm (I); possibly the loss of Cellach and so many of his warriors at Athelstan's hands was a crushing blow to his morale and reputation. But he had achieved the highest 'profile' and international importance of any of his line so far, in a remarkable reign of over forty years which speaks for his state's stability. He retired to be a monk at the abbey of St Andrews, possibly a genuine vocation as much as political 'neutering' by Malcolm as he had been noted for his involvement with the Church (e.g. as patron of St Andrews and of an expatriate Scots holy man, St Cradoc of the Rhineland). He died in 952, and as his father died in 878 he was at least in his mid-seventies and possibly older.

When King Edmund, Athelstan's younger brother who had fought at Brunanburh, regained control of the North in a campaign in Cumbria in 945 he drove Strathclyde's forces out of the area – traditionally by a victory over King Domnall at the pass of 'Dunmail's Rise' near Thirlmere. He may have taken the fortress of Carlisle, though if so Strathclyde was able to regain northern Cumbria (the pre-1974 counties of Cumberland and Westmorland) later as the border was eventually fixed at Stainmore near Kirkby Stephen. Edmund seems to have accepted Scottish rule of Strathclyde as a vassal-state as part of the two powers' agreement, and the final Viking attempt to rule York as an independent state (by ex-king Erik 'Bloodaxe' of Norway) ended in 954. Two years previously Malcolm of Scots had been defeated in a campaign in Northumbria, but it is unclear if he was attacking Erik in York or just trying to take over Bernicia from the local Angles. Driven out of York by King Eadred of England in 954, Erik was ambushed and killed on Stainmore while heading back to his ships and his Hebridean lands. His ambusher, Oswulf, the Anglian ruler of Bernicia, was appointed governor (Earl) of York and Northumbria by Eadred. The eastern border remained more or less fixed at the Tweed, though raiding continued and Kenneth II (r. 971–95) is supposed by the 'Chronicle of the Kings of Alba' to have raided Northumbria thrice; due to the distance from the English capital, Winchester, to the north the region was largely autonomous under its earls. By the late tenth century the earldom was held by Waltheof, of the dynasty which had ruled Bamburgh and usually been governors of Bernicia since the 880s.

King Malcolm I was killed in 954, probably in his fifties or sixties given his father's and grandfather's dates, and was succeeded by Constantine's son Indulf (r. 954–62). His name has an Anglian ending rather than a Gaelic one, and may imply Bernician or Lothian English descent – in the female line? He was supposed to have been the first Scots king to reside at Edinburgh after its capture from the Bernicians, so local descent may have added to his involvement in the region. His successor King Dubh 'the Vehement', son of Malcolm I, was killed at Forres by rebels in either July 966 (according to Andrew of Wyntoun) or 967 (the Irish version), with his son succeeding as first 'mormaer' of Fife but being excluded from the throne. The next king, Dubh's cousin and Indulf's son, Cuilean (Colin) 'the White', was killed in Strathclyde in 971, traditionally by their prince, Amdarch, in a family blood feud. Dubh's brother Kenneth, who was probably born around 930–35, then succeeded.

Kenneth II broke the strict line of rotation by killing his rival Olaf, brother of Cuilean, in 977 – he would normally have succeeded to the throne. The throne thence passed between the descendants of Malcolm I's sons, Kenneth himself and Dubh, and of Cuilean, while the family of Malcolm's brother Owain claimed Strathclyde. Cuilean's son Constantine III, nicknamed 'the Bald' according to John of Fordun in the fourteenth century, succeeded in 995 but only ruled for eighteen months. He was killed by a 'Cinaed/Kenneth mac Mael Coluim/Malcolm' – his successor Kenneth III was the son of King Dubh so the killer is uncertain. Kenneth replaced Constantine in 997 and associated his own son Giric with him as co-ruler (to keep out Cuilean's family?). He was killed at Monzievaird and succeeded by his cousin, Malcolm II (son of Kenneth II), in 1005 rather than by his younger son Boite or by one of Cuilean's line.

Malcolm, possibly born as early as 954 (and certainly with an adult daughter ready to marry before King Olaf Tryggvason of Norway died in 1000) so already well experienced, may have defeated a Viking army soon after his Coronation. He broke the rotation in the succession between the two lines of Malcolm I's family, despite only having two daughters, and married off his elder (?) daughter, Bethoc, to a native dynast (Crinan, 'thane' of Atholl and lay abbot of Dunkeld) and the younger (?), Donada, to his neighbour Jarl Sigurd 'the Stout' of Orkney. Possibly this was intended to combine the manpower of the 'mormaership' of Atholl and the Viking Jarldom of Orkney to support his own family against the excluded kin of Kenneth II in a succession struggle. He tried to wipe out the family of Kenneth III's younger son Boite in 1032.

English weakness during the Danish invasions by Cnut's father, King Swein 'Forkbeard', after 1002 enabled Malcolm II to reassert Scottish power; he attacked Durham in alliance with Owen of Strathclyde in 1006, taking advantage of the decline of elderly Ealdorman Waltheof of Bernicia (hereditary lord of Bamburgh), but was driven off by his vigorous son Uhtred. Uhtred was appointed to rule Bernicia by his grateful sovereign King Aethelred II ('Unraed', 'the Ill-Counselled'), and soon acquired southern Northumbria – based on York – too after the king treacherously murdered its earl, Aelfhelm.

Uhtred was a formidable warrior and Malcolm wisely left Northumbria alone for a decade, probably for the rest of Uhtred's period in office, despite the temptations of the Danish invasion by King Swein 'Forkbeard' and his son Cnut drawing off the earl and his army southwards. After securing the English crown by Aethelred's flight in late 1013, Swein died and Aethelred was recalled, with his more competent son Edmund 'Ironside' being aided in his heroic fightback against Cnut by Uhtred. When Cnut prevailed in 1016 Uhtred was seized, executed and replaced by a loyal Dane, Erik of Lade. It was probably at this point that Malcolm attacked Northumbria again, in 1018 according to Irish sources, though confusion has been caused by the mention of Uhtred as Malcolm's opponent as he was already dead. Did Malcolm attack in 1016, as some historians now claim, or did the sources mistake the name of the English commander? In any case, Malcolm won the Battle of Carham on the Tweed, and this secured Cnut's acceptance of his annexation of Lothian – it is unclear if this duplicated or confirmed the presumed English handover of the area to Scotland in 973. But Cnut had a large and experienced Anglo-Danish army which had been fighting in a war for rule of England for over a decade, plus Scandinavian resources in Denmark, and Malcolm could not push further south. Cnut restored English prestige and possibly regained some lands lost recently to Malcolm with an invasion of Scotland in 1031 (or else 1027). According to the saga of Cnut's enemy King/St Olaf of Norway, two kings – probably Malcolm II and his grandson Macbeth of Moray – and a Scottish/Irish dynast, Echmarcach (possibly ruler of Man), submitted to Cnut in 1031 and were confirmed in their lands. Until Malcolm's reign Strathclyde had remained separate from Scotland, but when his grandson and heir Duncan, ruler of the former, came to the Scottish throne in 1034 he united the realms. The Scots border thus extended south to include Cumbria, probably reaching the River Lune and Stainmore.

Having allied himself to the jarls of Orkney and seen his grandson Thorfinn become co-Jarl of Orkney from 1015, Malcolm passed the Scots throne on through his (eldest?) daughter Bethoc to her son Duncan (Irish/Gaelic 'Donnchad'). The latter, son of 'Thane' Crinan of Atholl, already held Strathclyde, which on Malcolm's death (1034) merged with

Scotland. His younger (?) daughter Donada had probably remarried after the death of her husband, Sigurd of Orkney, in battle at Clontarf in Ireland in 1014, to the 'mormaer' Findlaech (Finlay) of Moray – probably the most powerful of the kingdom's seven sub-'states' (the Tudor English chronicler Ralph Holinshed called him the 'thane of Glamis' – hence the appellation for his son Macbeth in Shakespeare's play.). Findlaech was later killed in 1020 – by his own people according to the 'Annals of Ulster', or by his cousin and rivals Malcolm and Gillacomgain (sons of Mael Brigte) according to the 'Annals of Tigernach'. Presumably Malcolm, who died in 1029, succeeded him in Moray – both Findlaech and Malcolm are named as 'Kings of Scotland (Alba)' but Gillacomgain is not, so did the latter fail to secure all of Moray when Malcolm died? If so he would have had to share it with Findlaech's son Macbeth, (?) Malcolm II's grandson, who is called 'King' in the account of Cnut's invasion in approximately 1031. The line of Moray were apparently descended from the ancient royal house of Dal Riada, via a junior branch who had last held the throne in around 700; there was possibly also a link to the line of Scots King Aed (d. 878). Traditionally Malcolm II lived to the age of eighty and was the oldest of his dynasty; his death at Glamis on 25 November 1034 was violent according to one source but not others.

Unlike in Shakespeare's play, the new king, Duncan, was not a respected elderly ruler but was at most in his thirties, and was quite possibly a controversial choice of heir by Malcolm and resented by his 'mormaers'. If the marital arrangements of Malcolm's daughters were meant to secure Orkney's and/or Moray's backing for the succession of the sub-ruler of Atholl's son, this backfired. Plausibly the fact that Gruoch, the daughter of Kenneth III's murdered son Boite, her first husband 'mormaer' Gillacomgain of Moray having been killed (by Malcolm's men?) in 1032, married his supplanter Macbeth (Gillacomgain's cousin and probably Malcolm's grandson), implies a move by Macbeth to secure the adherence of Kenneth III's family loyalists against Duncan. If so, the elderly Malcolm II's succession arrangements were broken up by inter-'mormaership' feuding and the Scots/Orkney clashes of the 1030s may imply that Jarl Thorfinn also backed Macbeth, his half-brother, against Duncan. The 'Orkneyinga Saga' has a naval clash between Thorfinn and a Scots or Moray ruler, won by Thorfinn, off Deerness on Orkney sometime in the mid–late 1030s. It is unclear whether Malcolm II aided or merely accepted Macbeth's takeover of Moray – he was probably the king's grandson but was a potential rival to Duncan.

In 1039/40 Duncan invaded England, probably to emulate his grandfather's exploits and present himself as a great war-leader, but according to the twelfth-century Durham monastic chronicle he met with defeat at that town from the earl of northern Northumbria, Ealdred (son of Uhtred). Duncan was killed within months by Macbeth (Mac Beatha, 'Son of Life') of Moray, in a battle at Pitgaveny near Elgin in 1040. The timing would indicate that the defeat at Durham, if accurately recorded later, inspired a rebellion in Moray; the place would indicate that Duncan invaded his challenger's lands and was certainly not the passive victim of a plot.

Gruoch, daughter of Boite and grand-daughter of Kenneth III, arguably had a stronger claim to the throne than her second husband. Her son by Gillacomgain, Lulach, was probably only around eight to twelve in 1040, so too young to rule. Unlike the later literary traditions of Andrew of Wyntoun (who first mentions the witches' prophecy of Macbeth's accession) and John of Fordoun, used by Shakespeare, the real-life Macbeth was a strong, just and 'modernising' ruler who visited Rome on pilgrimage in 1050 and distributed largesse to the populace there (according to the later chronicler Marianus Scotus). He seems to have been capable and widely supported, though either he or Duncan was presumably the Scottish king 'Karl Hundason' ('Churl, son of the Dog') who the 'Orkeyinga Saga' recounted as fighting Jarl Thorfinn at Tarbat Ness at the south end of the Dornoch Firth around 1040. Duncan's father Crinan of Atholl, evidently too strong to be removed in 1040, was killed fighting Macbeth in 1045, but Duncan's sons, Malcolm III and Donald, fled – according to John of Fordoun they took refuge in England at the court of King Edward.

In 1054 an English army under Earl Siward of Northumbria invaded Scotland. This time the attackers only seem to have secured Lothian (and probably Cumbria); John of Fordoun says that the invasion was designed to make Malcolm, son of the King of Strathclyde, ruler of Cumbria – this presumably means Malcolm III, as son of Duncan who had ruled Strathclyde as well as Scotland, though this is disputed. Plausibly it secured him rule south of the Firth of Forth. According to John of Fordoun, Siward was related to Malcolm's mother, an obscure woman whom the king-lists give the Gaelic name of 'Suthen' rather than an Anglo-Danish name so this remains unclear. According to the 'Anglo-Saxon Chronicle' Siward and Malcolm secured victory and large amounts of loot; but losses were heavy, including Siward's eponymous elder son and heir. This enabled King Edward and his chief minister Harold Godwinson to impose the latter's brother Tostig as next Earl of Northumbria when Siward died in 1057 – if Siward had left an adult son Tostig would have stood little chance of the earldom, but his surviving son Waltheof was too young. If the battle was at Dunsinane, as later alleged and used by Shakespeare, it represented an attack up the Tay from Perth towards Dunkeld, logically to link up with Prince Malcolm's family adherents in Atholl; and the battle left Macbeth as king, at least north of the Firth of Forth. In 1057 a second attack north of the Forth had more success and overthrew Macbeth.

3

The House of Dunkeld: 1057–1286

After Malcolm III killed Macbeth in battle at Lumphanan in Mar in 1057, Gruoch's son by her first marriage, Lulach, held out in Moray for a year. Malcolm is traditionally known by the sobriquet 'Canmore', i.e. 'Big Head' (or 'Great Chief'?) in Gaelic, though this was not contemporary and may have originally referred to his great-grandson Malcolm IV. He appears to have continued his predecessor's and his grandfather's policy of alliance with Orkney, a much-needed military ally for an insecure new regime; he married Ingebiorg, either daughter or widow of Jarl Thorfinn, by whom he had three sons (the eldest and survivor being Duncan). The 'Orkneyinga Saga' calls Ingebiorg the widow of Thorfinn and daughter of Finn, a former senior Norwegian 'thane' now exiled in Denmark; if this is correct she was probably older than her second husband. She appears to have died before 1066. After an initial raid on Northumbria in 1061, when Malcolm sacked the island monastery of Lindisfarne, he remained on good terms with the English government until his ally Earl Tostig of Northumbria, brother of King Edward's chief minister Earl Harold of Wessex, was expelled by his subjects in 1065 after alleged oppression. Harold (deliberately?) failed to restore Tostig, who was exiled as his foes demanded, and soon took the English throne when King Edward died on 5 January 1066. Tostig's supplanter, Morcar, was the brother of Harold's dynastic rival Earl Edwin of Mercia (grandson of Earl Leofric). In summer 1066 Tostig, who had taken refuge in Flanders with the kin of his wife Judith to hire ships, failed in attacks on Kent and East Anglia and turned up at Malcolm's court seeking aid to invade Yorkshire. Malcolm failed to help in person, but may have recommended him to try the aggressive King Harald 'Hardradi' of Norway who was now in the Orkneys with his fleet asserting Norwegian overlordship of the sons of Jarl Thorfinn (d. <1065), Paul and Erlend. The invaders landed in the Humber estuary, defeated inexperienced Edwin and Morcar and occupied York. But they were surprised, defeated and killed by Harold of England at Stamford Bridge near York on 28 September 1066. Within weeks Malcolm had to face an even more forceful, new King of England in Duke William of Normandy, who had killed the exhausted Harold at the Battle of Hastings on 14 October. William had the resources of Normandy to hand to add to his new subjects in England, including the new Western European military weapon of 'knights' fighting on horseback. The traditional Anglo-Scots conflict over demarcation of the Border was now to tip in England's favour, with the new Anglo-Norman government having large numbers of cavalry at its disposal. But it is possible that Malcolm was already used to Norman cavalry; he may have already fought Norman cavalry in Macbeth's army in 1054 or 1057.

With revolt seething in England, Malcolm was in a good position to assist rebels in Northumbria in the late 1060s. The new Norman earl, Copsi, was murdered within weeks in 1067 by Oswulf, whom King William replaced with Cospatrick – apparently the son of Maldred, Malcolm III's uncle, and so acceptable to him? There was a legitimist claimant to England to hand in King Edward's great-nephew Edgar 'Atheling', chosen to succeed Harold by the nobles in October 1066 but forced to surrender to William. In 1068 he fled north to assist rebels in Northumbria whom Cospatrick joined. Malcolm aided the rebellion and gave Edgar sanctuary in Scotland after it was put down. He assisted a second rising in Northumbria in person in 1069 after the new Norman earl, Robert de Comyn, was murdered, sending Edgar south to lead the rebellion. He raided south as far as Cleveland and, after William stormed York, Malcolm met up with Edgar and his family – his mother Agatha and sisters Margaret and Christina – as he was returning home with his loot. A storm later blew them to the Scottish coast so they joined Malcolm. The Danish fleet led by King Swein Estrithson, Cnut's nephew, arrived in the Humber and seized York with the aid of Siward's younger son Waltheof, now William's new Earl of Northumbria, but William swiftly and brutally recaptured it. Future risings in the North were prevented by the brutal Norman tactics in winter 1069/70.

Malcolm's marriage with Margaret in 1069–70 led to a disputed degree of 'Anglicisation' at the royal court, played up in the hagiography of Margaret by her chaplain, Bishop Turgot. His version had it that the highly educated and pious Margaret, a European princess brought up in Hungary with a German (not Hungarian as first claimed) mother, 'civilised' the uncouth Malcolm and introduced books to the illiterate king's court. Supposedly she also introduced royal deeds of Christian charity for the poor and had a zeal for justice, though this may place too much of the emphasis for a 'model' Christian kingship on her and undervalue Malcolm's capabilities. Turgot also had a dismissive view of the 'backward' native 'Celtic' Church, which he claimed Margaret Europeanised with new up-to-date Catholic appointments and practices. Certainly the first English/European-style abbey was founded at Dunfermline in Fife, close to the main royal residence, with the first Benedictine monks in Scotland running it according to Continental European practices. Traditionally Margaret founded the 'Queen's Ferry' at the eponymous crossing of the Forth to aid pilgrims' travel to Dunfermline and St Andrews. It is likely that Malcolm had spent part of his youth in England prior to 1057 and was less alien to his wife's culture than Turgot's version has it; he may even have met her at Edward the Confessor's court and considered a marriage with Margaret before his Orkney alliance of around 1059.

His second marriage must have alarmed the supplanter of Margaret's family in England, William, and added extra dynastic threat to his clearly long-term patronage of Edgar's family. In 1072 William invaded Scotland to enforce vassalage and Malcolm submitted at a meeting at Abernethy on the lower Tay (in September?), probably outnumbered and afraid of the Norman cavalry in a direct clash. It is probable that he had used 'scorched earth' tactics to lure the Normans into overstretched lines of communication. William insisted that Edgar and the ex-Earl of Northumbria, Malcolm's cousin Cospatrick, left Scotland for Flanders and that Malcolm handed over his eldest son Duncan as a hostage. Around 1074 the exiles returned to Scotland, once William was preoccupied with a war in Maine in France. Malcolm was emboldened by William's troubles overseas – in which his runaway eldest son Robert joined – to invade Northumbria again in 1079 and ravage as far as the Tees. King William's new and unpopular earl, Bishop Walcher of Durham, was murdered in January 1080 in another revolt, but any Scots support for this was rebuffed by the arrival of William's army, led by the reconciled Robert. The latter founded Newcastle as the principal Norman bastion on the lower Tyne, and advanced into Scotland as far as Fife before withdrawing that summer (probably after Malcolm renewed his homage to the king).

Even after Malcolm III's family monopolised the throne, from 1057/8, they still faced sporadic revolt from claimants from the rival line of Moray, with Lulach's son Maelsnechtai revolting in 1077 and Malcolm invading Moray and capturing his womenfolk and cattle but apparently not him. Moray was presumably ravaged and Maelsnechtai either fled or submitted; his death in 1078 ended the immediate threat to Malcolm's throne but, significantly, his heirs (probably his daughter's son Angus, underage) were not deposed.

In 1092 the new English king William II secured Cumbria for England by building a castle at Carlisle, confiscating the region from its mixed Anglo-Scottish ruler Dolfin – Malcolm's cousin, and brother of the deposed Earl Cospatrick of Northumbria (now Earl of Dunbar). Malcolm came south in 1093 to protest to William at Gloucester but was sent packing; his visit may also have involved a call by Margaret on his daughters, Edith and Mary, who were being educated at Romsey Abbey by her sister Christina (a nun there). On his way home he attended the dedication of Durham Cathedral. His retaliatory invasion of Northumbria to support rebel Robert de Mowbray led to his killing at the siege of Alnwick Castle on 13 November 1093; apparently the steward promised to hand over the keys and rode out to meet the king with them on the end of his lance, but ran him through with the latter. The garrison then set on the aghast Scots troops and routed them. Malcolm was probably in his early sixties. His reign had been the most 'high-profile' of the Scots kings' in terms of all-Britain importance, and this was due as much to his ambition, statesmanlike qualities and leadership as to his second marriage. With Edward, Malcolm's heir by Margaret, also killed in the battle, it appears that Malcolm's brother Donald 'Ban' – the correct heir under traditional Scots laws – proceeded to drive out Malcolm's other younger sons and seized the throne. Traditionally the news of the disaster caused the already ill Margaret, probably in her late forties, to collapse and die at Edinburgh Castle on 16 November; she was canonised in 1250. Was she weakened by devout fasting?

Duncan, Malcolm's son by Ingebiorg, was still in England, and William II decided to impose him as his client-king and lent him an army. He deposed Donald 'Ban' in spring 1094, but was unable to drive him out of Scotland and was murdered by his adherent, the 'Mormaer' of the Mearns, in September 1094 – probably aged in his early thirties. Donald then resumed the throne. Duncan's son by Earl Cospatrick's daughter Uhtreda, William Fitz Duncan, remained loyal to his uncles, the sons of Malcolm III and St Margaret, and did not claim the Scottish throne. His family became lords of Egremont in Cumbria; that region had previously been ruled by his uncle Dolfin. But his eldest son Donald Mac William seized Moray in revolt against the hapless King William 'the Lion' in 1181 and was not caught and killed until 1187. Donald's sons rose in rebellion against William and his son Alexander II in 1212 and 1215.

Malcolm III's fourth son by Margaret, Edgar (born *c.* 1074), was the eventual victor of the dynastic struggles of the mid-1090s with Norman help. The eldest, Edward, had been killed with his father at Alnwick in November 1093 and the second, Edmund, survived the attack but joined his uncle Donald 'Ban' against his 'pro-English' siblings. He ruled Strathclyde as Donald's ally in 1094–95, and was dispossessed by William II. He was forced to become a monk at Montacute Abbey in Somerset, a safely long distance away from his homeland to hinder any attempt to return. It is presumed that he was Donald's choice as his heir. It is not clear what happened to the third son, Ethelred, who should have succeeded rather than Edgar in 1097; he may have been regarded as mentally or physically incapable of the hard tasks of ruling the turbulent kingdom or could have chosen not to challenge Edgar, as the latter had a Norman army to back him. One document refers to him as 'Mormaer' (a title being Anglicised in the early twelfth century as 'earl') of Fife, but there was another contemporary earl, Constantine.

The non-Scottish names of Malcolm III's elder sons by Margaret seem to have been taken from the latter's Anglo-Saxon genealogy, presumably by her. Their eldest son Edward was called after her father (Edward 'the Exile', d. 1057), the second was Edmund after her grandfather (Edmund 'Ironside', d. 1016), the third named Ethelred after her great-grandfather Ethelred 'Unraed' (d. 1016) and the fourth was called Edgar after her great-great-grandfather Edgar (d. 975). The fifth, Alexander, was possibly called after Pope Alexander

II, and the youngest, David, was presumably named for King David from the Old Testament.

David I and 'Anglicisation': The Early to Mid-Twelfth Century

It is uncertain to what extent Donald Ban's takeover in November 1093 represented a reaction against the Anglo-Norman cultural practices and Church organisation that Margaret had introduced since the 1070s. But Donald, who had the support of one of Malcolm's and Margaret's younger sons (Edmund), was swiftly deposed by Prince Duncan; he returned later in 1094 but in 1097 was deposed again by an Anglo-Norman army sent by William II on behalf of Margaret's other sons. The second-eldest of the latter, Edgar, was installed as king as a dependent English ally and was duly succeeded by his brothers Alexander (8 January 1107) and David (23 April 1124). Edgar attended the crown-wearing ceremony of his patron William II at Westminster for the inauguration of Westminster Hall in April 1098, carrying the king's crown in the procession like a regular 'feudal' vassal. He abandoned claims to authority over the Hebrides to the resurgent naval power of Norway by agreement with King Magnus 'Bareleg', a frequent voyager to the area, in 1098, showing the Anglicised rulers' concentration on Lowland affairs to the exclusion of the Highlands. But as Scotland lacked a fleet this was only recognising a *fait accompli*, though the abandonment of sovereignty over the dynastic burial-place of Iona was symbolic, and the power vacuum as Norway lost control in the mid-twelfth century was to be replaced by the local Viking-Gaelic dynasty of Somerled mac Gillebride, a minor ruler from Argyll. Cumbria was returned to the Scots prince David as a personal grant by Henry I in 1107. David was married off by Henry in 1113 to his kinswoman Matilda who was the daughter of William I's niece Judith by the late

Earl Waltheof (Siward's son), who had been executed for treason in 1075, making her heiress to Waltheof's estates in Huntingdonshire. She was known as Countess of Huntingdon, and was widow of the king's baronial henchman Simon de St Liz (Senlis), Earl of Northampton; thus David became stepfather to her son Waldef (Waltheof), later abbot of his monastic foundation of Melrose. Sometime after Alexander's accession, that king married Henry I's illegitimate daughter Sibyl, who remained childless and died at Loch Tay in 1122. He was a patron of the Church like David, founding one new abbey at Scone and another on the Firth of Forth island of Inchcolm (traditionally after his vessel was wrecked there in a storm while he was out fishing). But Alexander was not as obviously Anglo-Norman in his politico-religious orientation, and carried out at least one recorded campaign against the restless Gaelicised north of his realm with a raid into Moray after his court was attacked. He may have opposed Henry's insistence of the grant of the south-west to David, as there is poetic record of discord between the brothers, and delayed implementing it (possibly until 1113). In 1114 he had to attend Henry's campaign into Wales as a vassal, providing troops which he led in person. There may also have been a need to keep an eye on the activities of his potential challenger in south-west Scotland, 'Lord' Fergus of Galloway, who had been seeking separate links to King Henry. Alexander died in April 1124 aged around forty-eight, probably at Stirling.

David ruled as 'princeps Cumbrensis' until he assumed the throne in 1124, and indeed tried out most of his pioneering 'Continental' (or Anglo-Norman) reforms in that region before following up in 'Alba', north of the Forth. The partly Anglian population and close trade links with England may have been crucial in this. His first 'modern', Anglo-Norman-style monastic foundation was at Selkirk on the Borders (1113) and his first two incorporated trading 'burghs' (towns) were at Roxburgh, his main residence and a pioneering Norman-style castle, and Berwick-upon-Tweed. He also introduced Anglo-Norman 'feudal' lordship to his lands, with men given land by legal grant, confirmed by charters, in return for service in a hierarchy of command; this replaced the usual Scots inalienable inheritance and secured the king's grip on his 'tenants-in-chief' (and theirs over their own subordinates). Among David's first feudal lords were the famous families of De Brus (Bruce) of Annandale; Stewart (founded by Walter FitzAlan, son of the Breton Alan Fitz Flaald) which was granted the 'Strathgryfe' lordship around Renfrew; and De Morville of Cunningham. Most of the founders were sons of Anglo-Norman barons in England. He also 'Normanised' the Church with men and procedures from south of the Border, reviving the Bishopric of Glasgow in the manner of an Anglo-Norman bishopric and attending the inauguration of the new Norman-style cathedral in 1136. Once David became King of Scots he extended his reforms to his new kingdom and also created the first network of royal sheriffs (shire-reeves, an Anglo-Saxon office) across the nation as the king's local representatives in the new counties which replaced semi-autonomous local lordships. He also created the 'Justiciarship' at the head of the Anglicised royal administration and legal system.

David founded new abbeys at Holy Rood in Edinburgh (1128) and Melrose in the Borders (1136) and, according to Ailred of Rievaulx, created around five new bishoprics. The abbey of the Holy Rood housed a reputed relic of part of the True Cross, brought to Scotland by David's mother Margaret and possibly inherited from her mother Agatha (a relative of the German Holy Roman Emperor Henry III). A network of bishoprics covered the country in the English pattern and in the 1130s he even installed a first Normanised bishop, Andreas, in remote and Norse-influenced Caithness. Ailred praised his justice as well as his religious zeal, and his clear reliance on a Continental template for the political, administrative and religious development of his kingdom was eulogised by non-Scottish contemporaries but led to subsequent nationalist historians denouncing David for his lack of patriotism. To some modern historians he was a Europeanised ruler, raised largely abroad and hostile to native traditions, though the pendulum of historians' opinion has swung back in his favour in recent decades. He is seen now more as a strengthener of the monarchy using up-to-date tools and an admirer of the Carolingian imperial and holy monarchy rather than an alien anti-Celtic figure. He was certainly 'nationalist' in his struggle for an independent Scottish Church, not a tool of his brother-in-law Henry – though he had been willing to act as Henry's tool in the south in 1113–24. The Archbishopric of York, held by Thurstan, attempted to enforce its powers as the 'metropolitan' of northern Britain by asserting supremacy over the Scottish bishops; the new Bishop of St Andrews (Kilrymound), prior Robert of Scone, was refused consecration by Thurstan unless he submitted to the authority of York. He and David refused to give in, and David seems to have attempted to create St Andrews as an autonomous Archbishopric for his kingdom. Thurstan also refused consecration to the new Bishop John of Glasgow in 1125, and David sent John to Rome to be consecrated by the Pope; the threat of papal backing for a separate Scottish Church brought Thurstan to Rome to protest and try to block this. Robert was eventually consecrated by Thurstan, without any submission; in 1151–52 David returned to the question of a new archbishopric for St Andrews and pressurised the visiting papal legate, Cardinal John Paparo, about it without effect.

David's main challenger – Malcolm, the illegitimate son of his late brother Alexander – attacked him within weeks of his accession and was defeated in two battles according to Orderic Vitalis. In 1130 Malcolm invaded again with a Gaelic northern army supplied by the current Earl ('Mormaer') of Moray, Angus, principal lord in the North and probably a descendant of the old royal house of Moray as grandson to Lulach. This was probably during David's absence in England, where the king attended an important trial at Woodstock in Oxfordshire as one of Henry's main vassals, and utilised criticism of David's lack of interest in the North. Malcolm and Angus were defeated and the latter killed on 16 April 1130 at Stracathro near Brechin, where around 4,000 rebels and 1,000 of the king's troops fell; the royal commander was an Englishman – Edward Fitz Siward, David's constable. By 1135 Malcolm was a royal prisoner at Roxburgh Castle; Moray was overrun by the royal army and a new earl was appointed, probably David's nephew William Fitz Duncan (who died in 1147). After this show of royal military strength David showed more interest in the North, and in 1139 was able to impose his own, half-Scottish Earl of Caithness and Jarl of Orkney – the underage Harald (later 'the Old') Maddadson. He only appears to have actually visited the North himself in 1150, when he founded Kinloss Abbey in person, and when he paid a visit to Aberdeen in 1150 or 1151.

David's work enabled Scotland to take its place among the mainstream of European nations and its representatives to deal easily with Continental kingdoms and the Papacy. He was later canonised. His marriage to Countess Matilda/Maud of Huntingdon (and Northampton by marriage) brought David's heirs English estates. This was mainly the 'Honour of Huntingdon' in the East Midlands, which passed to their son Prince Henry on Queen Matilda's death in 1130, and they also acquired a stake in the southern kingdom as barons. But there was a problem over the Scottish king having to do homage to the English king for these lands, which were given to a younger member of the royal family, not to the king, to avoid this humiliation, whenever possible.

The new 'Anglo-Norman' atmosphere of the Lowlands did not extend into the still 'Celtic' lordships of the North beyond the 'Highland Line' – or to isolated Galloway which had been partly settled by Vikings and politically dependant on Man in the eleventh century. Fergus (r. *c.* 1120–61), first known 'unifying' Lord of Galloway and apparently son-in-law of Henry I, was more of a Gaelic-Norse warlord like Somerled of the Isles than a mainland Anglo-Normanised baron, despite his uneasy fealty to David, and still claimed a kingly title. He may have been brought up at Henry I's court in the 1100s and met David as well as his future wife there, but if Henry intended him to be an English rather than a Scottish royal client this backfired. He was, however, open to Anglicising religious influences as David was, refounding the abbey and bishopric of Whithorn (site of the first Christian monastery in Scotland *c*. 400) around 1125. He also founded Dundrennan Abbey (1142), where his dynasty was to be buried. However, when he was forced into a monastery by his overlord King Malcolm IV in 1160 and replaced by his sons, Uchtred (East Galloway?) and Gillebride (West Galloway?), he chose Holyrood.

Taking advantage of the chaos in England from 1135 as his nephew and niece, Stephen and Matilda (children of his sisters, Countess Mary of Boulogne and Queen Edith/ Matilda of England), fought over the throne, King David tried to extend his borders further south from the Tweed and Cumbria to the Tees. Having been among the barons to swear allegiance to the queen's daughter, widowed Empress Matilda, as Henry's heir in 1127, he forced Stephen to grant him Northumberland as his price for recognising him – as a personal fief for his family within England, not as a part of Scotland, and excluding Newcastle, Bamburgh and the Palatinate of Durham. Northumberland was then turned into an earldom for his son Henry. David's attempt to swallow up more of Northern England as Matilda invaded England in 1138 involved a large and reportedly unruly army, including Islemen from the Hebrides whose victims accused them of assorted atrocities on the local countrymen. David's army roused patriotic resistance and was defeated by the local barons under Archbishop Thrustan at the celebrated Battle of the Standard near Northallerton, and he accepted peace with Stephen in 1139; Prince Henry did homage to the English king for Northumberland and married an English bride, Ada de

Warenne (*c.* 1120–78), sister of Stephen's loyalist Earl William de Warenne of Surrey.

In 1141 David ventured south to Winchester to assist Matilda's brief takeover of the whole kingdom after her army captured Stephen at the Battle of Lincoln. He arrived to find that Matilda had been driven out of London by a rebellion, losing her chance of coronation, and was besieging her cousin, Stephen's brother Bishop Henry of Winchester, in his palace in that city. David joined in, but had to retreat as Stephen's wife (the other Matilda) arrived with an army. He was nearly captured in the defeat of the empress's retreating forces during an ambush at Stockbridge, and fled. In 1149 he secured the agreement of Matilda's son Henry (II) to the annexation of Northumberland and Cumberland by his family when the teenage prince visited his court at Carlisle. David reaffirmed his backing for Matilda and Henry and knighted the prince, and in 1153 Stephen was forced to accept the latter as his heir. Henry succeeded to England in 1154, but went back on his agreement with David once he was militarily strong enough to resist the Scots claim (1157).

David's Descendants after 1153

Malcolm IV

Unfortunately David's son Henry died before him on 12 July 1152. David's eldest grandson Malcolm (IV), born in 1141, replaced him as heir, but was likely to succeed underage so David appointed Earl/'Mormaer' Duncan/Donnchad of Fife to become regent. David died at Carlisle on 24 May 1153, aged around sixty-nine, having firmly placed Scotland in a Western European orientation. Malcolm came to the Scots throne at the age of twelve – the 'Orkneyinga Saga' claims that there was great popular support for his rival William FitzDuncan's son, another William and also underage, to rule instead. His regent Donnchad died within a year, and the new regime was threatened by the support of the rising new naval Hebridean power of the Gaelic-Viking warlord Jarl Somerled, first 'Lord of the Isles'. Probable heir to a Gaelic lordship in Argyll with claims on the Inner Hebrides and rapidly expanding across the western seaways ready to challenge his neighbours, Somerled had claims on Kintyre and the islands of the Firth of Clyde, and a weak Scotland was to his advantage. Whether he had a cultural 'Gaelic' allegiance and so opposed David and Malcolm as 'Anglicisers' is more problematic. In 1153–54 he backed the claims of a pretender – the now-adult son of Malcolm's imprisoned uncle, 1124 and 1130 rebel Malcolm mac Alexander, or else an obscure Malcolm 'Mac Heth' – to the throne; one or other of these married Somerled's sister. However the threat passed; in 1157 Malcolm Mac Heth was pardoned and was probably given the Earldom of Ross. This would suggest that he was closely related to the late rebel 'Mormaer' Angus, and so to King Lulach of the Moray line. Luckily Scotland's potential Northern challenger, Jarl Rognvald of Orkney (co-ruler with Harald 'the Old'), was a foe of Somerled so the two were unlikely to combine, and in the mid–late 1150s he was away on Crusade.

Cumbria and Northumberland were granted to the new king's younger brother William as of 1152/3, but Henry II refused to accept this and handed Cumbria to Malcolm himself as his vassal; they were both forcibly retaken by Henry in 1157. Malcolm was to be noted for his vigour and martial enthusiasm by contemporaries, within a European rather than a 'Celtic' context, given his knightly enthusiasms, though his nickname 'The Maiden' (he remained unmarried) was interpreted in later centuries as implying effeminacy. He had to do homage to Henry II for Cumbria and for the Earldom of Huntingdon, and his failure to challenge Henry's 'land-grab' of 1157 was followed by a 'summit' between the two in 1158 when Malcolm appears to have been refused his requested dubbing as a knight by his neighbour and overlord. In 1159, however, he meekly obeyed Henry's summons to join his army for their attack on Toulouse in southern France (as vassal earl or as vassal king?). His brothers William and David accompanied him. He was using the expedition to gain invaluable military experience and was knighted, but in his absence there was a major conspiracy – plausibly he was regarded as too obedient to Henry. In 1160, returning home, he was attacked and besieged in Perth by six rebel earls/'mormaers', led by Earl Ferchar of Strathearn. He drove them off and peace was restored with the Church mediating, but it clearly signified major discontent.

Malcolm restored his reputation with at least one and possibly three major campaigns in 1160 against his most powerful Southern Scots vassal, Fergus of Galloway. Not definitively linked to the attack on the king at Perth but a threat due to his autonomy and large manpower, Fergus was eventually overwhelmed and forced to abdicate and become a monk; his sons Gille Bride (elder but probably illegitimate by Catholic canon law) and Uhtred divided Galloway between them. Malcolm's triumph was probably undermined by declining health, as he was seriously ill in 1163 and apparently suffered from pains in his head and legs – it has been suggested that if the epithet 'Canmore' ('Great head') referred to him not to Malcolm III, it implies an unusually large head and so to Paget's Disease. His concern for good works, charity and the Church in the early 1160s may reflect an awareness of his physical decline, and he founded the abbey of Coupar Angus in 1164.

Around 1163 another revolt against Malcolm followed, this time during his absence in England when he was lying ill at Doncaster and involving the men of Moray. During this stay in England he did homage to Henry at his court at Woodstock, along with assorted Welsh princes, and was required to leave his youngest brother David behind when he returned home as a hostage for his good behaviour; David was to stay in England until 1175 and to become thoroughly Anglicised in his choice of residence and baronial friendships.

On Malcom's return he reportedly ravaged the province and deported large numbers of its inhabitants, probably increasing Anglicisation and royal control. His final challenge came in 1164 from Somerled, who was attempting to seize control of Bute and Rothesay in the Firth of Clyde and was in dispute with the local royal 'strongman', Walter Stewart the Lord of Renfrew. Malcolm backed Walter up and Somerled retaliated by supporting the claim of the king's cousin – William, the son of William Fitz Duncan – to the Scots throne. Whether this implied a serious threat or was just a tactic for intimidation, Somerled invaded the mainland with an army in reportedly 160 ships. The great commander marched on Malcolm's army at Renfrew, but was attacked en route by the royal force commanded by Walter FitzAlan and the Bishop of Glasgow. The events of this Battle of Renfrew (in April 1164?) are unclear, but Somerled's men had the worst of it and he was either mortally wounded by a javelin in the leg during the battle or was treacherously attacked and cut down during a ceasefire. His sons took the fleet home and the threat ended.

William I, 1165–1214

Malcolm died on 9 December 1165, aged twenty-four. It is probable that his brother and successor William 'the Lion' (called this by later writers from his banner, not due to personal qualities) was even more 'Europeanised' and less interested in Gaelic Scotland than his predecessor; he had been on the Toulouse expedition in 1159, was known for his knightly prowess, and seems to have been highly concerned to have his confiscated Earldom of Northumberland within England returned. By contrast his early reign saw minimal action to assert his power within Scotland. He was often referred to in contemporary Anglo-French chronicles as 'De Warenne', i.e. as one of his mother's rather than his father's family – was this how he saw himself? In 1166 he went to Henry's court in a vain effort to have Northumberland returned, and appears to have approached Henry's rival Louis VII of France for help in 1168 in retaliation for Henry's stonewalling, allegedly causing the English king to roll on the floor in a rage when he found this out. He did homage to Henry's son the 'Young King' at the latter's Coronation in 1170, and probably formed a personal friendship with him given his decision to support him when he rebelled in 1173. He was seeking the reconquest of Northumberland and Cumbria again; the two counties and lands in Cambridgeshire (for the Earldom of Huntingdon) had been promised him by the 'Young King'. He gave Henry II a final warning to return 'his' lands or face withdrawal of his allegiance, and was ignored. His brother David was currently in England, and aided the rebels in the Midlands through 1173–74. However, William was a poor general and his 1173 invasion petered out with unsuccessful attacks on Warkworth Castle, Alnwick Castle, Newcastle and Prudhoe, after which he moved west to attack Carlisle. He had to give up and return to Roxburgh as Henry sent loyal troops north, and Henry's senior adviser and 'Justiciar' Ranulf de Glanville sacked Berwick in reprisal; a truce was arranged until March 1174. In spring 1174 he returned to the attack with reportedly up to 80,000 men (probably an exaggeration), failed to take Prudhoe again and split his army into three sections to head north and attack Alnwick Castle, principal stronghold of the royal loyalist Percy family. Earl Duncan of Fife's contingent was absent, sacking Warkworth when Ranulf de Glanville arrived after a hasty overnight ride on 13/14 July 1174. A poor general, William was ambushed and captured in thick fog by Glanville's men on the 14th outside Alnwick Castle; his men fled and he was taken off to Newcastle with his feet tied beneath his horse's belly like a common captive.

Deported to Falaise in Normandy as a prisoner, the humiliated king had to buy his freedom and become Henry's vassal – definitively as King of Scots not as an English earl – in the Treaty of Falaise (December 1174). He was thus fitted into the neat administrative framework of the so-called 'Angevin Empire', as one of the 'second-ranking' tier of subordinate rulers to the royal house of England, Normandy and Anjou – with the princes of Wales and kings of Ireland. He also had to hand over the main castles of Southern Scotland – Edinburgh, Stirling, Roxburgh, Jedburgh and Berwick – to English garrisons. Henry confiscated his Earldom of Huntingdon, which was handed to David I's stepson Simon de Senlis but was returned to William's brother David when Simon died. He returned to Scotland humiliated in February 1175 to face rebellion. His ally Uhtred the co-ruler of Galloway was attacked, blinded and castrated (to make him ineligible to rule), and later murdered by the men of his half-brother Gillebride who then offered to transfer his allegiance to Henry and thus lose Galloway to Scotland. Luckily Henry II's envoys to Galloway (including the chronicler Roger Hoveden) were so disgusted at their discovery of the way that Henry's ally Uhtred had been dealt with that when they reported it to Henry he rejected Gillebride's offer.

William's humiliation continued for the rest of Henry's reign, as he was kept under strict ties of feudal vassalage. In June 1175 he did homage to Henry at York to confirm the terms of the Treaty of Falaise, explicitly for Scotland; and once this precedent had been set the English kings would keep returning to enforce it. He even had his bride – Ermengarde de Beaumont, daughter of Viscount Richard of Beaumont-le-Vicomte (a middle-ranking Norman baron) and an illegitimate daughter of Henry I – selected for him by his overlord the king. He married Ermengarde at Woodstock in Oxfordshire on 5 September 1186, but they did not have a son (Alexander) until 24 August 1198; if a daughter succeeded, her marriage legally needed the permission of her father's overlord. The Scots royal family were now operating within the family and social circles of the senior Anglo-Norman nobility. William's illegitimate daughters were, however, married to senior southern Scots nobles – Isabella to Robert de Brus (II), Lord of Annandale, in 1183 and another daughter to Patrick, Earl of Dunbar, in 1185. William's brother and presumed heir David, Earl of Huntingdon, also married an Englishwoman, Matilda of Chester, in August 1190, as chosen by his patron Richard I.

William was able to reassert his military power in the North, campaigning with his brother David in Easter Ross in 1179 to build new castles at Redcastle and Dunskeath and restrict the local power of the jarls of Orkney to Caithness. David was installed as Lord of Garioch and Strathearn to build up royal power in the central Highlands. A more confident William also took on the power of Pope Alexander III in protection of his 'rights' to nominate bishops, an ironic imitation of his nemesis Henry II. When Bishop Richard of St Andrews died in 1178, William refused to accept the cathedral monks' election of their own candidate, John, and nominated his chaplain Hugh; the two sides eventually accepted papal mediation and in 1180 a legate, Alexius, came to hold a Church Council at Holyrood but backed John. William refused to accept it and sent John into exile, for which the Pope placed Scotland under an Interdict which prevented the clergy from carrying out any functions. The image of a 'nationalist' king defying the Papacy was presumably useful to restore William's prestige, the Pope's wrath being less dangerous than King Henry's. The Interdict was lifted by the next Pope, Lucius III, in 1182.

In 1181 the latest challenger from the line of Malcolm III's eldest son Duncan, Donald Mac William, seized control of the Earldom of Ross and defied the king. Possibly involved with the 1179 troubles and claiming Ross as the heir of William Fitz Duncan who had been earl in the 1130s, he could not be removed by the evidently weak Royal army and held on to Inverness until his death in 1187. Earlier that year a royal military expedition defeated him at the Battle of 'Mam Garvia' (near Dingwall?) but failed to dislodge him. However, William did have more success in the south-west. Unreliable Gillebride of Galloway died in 1185 and his young sons, led by Donald (a former hostage in England and so a protégé of Henry II), were driven out by their uncle Lochlann/Roland, a friend of William's. Henry angrily told William when he next visited his court to remove Lochlann but he failed to act so the English king brought his army to Carlisle ready to invade Galloway. Luckily Henry had other, Continental priorities and accepted Lochlann's politic submission, and William escorted Lochlann to Carlisle in July 1186 to meet Henry. William and Henry confirmed him as lord (this was in itself an interference in Scottish affairs).

Henry died during a revolt by his eldest surviving son Richard in July 1189, and the latter had the Third Crusade as his priority. Richard was desperately raising money to fund his army; accordingly William was able to pay him 10,000 marks to cancel the Treaty of Falaise. He was released from his vassalage and the Scottish castles were returned to him. Richard was absent from England until 1194 and William resumed effective independence. He loyally refused to aid the machinations of Richard's brother John to seize the throne after Richard was captured en route home from the Crusade and imprisoned by Emperor Henry VI, and contributed to Richard's ransom. He turned up at the king's court when he returned home after the money had been paid to help him defeat John's revolt, a campaign in which Earl David also assisted. But William seems to have been more concerned about the return of his beloved Earldom of Northumberland, and he asked Richard for it to be told that he could have the lands without their strategically vital castles which the Bishop of Durham would retain. On 17 April he carried one of the three swords of state at Richard's crown-wearing ceremony at Winchester, and David went to Normandy in 1196–97 to aid Richard against King Philip II of France.

In the meantime, the mid–late 1190s saw several campaigns by William in Ross, Sutherland and Caithness to build up royal power in the far north and diminish that of the jarls of Orkney, with new castles being founded and lands granted to loyal vassals on condition of military service. Probably the king's illness in 1195 had emboldened the autonomist endeavours of long-serving Jarl Harald 'the Old', and the latter's recent marriage to a MacHeth lady, Hvarflod, would have implied a threat to the Scots dynasty as well as possible claims on Ross or Moray. In 1196 Harald's son Thorfinn invaded the mainland, aided by an unknown magnate called Ruari, and fought a battle in Caithness with royal troops. In 1197 William marched into Caithness with the first royal army ever seen that far north, and forced Jarl Harald to come to him at Nairn to surrender. Harald was held hostage until his son Thorfinn surrendered and took his place; he also gave part of Caithness to Harald's pro-Scottish dynastic rival, Harald 'the Young', grandson of Harald's late rival co-ruler Rognvald 'Kali'. After the elder Harald killed the younger and reunited the jarldom in 1198, William seems to have used another Hebridean rival, Rognvald of Man, against him. A subsequent revolt against the king in 1201 saw Harald seizing castles in Caithness and arresting and mutilating Bishop John of Caithness, a royal nominee, for stirring up the king against him. This led to Thorfinn's fatal blinding by the angry king and another major royal campaign in 1202. This time the Orkney principality explicitly and permanently accepted a Scots presence in Caithness, and Harald submitted to the royal army and handed over a quarter of the revenues of Caithness to the king. William had also secured the bonus of papal recognition of the full independence of the Scots Church from the Archbishopric of York in the bull 'Cum Universi' in March 1192, halting English ecclesiastical claims.

Richard's sudden death during a minor siege in April 1199 saw the surprise exclusion of Arthur of Brittany, the son of his next, deceased brother Geoffrey, as his youngest brother John seized the English throne. William attempted to play the two off against each other; John prevailed and on 21 November 1200 William did homage to John at Lincoln. After Arthur's death the angry French King Philip II invaded and retook almost all of John's French lands (1204), and as a result John was driven back on his British mainland and Irish resources. He was keen to resume the role of overlord of Scotland,

Wales, and Ireland and William's position came under threat again. In 1208 John built a new castle at Tweedmouth on the border without consulting William, who retaliated by sending men to pull it down – an insult that John would not tolerate. John threatened to invade Scotland if William did not turn up for a 'summit', probably requiring his aid against the plotting English barons. William refused and gathered an army at Roxburgh but fell ill, which postponed a confrontation. The two kings' armies faced each other across the Tweed near Norham, neither daring to make the first move. A prolonged stalemate ended on 9 August with the 'Treaty of Norham' whereby William renounced his claims to Cumberland and Northumberland and paid John 15,000 marks. He was required to hand his two elder daughters, Margaret and Isabella, over as hostages for his good behaviour; they were installed in the ultra-secure Corfe Castle in Dorset and John later found them husbands. William's son and heir, Alexander, was promised Cumberland and Northumberland when he was adult, but only as an ordinary English earl. When the treaty was renewed in 1212 John formally promised the hand of his daughter Joan to Alexander, who spent some months in England as an effective hostage at John's requirement. William was too old to take advantage of the threat John was under from the Papacy in 1213, France in 1213–14 and rebellious barons in 1215, but the abortive settlement between John and the barons of 'Magna Carta' promised justice for his claims on English lands and suitable marriages for his two elder daughters (which John was supposed to have arranged by now). In August 1214 William made a final journey north to Elgin, to meet the new Earl John of Caithness – a threat as he had MacHeth blood – and to take his daughter into custody as hostage for his good behaviour. He died on 4 December 1214 at Stirling, probably seventy-one. His later years had seen a restoration of royal power within Scotland after the humiliations of the mid-1170s, at least as long as a direct confrontation with England was avoided, and William's poor reputation was partly due to circumstances in England beyond his control – when a Scots king faced a weaker English ruler, as David did with Stephen or Alexander II did with Henry III, they could appear more independent. He was to be called 'The Lion of Justice' by the fourteenth-century historian John of Fordoun. But William's early concentration on the southern not the northern part of his realm was arguably a serious miscalculation.

Alexander II, 1214–49

Alexander II was crowned at Scone on 6 December 1214, aged sixteen. John was distracted by the major rebellion that followed his attempt to retract his agreement to 'Magna Carta', and as the husband of his niece Blanche, Prince Louis of France, was offered the English throne by the rebels the new Scots king was put in a highly advantageous position. But first he faced another attempt to drive the 'Anglicised' line of Malcolm III and St Margaret from the throne, as the Mac Heths linked up with the Mac Williams in the far north – a dangerous combination. Cinaed Mac Heth and Domnhall/Donald Mac William invaded Ross in 1215, but were defeated and killed by the local loyalist 'strongman' Ferchar (Mac Taggart?), future Mormaer/Earl of Ross. Joining the rebel league against John, Alexander invaded Northumberland, took Norham Castle on 19 October 1215 and sacked Berwick. The rebels offered him Northumberland, Cumberland and Westmorland, but John led an army swiftly north and sacked Newcastle. Boasting that he would 'drive the fox-cub from his earth', John took Berwick in January 1216 and marched as far as Haddington in Lothian before his dire position in the South forced him to retreat. Alexander chased him as far as Richmond in Yorkshire, and then led his army south to aid rebel barons and Prince Louis. In September 1216 Alexander and his army arrived at the rebel siege of Dover Castle after a remarkable foray across a chaotic England, and Alexander did homage to Louis as rightful King of England.

The infuriated John died weeks later and, with him gone, many affronted barons had second thoughts about backing the French against John's uncontentious nine-year-old son Henry III; the pendulum swung back to the royal cause and in 1217 the rebels suffered major defeats at the hands of the regent, William Marshal. Louis agreed a treaty with Henry's ministers, and abandoned his claim and went home. Alexander held out but Scotland was placed under an Interdict again by the papal mediator, Legate Gaula, and he had to come to terms. On 1 December he surrendered Carlisle to the English in return for the Interdict being lifted, and the Scots recognised Henry as rightful King of England. Alexander did homage to Henry for his English lands of Huntingdon and Tynedale at Northampton. On 18 or 25 June 1221 Alexander married Henry's sister Joan at York Minster, and his eldest sister Margaret was then married to Henry's chief minister Hubert de Burgh, successful defender of Dover Castle against Alexander and Louis in 1216.

However, Alexander's marriage was to be childless and, as annulling it would probably cause war with England, the realm remained without a clear heir for decades. Alexander had only sisters, married off to English nobles; the original plan of 1221 was for Henry III to marry the youngest, Margaret, himself but instead she was married to the leading Marcher baron Gilbert Marshal, Earl of Pembroke and son of the ex-regent, in an effort to bind him to the royal cause. Alexander's uncle Earl David (d. 1219) had a son, John, who succeeded his mother's kinsman Earl Ranulf as Earl of Chester and was married to the daughter of Prince Llywelyn of Gwynedd but died young on 6 June 1237. After John came the claims of his sisters: Margaret (married to Alan, Lord of Galloway), Ada (married to Henry de Hastings) and Isabella (married to Robert de Brus/Bruce, 4th Lord of Annandale). The question of which of these sisters' descendants was rightful heir to Scotland was to overshadow Anglo-Scottish politics for a century; but for the moment Queen Joan's death on 4 March 1238 (in England, in Essex) enabled Alexander to remarry. On 15 May 1239 he married Marie de Coucy, of a minor North French comital dynasty, at Roxburgh despite English objections; they had a son, Alexander, born at Roxburgh on 4 September 1241.

Alexander resumed his father's sporadic attempts to overawe his restive, great territorial nobles, suppressing a rebellion in Argyll in 1222. He certainly showed more interest in the Hebrides than his father had done, though as yet to no major effect given Norwegian control of its local lords. He was also overshadowed in his south-western lands by 'Lord' Alan of Galloway (r. 1200–34) who in practice had more men under his command than the king did and only had a sketchy allegiance to him. In 1228 Alan was able to intervene in the long-running dynastic dispute over rule of the Isle of Man and its Hebridean island territories between the sons of King Godred (d. 1187), the illegitimate but older Ragnald and the legitimate but younger Olaf. Olaf, born in 1177, had been forced to accept rule of the Northern Hebrides alone by his sibling in 1187 and been deposed and handed over to King William of Scots as a hostage in 1207; he remained in this status until William's death but was released by Alexander II and left for the Fifth Crusade. Olaf succeeded in invading Man and forcing his brother to accept him as co-ruler in 1226, but during his absence in 1228 Ragnald secured Alan of Galloway's aid to seize full control. Alan imposed his own officials in Man as co-ruler, thus starting to create his own seaborne mini-state without reference to King Alexander, but his men were driven out and Ragnald was killed in February 1230 when Olaf returned. Alan of Galloway died in 1234 without a legitimate son, and his vast estates were divided between his daughters' families by order of Alexander as his overlord; the Anglo-Norman Balliols and Comyns had the greatest share. Alan's adult but illegitimate son Thomas, who would have normally succeeded under the looser Gaelic inheritance laws, was excluded and led a major rebellion in 1235, ravaging the king's lands. Alexander invaded but faced difficulties in unfamiliar and hostile country and had to be rescued by Earl Ferchar of Ross. After Thomas was overwhelmed, Galloway was divided between the king's candidates, all loyal Anglo-Norman barons, and in effect joined the 'mainstream' feudalised world of Southern Scotland. Walter Comyn, a major landholder in Buchan and the leader of a baronial faction at Alexander's court opposed to the Earls of Dunbar, became governor of Galloway.

In 1237 Alexander tried to reclaim Cumberland and Northumberland from Henry III, whose relations with him had been soured by the king marrying Eleanor of Provence, not Alexander's sister Margaret, and in reply the English king demanded homage from him. Armies were raised, but a compromise was reached between negotiators at the 'Treaty of York' which settled the borders permanently at the River Tweed in the East and the Solway Firth in the West. The border became what it has remained (with minor adjustments) for over 770 years. An uneasy peace at Newcastle in 1244 ended subsequent tensions and held as Henry turned his attention to regaining lost border lands in Wales; and Alexander turned his attention to the long-neglected west of Scotland.

The north-western islands of the Inner and Outer Hebrides had remained under their own lords or the Kingdom of Norway, with Edgar abandoning claims to the area to Norway (1098). After the 1164 invasion of Renfrew there was no major Scots involvement in the Hebrides until the end of Alexander II's reign. The latter tried to persuade Ewen Mac Dougall, Lord of Lorne and descendant of Somerled's son Dugald, to transfer his 1248 oath of loyalty to the King of Norway, Haakon IV, to him instead. On Ewen's return from Norway he was summoned to meet Alexander, and was probably at this point extending his largely mainland, Lorne domains onto the Inner Hebridean islands as Haakon's local viceroy after the recent drowning of his rival Jarl Harald of Orkney. Ewen met Alexander as ordered but refused to abandon his oath to Haakon, and Alexander raised an army and fleet. He sailed round Kintyre to the Inner Hebrides in summer 1249 – the first known Scots royal expedition there – to 'show the flag' of the Scots monarchy and force Ewen to submit, but died on 6 July 1249 on the island of Kerrera (off Mull) en route to attack Lorne. According to legend he was 'warned off' his campaign by a trio of Hebridean protector saints, led by St Columba, in a dream but ignored them. He was fifty; his son Alexander III succeeded aged seven. Alexander II had been a far more successful ruler than his father, though he had been luckier in facing a weaker King of England, and if he had not died suddenly he would probably have added the Inner Hebrides to his dominions.

Alexander III, 1249–86

Alexander III's long regency through the 1250s was dominated by two rival great nobles. One, Alan 'Durward' (the 'Doorward'/'Hostarius' or 'Usher' of the royal Household, a hereditary post in charge of the latter, which his father Thomas had held before him), was the paternal grandson of Gillechrist, Earl of Mar, and maternal grandson of Earl/ Mormaer Malcolm of Atholl, and had claimed the Earldom of Atholl in the 1230s; he was 'Justiciar of Scotia' (chief legal official and head of the government administrative machinery) with Earl Alexander Comyn of Buchan in 1244–51. The other regent, with whom he clashed sporadically, was another of the increasingly powerful Comyns, now powerful in both Buchan and Galloway – Walter Comyn (d. 1258), Lord of Badenoch and husband of Countess Isabella of Menteith. Their bickering rule lasted until Alexander's majority in 1262. Durward, as husband to an illegitimate daughter of Alexander II, was open to charges that his attempt to have the Pope legitimise her implied ambitions on the throne, which the Comyns exploited. He attempted to secure political leeway over his new king by proposing that he should be the man to knight him at his Coronation, but Comyn led alarmed nobles in vetoing this. Durward nevertheless became senior on the regency council. The uneasy alliance with England continued and was cemented by the king's marriage to Henry

III's daughter Margaret (1240–75), which took place on 26 December 1251 at a grand ceremony at York Minster; the previous day Henry had knighted his fellow sovereign. The sumptuous festivities were spoilt by an unsuccessful attempt by Henry to bully Alexander into doing homage for his kingdom of Scotland; he politely but firmly only did it for his English lands. Margaret gave Alexander three children – Margaret (February 1261–1283), whose marriage treaty with King Erik II of Norway at Roxburgh in July 1281 crucially provided for their heirs to succeed to Scotland; Alexander (21 January 1263–28 January 1283), born at Jedburgh; and David (20 March 1272–June 1281).

Once he had attained his majority Alexander returned to his father's attempt to wrest back the overlordship of the Hebrides from Norway, and in 1261 sent an embassy to King Haakon IV, 'the Good', of Norway demanding the cancellation of the treaty between King Edgar and King Magnus 'Bareleg' of 1098. He offered to pay for the redemption of the islands, but Haakon refused. The Scots were even arrested and not allowed to leave the Norwegian court for trying to depart without permission. So Alexander launched a major expedition to regain control of the Hebrides and sent the Earl of Ross to invade Skye in 1262. This challenge caused Haakon to raise a huge fleet of possibly 120 ships, reputedly the largest ever seen in the region, and to sail via Orkney to the Outer and then the Inner Hebrides in summer 1263 to force the submission of the local lords. The size of the Norwegian expedition forced compliance from most, apart from Ewen Mac Dougall of Lorne who evaded battle. Haakon then moved on round the Mull of Kintyre, like Somerled had done in 1164, to attack the islands of the Firth of Clyde.

This expedition ended with a confused battle with the Scots on the beach at Largs in Ayrshire – not a 'full-on' invasion of mainland Scotland, but a temporary landing to retrieve ships driven ashore at Largs in a westerly storm after being blown from their moorings off the island of Great Cumbrae on the night of 30 September/1 October. The Norse landed men to refloat the ships on 1 October, and local Scots levies attacked them; this was probably a series of limited skirmishes. On the 2nd, the local Scots plus a section of Alexander's army (based at Ayr), probably led by the hereditary 'Steward' Alexander Stewart of Dundonald, attacked the Norwegian salvage work in a pitched battle. The Scots apparently had the advantage of around 200 mailed horses and could launch a cavalry attack across the beach. One part of the Norwegian force, around 200 men under Ogmund 'Crows' Dance', set up a position on a nearby hillock, and were forced back onto the beach; their retreat was seen as a defeat by some of the main Norwegian force, around 700–800 men on the beach led by King Haakon, and panic spread. The Scots chased the Norwegians back to their ships, but Norwegian reinforcements landed and retook the hillock. As part of Haakon's fleet had sailed off to raid the Lennox coast, he was unable to bring his full force to bear, and on 3 October the ships were refloated safely and the Norwegians left; in effect the battle was a draw. But the Norwegians returned to the Outer Hebrides and thence Orkney without further clashes with the Scots, and on 15 December 1263 Haakon died at the Bishop's Palace at Kirkwall. Thus in retrospect the expedition was seen as the 'swan-song' of the Viking/Norse presence in the Hebrides, and the revival of Scots control over the area followed. In 1264 Alexander sent Alan Durward and the earls of Buchan and Mar to ravage the nearer Hebridean islands and punish those chiefs who had taken Haakon's side in 1263, and most seem to have submitted and become his vassals. He also assembled a fleet to invade the Isle of Man, Norway's most southern vassal and formerly part of Somerled's 'empire', but King Magnus hastily sent envoys to sue for peace and came to Dumfries to do homage to Alexander. He transferred his vassalage from Norway to Scotland and agreed to supply warships to Alexander's fleet, and when he died in 1265 a Scottish expedition took over the island. From now on royal 'baillis' ruled Man as a Scottish dependency.

Haakon's son, Magnus IV, agreed to talks with Alexander. Eventually talks succeeded, and Alexander was able to secure nominal control over the Hebrides in the resulting 'Treaty of Perth' on 2 July 1266. Norway relinquished its claims to the Hebrides and Man in return for a Scots payment, and the princes of Somerled's family were transferred to vassalage to Scotland but were given immunity for past defiance. From this date Scots control existed over all the region except for the Jarldom of Orkney, and in 1281 Alexander married his sole daughter Margaret to King Erik II of Norway, overlord of Orkney.

Alexander offered military support to Henry against the rebel baronial faction led by Simon de Montfort, Earl of Leicester, who defeated the king and his son Edward at Lewes in 1264 and forcibly imposed political reforms under their control. The prince escaped and joined in a Welsh Marches rebellion, and de Montfort was defeated and killed at Evesham in August 1265 without any need for the Scots to intervene. The civil war, not ended until 1267, and the resulting weakness of royal government as Henry aged and Edward departed on Crusade was ended with the latter's return as King Edward I in 1274. As vigorous and determined in asserting his rights by legal manoeuvre and brute force as Henry II or John, Edward was to prove as catastrophic a neighbour for Scotland as for the Welsh principality. For the moment, an uneasy peace was kept and Alexander attended Edward's Coronation in August 1274. On 28 October 1278 he did homage to Edward, but only for his English lands – no doubt to the latter's annoyance.

The Scots kingdom's security was seriously imperilled when the direct royal line unexpectedly died out. Alexander III survived both his two sons and his daughter, who all died in 1281–83. The only direct heir he now had was his daughter's daughter, Princess Margaret of Norway, born early in 1283. His first wife, Margaret of England, had died on 26 February 1275, and his second marriage, to secure further heirs, followed his children's deaths; he was only in his early forties and his father and grandfather had not had sons until they were older so the problem was not unprecedented. On 15 October 1285 he married Yolande of Dreux (1263–1330), daughter of Count Robert of Dreux (a cadet of the French royal family) and of Countess Beatrice of Montfort l'Amaury, at Jedburgh Abbey. Later legend had it that the marriage feast saw a vivid portent of doom appear to the prophet Thomas 'the Rhymer' of Ercildoune (Earlston near Jedburgh), a local poet of subsequent mythical stature who was probably the author of the first Scots translation of 'Tristan and Iseult' and was later supposed to have been abducted to the Otherwold for seven years by the 'Queen of Elfland' on the Eildon Hills. Yolande quickly became pregnant, but this was followed by Alexander's sudden death at the age of only forty-five on the night of 18/19 March 1286. In an avoidable accident his horse threw him at Kinghorn beach, Fife, in the dark while he was travelling from a council meeting at Edinburgh Castle to his new wife's residence there to celebrate her birthday next day. As his wife probably miscarried, the subsequent meeting of Parliament on 2 or 28 April elected Margaret 'the Maid of Norway', his late daughter Margaret's daughter by Erik of Norway, as queen under a regency, aged three and named by Alexander as heir in 1284. Alexander's long and mostly peaceful reign compared to the disasters that followed gave it a golden glow to subsequent chroniclers, as it could be seen as a halcyon time before chaos and conquest. In that, it acquired a mythical quality like the reign of Edward the Confessor in England – and it was similarly played up for political reasons, with the Bruce regime from 1306 presenting their government as trying to restore this golden age. Alexander was lucky in that he did not have to face Edward I at his most demanding, as during his lifetime that king was concentrating on Wales and Gascony. His Hebridean/Manx achievement was substantial, though it only replicated what his father would probably have done had he not died early. But Alexander's casual attitude to his safety and unlucky demise is perhaps an appropriate comment on his governance.

4

The Wars of Independence and the Bruces: 1286–1371

Margaret (1286–90) and the Competition for the Empty Throne (1290–92)

Following Alexander III's funeral at Dunfermline Abbey on 29 March 1286, an assembly of the Scottish nobles and prelates was held at Scone to determine the succession. His widow, Yolande of Dreux, was pregnant according to some sources, but if so she appears to have lost the baby; within a month the succession had been settled on the late king's grand-daughter Margaret, motherless daughter of King Eric of Norway (d. 1299). Eric's heir to Norway was his brother Haakon, so there was no problem of the queen inheriting Norway too. The accession of Scotland's first Queen Regnant was not openly contested; however her accession presented the problem of who was to marry her and hold the powerful role of consort. Given contemporary views on a woman's subjection to her husband and the necessary male role of war leader, it was implied that the queen's husband would be 'de facto' king whether or not he was crowned. The role was soon being eyed up by the ambitious Edward I as suitable for his only surviving son, Edward of Caernarfon (born 1284), who could thus unite the two kingdoms and in practice merge Scotland into England. This proposal was bound to arouse intense unease – and as the new queen was the daughter and ward of King Eric, Edward could negotiate with him without consulting the Scots.

For the moment the infant 'Maid of Norway' had to stay in her father's land under his supervision, and was too young to marry (even nominally) even by medieval standards, which provided an excuse to delay a potentially contentious decision. A board of six 'Guardians' ruled Scotland on her behalf, including Robert Bruce of Annandale and John Comyn, 'the Black'. Robert Bruce was the son of the daughter of William I's brother Earl David of Huntingdon (and recognised as heir to Alexander III before the latter had children), and John Comyn was Lord of Badenoch and married to Edward I's cousin. Comyn held lands in Galloway as well as the Gaelic North, and was thus a counterbalance to Bruce as Lord of Annandale. But he was also a rival claimant to the throne to the Bruces, as he was descended from a daughter of King Donald 'Ban' (deposed 1097), and was brother-in-law and ally to the Bruces' most serious rival, John Balliol, son of the 5th Lord of Barnard Castle in County Durham (England) and of Devorguilla, daughter and senior heiress of 'Lord' Alan of Galloway. Balliol (born *c.* 1248), a generation younger than Bruce, was the great-grandson of Earl David of Huntingdon; his grandmother (Isabel of Huntingdon) had been David's eldest daughter and Bruce's mother had been the second daughter. He was thus the closest heir to the House of Dunkeld as Earl David's eldest daughter's heir; Bruce was its 'heir proximate' as closest by descent.

For the moment the two great 'power blocs', Bruce and Balliol/Comyn, circled each other warily; meanwhile Queen Yolande returned to her native France, contracted a second marriage (to Duke Arthur II of Brittany) in 1292, had children, and lived on until 1330. Edward I had other priorities on the Continent – protecting his lands in Aquitaine from the aggressive, young French King Philip IV – and as he held court in Bordeaux King Eric sent envoys to him in May 1289 to discuss a marriage between Edward's son and

Queen Margaret, and the queen's move to Scotland. The talks continued after Edward returned to England, and in October 1289 the 'Guardians' sent an embassy to join in and ensure that Scotland's interests were protected. Given Edward's single-minded determination to secure the agreement he wanted and the threat of him invading now he had subdued the Welsh, the Scots could only play for time. The Treaty of Salisbury duly agreed that Margaret would come to Scotland or England before 1 November 1290 and then an agreement would be finalised; meantime Edward had despatched a delegation to Rome to secure a papal dispensation for the two cousins to marry, which Pope Nicholas granted weeks later. The agreement was backed up by an Anglo-Scots treaty at Birgham on the Tweed on 14 March 1290, where it was agreed that Margaret would not be married without the joint consent of Edward and Eric; English and Norwegian representatives would assist the 'Guardians' in ruling Scotland during the queen's minority. A further agreement was then made at Birgham on 18 July guaranteeing Scots independence and the complete separation of the two realms' administrations. The English king also negotiated separate agreements with the inhabitants of Man and the Hebrides without any reference to their overlords in Scotland, as if transferring them to his direct overlordship.

Eric eventually sent his daughter from Bergen, the nearest Norwegian port, to Scotland the following summer, but the adverse weather en route appears to have given the seven-year-old serious illness, possibly pneumonia. She was delayed at Kirkwall on Orkney, too ill to proceed further, and died on 26 September without ever seeing the country of which she was queen. Remembered as 'the Maid of Norway', she was returned to Bergen for burial but her isolated demise gave rise to a pretender in 1300. The 'False Margaret', appearing to be considerably older than the late queen and with a husband in tow, arrived in Bergen claiming to have been smuggled abroad to Germany to save her from the English marriage; by then her father was dead and his brother and successor King Haakon promptly had her arraigned as an impostor and burnt at the stake. It seems unlikely that she was genuine.

The Scots throne was now definitively vacant, and the delicate question had to be faced – would either the Bruces or the Balliols accept the other's candidate as king without a civil war? An election by the senior nobles was the logical means to proceed, but the defeated candidate was likely to claim it had been 'fixed' and to have the manpower to resist it. For the moment, the 'Guardians' had to continue their regency, with most of the nobles now assembled at Perth ready for the queen's arrival. Bruce, who had a weaker genealogical claim (see above) but had been recognised as heir by King Alexander, attempted to force the issue in his favour by a coup as he led an armed posse of his tenants to Perth – near the coronation site at Scone. But he was resisted by the local bishop, William Fraser of St Andrews, who appealed to Edward I to act as adjudicator of the succession and to come to the Border ready to add his weight to the decision made by the nobles. Edward's queen's death prevented this.

The Balliols now emulated Bruce and, assisted by John Comyn's son John (the 'Red Comyn'), staged a revolt in their power base of Galloway to seize the royal castles. Bruce 'the Competitor' with his son Robert – husband of Marjorie, the heiress of Carrick, and Earl *de iure uxoris* – and the Stewarts led an army to drive them out. For the moment the regency regime stalemated the Balliol/Comyn attack, and the latter had to emulate Bruce and try to secure the throne by negotiation among their peers. A small group of four 'Guardians' was appointed to oversee the succession rather than the six who had held power in 1286–90: Bishop Fraser, Bishop Robert Wishart of Glasgow, James the 'High Steward' and John Comyn 'the Black'. They were later to be joined by two English lords representing Edward I, who pressed his legal claim to act as a feudal lord had a right to do in the lands of his vassal. Edward's summons brought a large contingent of Scots nobles and bishops to Norham Castle near the Tweed for legal hearings on the succession to open on 10 May 1291, and all potential claimants were required to submit their claims there. The three most serious claimants were Balliol and Bruce – as representing the descent from Earl David of Huntingdon's two elder daughters – and John, Lord Hastings, grandson of Earl David's third daughter. He based his claim on the shaky grounds that the Scots kingdom was not a normal, legally recognisable European kingdom as its kings were not crowned or anointed in the established manner; therefore it was an 'estate' and by feudal law where there was no male heir to a lord the heirs of his daughters divided it up. The other main claimants were:

John Comyn 'the Black' – as representing the line of Donald Ban's daughter.

Count Floris of Holland – the great-great-grandson of Ada the daughter of Earl Henry of Huntingdon (William I's father).

Patrick, Earl of Dunbar – the heir of the direct male line from King Duncan's brother Maldred.

William, Lord Vesci – descended from Margaret, the daughter of William I.

William, Lord Ros – descended from Margaret's sister Isabella.

Nicholas de Soulis – grandson of Alan Durward and Marjorie, daughter of Alexander II.

Edward I had a claim himself, as descendant of Malcolm III's daughter Edith/Matilda. But the front runners were Balliol, who submitted his claim on 6 June, and Bruce. Given the complexities of dynastic interrelations north and south of the usually peaceful Border, both men had inherited lands in

England though Balliol had a larger patrimony there, based in County Durham, and so could be reckoned to be less likely to stand up to Edward. Bruce had served in Edward's invasion of Wales, and was fully aware of his ruthlessness towards wayward 'vassals'. The Scots nobles refused Edward's demand that they recognise him as the overlord of Scotland as a preliminary to the proceedings, and claimed that they had no right to rule on such a weighty matter except when their own king was present. Edward and his lawyers decided to require all the candidates to recognise him as the overlord of Scotland and required custody of all the royal castles in Scotland. Once Edward had secured his requirements, a court of 'auditors' was set up – forty nominated by Bruce, forty by Balliol, and twenty-four by Edward.

The other candidates were thus marginalised from the start as the hearings opened at Berwick in August 1291. However, Count Floris alleged that the two principal claimants' ancestor Earl David had resigned his rights to the throne in return for a grant of land so they had no valid claim. Unfortunately he could not provide documentation. Floris and Bruce made an agreement whereby each would help the other financially if he was successful, evidently anticipating that Balliol would be their principal joint challenger. In the event, the court decided in Balliol's favour on 17 November 1292; on 19 November Edward gave orders for Balliol to be given possession of his new kingdom. The new king was inaugurated at Scone on 30 November (St Andrew's Day), being crowned by the English bishops Bek and St John instead of the usual Scots Earl of Fife (who was underage). Balliol did homage to Edward on 26 December – explicitly for the whole kingdom of Scotland.

The Fall of John Balliol – 'Toom Tabard', 'Empty Coat' (1292–96)

Balliol was in a more difficult position than most founders of new dynasties, given the predatory attitude and relentless pressing of English royal rights by Edward. The threat of an English invasion and deposition for breach of his 'duties' as Edward's vassal lay in front of him, with the Scots nobility and Church having had to concede (in writing) far more than any previous treaty had done. Edward could claim that any resistance to him was a breach of legal rights and sworn faith, though this was of more importance abroad (e.g. with the Papacy) than in Scotland, and Edward's French foe Philip IV had political reasons to encourage Scots defiance. Balliol's ability to rely on the Bruces was in doubt, and he was the head of one powerful faction of nobles rather than a consensual figure. On a personal level, he is a somewhat obscure figure and we do not even know if his (English) wife Isabel de Warenne was still alive in 1292; but he had a son ready to succeed him, Edward (probably born around 1280/85).

Edward had ruthlessly used his legal rights as suzerain of the Welsh principalities in the late 1270s and early 1280s to have his officials sit in judgement on legal appeals from the princes' courts and to summon his vassals to answer lawsuits like normal plaintiffs. This legal centralisation was now applied to Scotland, starting in Berwick within days of Balliol's Coronation. 'Test cases' were arranged and lawsuits encouraged – though at the time it was a norm for an overlord to relentlessly use his rights in order to display them and the kings of France were to treat the English Crown in its fief in Gascony in a similar way. Balliol had to absolve Edward from his earlier promises not to interfere in Scots affairs. At Christmas 1293 Balliol had to appear at the English parliament to defend a case of a stolen inheritance brought by MacDubh (Macduff), the son of the Earl of Fife, while Edward granted rights and pensions within Scotland without reference to him. In summer 1294 Balliol was required to bring an army to take part in Edward's war with France over the control of Gascony – by form of a feudal summons as King of Scotland, not on account of his lands held within England. The war, however, gave Balliol an opportunity to retaliate against

Edward by threatening to come to an agreement with Philip and thus obtaining French military help if Edward invaded. But Balliol appears to have hesitated, to the detriment of his subsequent reputation; the issue was forced by the more belligerent nobility who met to set up a new governing council, an unprecedented step for an adult Scots king to face but in line with the English nobility's manner of dealing with Edward's irresolute father Henry III in the 1250s and 1260s. The council then arranged a new treaty of alliance with France (February 1296), providing for French aid and threatening Edward with a war on two fronts. Both countries mustered their armies – the English first.

The question is whether the treaty or the Macduff case was the prime reason for the outbreak of the war, after which there was to be near-permanent retaliatory raiding over the Border – until now a largely peaceful zone – right up to 1560. Border warfare and regular pillaging became the norm, and duly increased the importance and the lawlessness of the Border dynasties on both sides. As the war opened at Easter 1296, Edward moved his troops up from Newcastle to Berwick and the Scots made the first move in the west. John Comyn, Earl of Buchan, led an expedition to attack Carlisle, but they failed to take it by surprise and they lacked siege equipment so they had to return empty-handed; the town was defended by Robert Bruce, former Earl of Carrick (which had passed to his son Robert, the future king, on his wife's death in 1292). His octogenarian father, the 'Competitor', had handed the lordship of Annandale to him and died in 1295 – and was buried with his De Brus ancestors in Yorkshire, not in Scotland. The younger Bruce had clearly thrown his lot in with Edward – in case Edward was looking for a new king? – and as Lord of Annandale was a crucial strategic 'bonus' for English access to Galloway.

Edward moved his army up to Berwick, the commercial *entrepôt* for the prosperous Southern Uplands and one of the largest towns in Scotland, to open the attack on 30 March, after Easter. But his over-eager sailors mistook the signal for an attack and crossed the river towards the town's port before the army was ready to assault the walls. One ship ran aground and was burnt and as two more caught fire the rest retreated to safety; the infuriated Edward ordered an immediate assault on the town's wall (really only a palisade as Berwick was unused to warfare), which was quickly stormed. There was little resistance but the king made no attempt to halt the resultant bloodshed and had the town's menfolk massacred as a warning to the Scots of what awaited any who defied him; up to 11,000 may have died.

The English under John de Warenne, Earl of Surrey (Edward's cousin and brother of Balliol's late wife), besieged Dunbar, and the defenders sent urgently to Balliol, at Haddington with the main army, to come to their rescue. As he arrived the defenders broke the truce, but the Scots army mistook Warenne's preparations for a clash for retreat, charged at his ranks without any plan and were routed by the more disciplined English. Dunbar surrendered as Edward arrived.

Following Dunbar, Balliol retreated with his demoralised army, James the 'High Steward' surrendered Roxburgh and Edward and his huge army could march on across Lothian into Fife unopposed. Balliol received Edward's envoy, Warenne, and tried to negotiate an English earldom for himself in return for his abdication – the terms which Edward had offered the equally outnumbered Llywelyn ap Gruffydd of Gwynedd in 1282. This time Edward, less generous, demanded complete surrender and Balliol chose to obey, as the English army marched as far north as Elgin without resistance. Edward heaped unnecessary humiliation on Balliol, drawing out the process of legal negotiation of his submission to punish him. In the symbolic climax of the surrender at Brechin, Balliol's heraldic surcoat bearing his 'arms' was stripped off him – hence his nickname 'Toom Tabard', 'Empty Coat'. He was sent to the Tower of London, and the Scots regalia and administrative records were deported to London too to emphasise that Scotland had ceased to exist as a legal entity.

Annexation and Revolt

This was not the usual 'union of crowns' that occurred when two states were dynastically united in contemporary Europe (e.g. Castile and Leon), where the sole ruler used the title of king of both his kingdoms and kept the institutions of his new realm intact. This was outright absorption into the English legal system as Edward had imposed on the Welsh principalities between 1277 and 1287 (and as was being done as far as possible in Ireland after the 1172 invasion). Whether Edward had intended this all along, and provoked the Scots by constant legal assertion of his rights hoping for 'treasonable' resistance, is debateable. The timing of the annexation, in the middle of the French war, was unwelcome. For the moment, the Scots nobles queued up to submit and swear allegiance to Edward, at his next Parliament at Berwick in August 1297. Among those who swore allegiance at Berwick and put their names to the so-called 'Ragman's Roll' of submissions were the two Robert Bruces, senior and junior. Scotland was put in the charge of English officials, led by the 'Keeper' Warenne and the fat and greedy treasurer, Hugh Cressingham, who had no experience of what amounted to a 'colonial' government and were there to enforce norms of English law. The Scots were expected to provide substantial amounts of men and money for the English king's French wars – a level of commitment unknown in a state unused to such demands. The resulting resistance can be seen as part of the similar objections made by secular and religious leaders in England to the scale of Edward's demands in spring 1297.

The resistance that broke out in Scotland to the king's extortionate officials was to consist of apparently spontaneous outbreaks and to be led by the lesser gentry and farmers, not the great nobility. But does this mean that, as some nationalist historians have claimed, they were more patriotic, more willing to stand up to Edward and the English than the culturally 'internationalised', Anglo-Normanised nobles (with their estates to protect) were? This debate has been muddied by the fictional accounts of the revolt which followed and the 'hero-cult' of its main leader, William Wallace, which was first presented as the national epic in 'The Acts and Deeds of Sir William Wallace, Knight of Elderslie' by Blind Harry in around 1470. It is best known now to non-historians from the highly inspiring but often inaccurate film *Braveheart* (where Mel Gibson's warriors anachronistically paint themselves with woad like Picts). It can also appear as a 'people's revolt' where the aristocrats, such as future king Robert Bruce, often remained aloof or were quick to change sides. Little is known of Wallace's origins (probably a minor gentry family, the name meaning 'Welshman' i.e. a Strathclyde Briton?) or even whether he came from Elderslie in Renfrewshire or Ellerslie in Lanarkshire; he possibly had some experience as an archer. In May 1297 Wallace was responsible for the killing of William de Haselrig, the English sheriff of Lanarkshire, one of a number of violent attacks on the new king's officials across Scotland, and he led a local revolt in Renfrew; he then joined William, Lord of Douglas, for a raid on Scone. Andrew Moray of Petty, son of his namesake the former 'Justiciar' of the North (one of those nobles deported in 1296), was leading a rising in Moray. His exploits are much less known than Wallace's. However, he appears to have been able to ravage around Inverness and Elgin and hold back the local Anglophile sheriff, Sir Reginald Cheyne. By the end of the summer Moray had secured all the north except for Dundee, which he and Wallace were besieging.

A number of great southern nobles, including the two Bruces and the Steward, joined in Wallace's revolt but subsequently failed to fight a larger royal army under Percy and Clifford (two senior Northern English nobles) at Irvine in July and abandoned Wallace to negotiate their surrender. But the outbreaks of rebellion continued across the country, with English officials chased from their posts and Warenne mostly south of the Border and failing to give any leadership.

The delay in Warenne leading a substantial army north gave Wallace and Moray time to link up their forces and train their men to face professional soldiers. As Warenne moved north they came south to Stirling to meet him. On 11 September 1297 Warenne, belatedly moving north with around 3,000 cavalry and 8,000–10,000 infantry, arrived at Stirling, the only route from Lothian into the Highlands. Wallace and Moray were waiting, and attacked the English as they were crossing the bridge over the Forth. The English superiority in numbers was a disadvantage; only three men or so could cross abreast, and the time it would take to get the army across left those who crossed first in danger of being attacked while they were the smaller force. The infantry crossed first, rather than the cavalry who could have ridden down the Scots infantry. Wallace and Moray then formed up their famous 'schiltrons', tightly packed knots of pike-wielding infantry whom the English infantry could not penetrate, and pushed the English advance guard back onto the bridge; the crush prevented the cavalry from being used. The bridge broke under the weight of the English and hundreds of men were drowned or killed in the rout that followed. Cressingham was caught and was contemptuously flayed like a pig, and Warenne had to abandon Lothian and flee south.

Most of Scotland now accepted the leadership of Wallace (who was not even a knight until this was rectified) and Moray as 'Guardians' for the absent King John Balliol, though it is unclear if Moray was badly wounded at Stirling (or soon after?) as he seems to have died within months. Problems in England and Gascony meant that Edward could not launch a counter-attack until summer 1298. The royal household administration, which normally organised campaigns, was in Flanders and great nobles had to be offered an inducement to fight in winter after the recent 'strike'; in the event the new army mustered at Newcastle had to be content with relieving the Scots sieges of Berwick and Roxburgh.

Wallace and the often overlooked Moray were masters of

guerrilla warfare and unconventional tactics, but they had fought a larger English army on unusually favourable terrain at Stirling Bridge and Edward himself would be in charge of the next invasion. The English army which mustered at Roxburgh on 25 June consisted of around 3,000 cavalry, 14,800 English infantry and 10,900 Welsh infantry. The Scots nobles refused Edward's feudal summons to join up, so he could brand them as traitors and confiscate their estates. Wallace duly retreated ahead of Edward's army as it crossed Lothian, and the English were hindered by problems with their food supplies, a mixture of inadequate preparations and contrary winds holding up their ships. A load of wine did arrive and the Welsh contingent became drunk and rioted. But as Edward was moving back for supplies he was informed that the Scots were nearby at Falkirk, and quickly moved in to attack them. The resulting Battle of Falkirk on 22 July 1298 (St Mary Magdalene's Day) saw Wallace using his 'schiltrons' again, this time four of them and protected by ropes connecting stakes driven into the ground. His cavalry were left outside the perimeter and routed, and the charge of cowardice or worse was later levelled against the Comyns for fleeing (possibly a result of propaganda by their successful Bruce rivals after 1306?). The English gradually prised the 'schiltrons' open by a mixture of archery, hand-to-hand combat and probably a cavalry attack from the rear. This battle was much more evenly matched than Stirling Bridge and possibly 2,000 English were killed; the Scots casualties were far higher but most of the nobility were on horseback and escaped. So did Wallace, but after this serious psychological setback he was short of men and was reduced to 'hit-and-run' tactics again; the Scots did not dare to meet the English in the field.

Edward marched on and sacked Perth, and English administration was restored with the lands of assorted Scots nobles who had been at Wallace's side at Falkirk being given to militarily experienced knightly or noble Englishmen. These confiscations did not include the Bruce lands of Annandale or Carrick, although the younger Robert had rejoined the Scots rebels after Stirling Bridge and when Wallace resigned as 'Guardian' after Falkirk, he and his rival John 'the Red' Comyn were appointed the new 'Guardians'. William Lamberton, Bishop of St Andrews, was added in August 1299 after a reputedly violent quarrel between Bruce and Comyn at a council at Peebles; the two evidently already distrusted each other. Possibly Edward, not usually a man to forgive rebellion, still had hopes of luring Bruce back to the English cause – or wanted that possibility to be suspected by Bruce's rivals so he could not lead a united Scots resistance. By May 1300 Bruce had resigned as 'Guardian' and been replaced by a friend of John Balliol's, Sir Ingram d'Umfraville, and a year later John de Soulis took over as sole 'Guardian'.

The Scots leadership remained loyal to their deposed king despite his poor governance, perhaps not wanting to choose between Bruce and Comyn as his replacement and thus alienating the superseded party. Edward continued to threaten to ravage Scotland from sea to sea as long as it resisted him and increasingly bloody and bitter guerrilla war resulted with neither side able to secure a decisive blow. A substantially lengthy truce followed in 1302. Meanwhile Master Robert Bisset's team of Scots lawyers successfully argued in Rome that Edward had no rights to Scotland, its independence resting on the factors of papal privilege, a separate common-law system, past history and documentary evidence that its kings had only done homage in England for their lands there. Pope Boniface was convinced and Edward agreed to hand over Balliol to his custody (summer 1301); the ex-king's luggage was opened as he was leaving England and the Scots crown and royal seal were confiscated. Balliol was settled on his family estates in Picardy and was to die there around November 1314 without making any effort to reclaim his title; the family claim was left to his son Edward.

The fact that within months the younger Bruce, Comyn's future arch-enemy, temporarily abandoned the Scots cause in return for promises of his family's lands and future favours as to his 'rights' from Edward has been seen as an embarrassment to the future hero king's reputation. From Bruce's point of view the elderly king showed no signs of flagging in his war, let alone dying, and the war was turning into a stalemate. From Edward's point of view, it is possible that he feared the Pope and King Philip would recognise Balliol as King of Scots so it was wise to have his potential challenger at hand to set up as a puppet if needed – and he could play him off against Comyn. The fact that Bruce joined Edward's side gave him invaluable military experience for the future in the well-organised English army.

Berwick, Roxburgh, Jedburgh, Edinburgh, Linlithgow, Dumfries and Lochmaben provided the backbone of Edward's garrison across the south from 1299 onwards, with Scots-held Stirling Castle blocking the way north until the summer campaign of 1303 when Edward succeeded in setting up a 'bridge of boats' over the Firth of Forth to land in Fife. Luckily for the Scots, he did not have the men, money or materials to construct a network of untakeable new castles to dominate the landscape that he held as he had done in Gwynedd in 1283–84; instead his large army marched unchallenged as far as Brechin, Aberdeen, Banff and Elgin to winter in Fife. Reinforcements arrived from Ireland under Richard de Burgh, Earl of Ulster, to back up Aymer de Valence's army in the south-west; if Wallace was back in Scotland by now he was marginalised into an isolated guerrilla leader. Early in 1304 John 'the Red' Comyn and most of the other 'rebel' nobles agreed terms with Edward at Strathord near Perth, whereby most were able to repurchase their confiscated lands now or after a short period in exile as punishment for their recent 'treason'. The laws of Scotland as they had existed under Alexander III were guaranteed. Later in 1304 Edward personally besieged and took Stirling Castle. But the fact that Edward had already granted many estates away to Englishmen meant that he could or would not return them to their Scots owners when these men surrendered, storing up animosity.

Wallace's capture by a Scots defector, John of Menteith, at Robroyston near Glasgow in August 1305 seemed to show that open resistance was crumbling. Wallace was taken south for a speedy treason trial at Westminster Hall, London, which made the most of his atrocities against civilians; he argued that he could not commit treason against Edward as he was not his subject but was predictably ignored. He was hanged, drawn and quartered at Smithfield Market as a traitor and his head was placed on London Bridge. In the meantime the 1305 parliament put in place long-term plans for the governance of Scotland, under a 'King's Lieutenant' (John of Brittany, a royal kinsman), an English Chancellor and Treasurer, and four pairs of English and Scots justices. Scotsmen dominated the new council and held some, but not the crucial, appointments as castellans. Their law was to be partially reformed in line with customary English/Continental practice and some 'barbarous' practices outlawed; it was a more conciliatory policy than that of the mid-1290s but the king's insistence that Scotland was a subject land like Wales and Ireland, not a kingdom, was followed in the documentation.

Bruce Claims the Throne but Is Driven into Exile, 1306

The settlement could have been expected to last for the ageing king's lifetime, with his young and unwarlike son's accession the likely point for rebellion to break out. But instead the next revolt resulted from a violent end to the mutual mistrust of the younger Robert Bruce (who succeeded his father as Lord of Annandale in 1304) and the 'Red' Comyn, rival contenders for the abolished crown. The two men apparently took the sensible course of trying to resolve their rivalry so the next rising would have a united leadership, with Scots sources saying that in summer 1305 Comyn agreed to waive his claim to the throne and fight for Bruce's in return for receiving the Bruce estates once the rebellion began. Bruce's motives for preferring alliance with his arch-enemy to waiting for Edward to die are unclear, but possibly he feared being 'left out' of a revolt. The speed with which churchmen such as Bishop Wishart of Glasgow rallied to Bruce in February 1306 suggests that they were in the plot too; Bishop William Lamberton had signed a secret pact with Bruce to back him against all others (which Edward I acquired in 1306 and sent to the Pope to try to get him dismissed) and this presumably included a Bruce-Comyn struggle for the crown. But at this distance it cannot be stated that Bruce was more 'treacherous' to his sworn lord, Edward I, than Comyn; the latter may have been planning revolt on his own behalf too.

Someone (the double-crossing Comyn?) tipped Edward off while Bruce was at the English court early in 1306. Warned of his arrest by his friend Ralph de Monthemer, the king's son-in-law, Bruce rode back to Scotland in time, gathered some men, and confronted Comyn in the chapel of the Greyfriars Monastery in Dumfries on 10 February. The meeting ended with high words, an accusation of treachery by Bruce and Bruce stabbing Comyn to death at the High Altar, an act for which he would inevitably face excommunication and international Church censure – which suggests that it was not premeditated. According to the 'Scotichronicon' he staggered outside dazed to tell his followers, 'I doubt [i.e. think] I have killed the Red Comyn', whereupon his friend Sir Roger Lindsay remarked practically, 'You doubt? Then I'll make sure' ('mak siccar' in the original dialect) and rushed inside to complete his work. His followers then helped him to attack and capture Dumfries Castle from its English garrison, and he rode to Glasgow to be absolved of his crime by Bishop Wishart before heading to Scone to hold an impromptu coronation.

The official English response, successfully seeking his excommunication, claimed it had been a careful plan to murder his rival unawares and seize the throne in midwinter, an act of blatant treason to his lord, King Edward. It is likelier that the decision to seize the throne so quickly had been planned only as Bruce fled London, knowing that it was 'now or never'. On 25 March he was crowned at Scone by Bishop William Lamberton of St Andrews, who was to be his most faithful clerical ally, with the bishops of Moray and Glasgow and the earls of Atholl, Mar, Menteith and Lennox (four out of the seven original 'Mormaers') in attendance and the royal robes, hidden from the English, used. His second wife Elizabeth de Burgh (whom he had married in 1302), daughter of Edward's Anglo-Norman Irish 'strongman' the Earl of Ulster, was also crowned – and is said to have quipped that the royal couple were only 'King and Queen of the May', that is an insubstantial nine-days' wonder. It is a moot point whether or not the 'Stone of Scone', the ancient granite coronation seat kept at the abbey, had been carried off to Westminster Abbey along with the rest of the regalia; this stone was at the abbey until 1996 but some Scots sources maintain that this was a fake passed off on Edward's men and the original was used by Bruce. The traditional Scots noble who performed the act of crowning, the Earl of Fife, was underage and a hostage in England, so when his sister Countess Isabel of Buchan arrived next day she did the honours at a second ceremony – as the only female 'crowner' in Europe.

It should be noted that the mixed Gaelic and Anglo-Norman ethnic descent of Robert Bruce was to be an important factor in his future career, although his 'coup' of February–March 1306 was a political move involving a faction of the Lowlands nobility and clergy against both the English overlord and the still-active rival claim of John Balliol. Bruce's direct paternal ancestry was, as has been said, Anglo-Norman; the family name came from Bruis near Cherbourg in Normandy, whence the first Robert de Bruis sailed to England in 1066. The Bruces still maintained lands in England, as did many of the Anglo-Norman nobility who moved easily in a world of international knightly chivalry which was culturally Norman-French. In that, they were no different from the Balliols from Picardy, though they had less landed property in England than the latter. Robert's mother, Countess Marjorie of Carrick, was supposed to have had a determined if not reckless nature, allegedly deciding to have Robert's father as her second husband when he returned from the Crusade in 1271 to bring the news of her first husband's death – and locking him in her castle until he agreed to marry her (this was probably a later story, and the timing makes it unlikely that the elder Bruce ever went on Crusade then). By his grandfather's marriage into the De Clares, Robert was descended from the renowned William Marshal, Earl of Pembroke, the 'greatest knight in Christendom', who had saved the English crown for the Plantagenets as regent for Henry III in the 1216–17 civil war. Robert Bruce seems to have inherited his strategic genius. The new king's mother, Countess Marjorie, was a direct descendant of Gilbert, ruler of Galloway (d. 1185) and son of 'king' Fergus, and through them was descended from the Irish kings. Thus Robert and his heirs were linked to the great dynasties of Ireland as well as Scotland, and this enabled him to call on Irish as well as Scots support – and after 1315 to embark on an attempt to drive the English out of Ireland too.

Bruce lacked the men to hold out against the local English and Anglophile Scots lords who now rallied to Edward's cause – quite apart from having alienated the large Comyn affinity. Even in spring 1306 the English loyalists in Southern Scotland under Aymer de Valence could outmatch his small army, and Valence's troops routed Bruce at Methven near Perth in a surprise attack on 19 June. He retreated West to the mountains, but was ambushed by Edward's local allies, led by John Mac Dougall (the son of Alexander, Lord of Lorn), at Dalry near Tyndrum in Strathfillan and routed. With his army broken up, guerrilla warfare was his only hope and he sent his womenfolk – his second wife Elizabeth de Burgh, his daughter by his first marriage Marjorie, his sisters, Mary and Christina, and the redoubtable Countess of Buchan – to sanctuary at Kildrummy Castle in Buchan, whence they had to flee as an English army under Prince Edward marched north. Neil Bruce, Robert's brother, and his party of Bruce womenfolk fled over the Great Glen and hid at the sanctuary of St Duthac at remote Tain in Ross, but were rounded up there by 'Mormaer'/Earl William (Uilleam) of Ross, local 'strongman' and a kinsman of the Comyns. They were taken to King Edward, who had Neil executed, sent Elizabeth and Christina to isolated English estates safe from rescue and considered placing Marjorie in a cage in the Tower (a security measure also used for the underage sons of princely 'traitor' David of Gwynedd in the 1280s) but relented due to her age (ten) and placed her at Witton nunnery near Beverley instead. Luckily for Elizabeth, the vengeful king was a friend of her father, who was a capable general and had a semi-autonomous lordship with plenty of warriors at hand in Ulster and was not to be alienated. Her place of confinement was to be moved around the south for years; by 1314 she was at Rochester Castle, one of the strongest fortresses in the kingdom, as a valuable hostage. Edward exhibited Mary Bruce and the Countess of Buchan in cages on the walls of Roxburgh and Berwick Castles – an unusual act of savagery towards women even for that era (but not complained of as such by contemporary writers). The Earl of Atholl and other captured senior combatants were executed as traitors; among those lesser captives who were spared and temporarily changed sides was Bruce's nephew, and later lieutenant, Sir Thomas Randolph; Bishop Lamberton was spared on account of his clerical rank so as not to anger the Papacy but was not allowed north of the Border.

Bruce, his other brothers (Edward, Thomas and Alexander) and a handful of loyal followers dispersed into hiding, and their whereabouts over winter 1306/7 are unclear. Bruce probably fled by sea to the MacDougalls' hereditary foe, Angus 'Mor' ('the Great') Mac Donald, Lord of Islay and Lochaber, on Bute. His destination then is unclear – possibly the

MacDonald kinswoman Christina Mac Ruari of Garmoran in the Inner Hebrides, or else Northern Ireland (or even his other sister Isabel, widow of King Eric II of Norway, at Bergen?). Legend places him at one point on Rathlin Island off Ulster where the famous incident with the inspirational spider, who showed him how persistence against hopeless odds pays off, is supposed to have occurred. In the meantime, Scotland was temporarily cowed and quiet.

The Reconquest of Scotland: 1307–1314

Bruce's first attacks on Galloway from February 1307 were beset by problems. He and his brother Edward landed successfully at his own estate, Turnberry, and escaped into the hills but his brothers, Thomas and Alexander, with around 1,000 mercenaries from Ireland and Kintyre, landed at Loch Ryan to be intercepted by the local Balliol lieutenant Dugald Mac Dougall, captured and executed at Carlisle (9/10 February). The English king's bloodbath was clearly designed to intimidate resistance, but Bruce knew the Ayrshire countryside far better than his pursuers and he eluded capture in the hills and started ravaging the local lands of the Balliols. He soon emerged to stage ambushes, starting with the defeat of Philip Mowbray in Glen Trool in April, and Aymer de Valence was called in to deal with him. Meanwhile, Bruce's best general, the brilliant and ruthless guerrilla leader Sir James ('the Good') Douglas, moved onto his confiscated estates in Douglasdale to tackle the English occupiers and sacked Douglas Castle, which belonged to his own family. His deliberately brutal treatment of the garrison – cutting off their heads and piling the bodies on a heap of food and wine in the cellars that was then set afire in the 'Douglas Larder' incident – showed what the independence fighters were prepared to do both to the enemy and to their own property in this increasingly vicious war.

Bruce's first major success, defeating De Valence at Loudoun Hill on 10 May 1307, saw him digging pits along the 'front' of his line so that the advancing English troops were forced into a narrow zone where he could take them on more equal terms. His success led to the ageing Edward I calling out his vassals for another major campaign, with a muster to take place at Carlisle in July. The sixty-eight-year-old king marched on Scotland again to destroy Bruce, but died en route at Burgh-by-Sands on the Solway Firth sands. He allegedly ordered his son Prince Edward to boil his remains and take them at the head of the army so he could still participate in the campaign, but the new king notoriously preferred the comforts of his court (and his friend and alleged lover Piers Gaveston) and went home for his Coronation. Edward II only returned to Southern Scotland in 1310, in an unsuccessful attempt to rebuild his reputation with his distrustful barons as a leader by defeating Douglas who was now based in the Ettrick Forest launching 'hit-and-run' raids. Needless to say the latter would not risk battle against a vastly superior force and kept carefully out of contact, wearing down Edward's army with skirmishes until they ran out of time and food and returned home.

As Bruce's initial successes in Galloway became more formidable he gained growing numbers of adherents among those great provincial lords who had stayed aloof at first out of family jealousy of the Bruces or fear of English vengeance. He was then able to leave his surviving brother Edward in charge in the south-west and move on to the Western Highlands, in alliance with Angus 'Mor' MacDonald and the Mac Ruaris of Garmoran who supplied ships, and start a campaign in the Great Glen. The local English allies, the Mac Dougalls of Lorn, were unwilling or unable to stop him – due to the threat of invasion from the west by the rest of 'Clan Donald' at their rear if they left Lorn unprotected? As the Bruce/MacDonald fleet sailed up Loch Linnhe past their lands, Bruce's old foe John MacDougall, deputising for his sick father Alexander, secured a truce. Bruce's army of around 3,000 Islemen (and Irishmen?) plus locals moved up the Glen unhindered; Inverlochy and Urquhart castles were taken, and then Inverness and Nairn were sacked. Only Elgin held out as Earl John Comyn of Buchan, cousin of the murdered 'Red Comyn' so at blood feud with the Bruces, mustered his tenants to the east to stop the Bruce advance. The Earl of Ross, lord of the lands north of the Great Glen and at risk of vengeance for handing over Bruce's womenfolk and brother Neil to the English in 1306, came to terms and was judged too valuable an ally to be punished despite his Comyn links. The only other setback was an unspecified illness that detained Bruce for some weeks as he advanced on Banff in late 1307 and held up his campaigning, possibly an early sign of his later skin disease. But he recovered despite the problem that many of his troops had drifted home due to the lack of action or loot, avoided a clash with the larger army of the Earl of Buchan and moved back across Moray, taking Balvenie and Duffus.

May 1308 saw Bruce's return to Buchan, probably with a larger force but still physically weak – he had had to be carried in a litter by his men for weeks. He defeated the earl at Inverurie on 10 May, when Bruce's army was caught unprepared in the early morning as Buchan's lieutenant, David Brechin, attacked the town, but he rallied his men to drive the attackers out. Buchan was not ready to follow up Brechin's raid so missed a great opportunity, and when he did draw up his men by the Hill of Barra they appear to have been dismayed to find that Bruce was able to sit on a horse. They were routed, and the earl fled to England without trying to save his estates. Bruce was able to ravage the Comyns' lands across the area and end the Comyn obstacle to his plans by driving the family out of their hereditary lands. The 'Harrying of Buchan' both extinguished the Comyns as a power in the land and denied the manpower and supplies of the region to the English, and Bruce followed it up by defeating the English garrison at Aberdeen.

Next Bruce took on the MacDougalls in Argyll rather than moving south, preferring to build up an unchallengeable position north of the Tay than to directly attack the remaining English garrisons. The MacDougalls, pro-English branch of the 'Sons of Somerled', were defeated at the Battle of the Pass of Brander, probably on the bank of the River Awe below the slopes of Ben Cruachan though the site and date are disputed (August 1308?). John Mac Dougall was in command of his clansmen again, and tried to stage an ambush by hiding his men up on the hillside above the pass; however Bruce sent Sir James Douglas and his men up the mountain to take them by surprise from above. The MacDougalls' main castle at Dunstaffnage was besieged and taken, and Alexander surrendered as John fled by sea to England; Argyll was overrun and the MacDougalls, like the Comyns, were expelled; local power now passed to the MacDonalds west of the Great Glen and to the Campbells, the family of Bruce's close follower Sir Neil Campbell, in Argyll. Alexander joined his son and the Comyns in exile as dependants of Edward II. One of the Scots lords fighting for the MacDougalls who was captured and changed sides was Bruce's nephew Thomas Randolph, captured by the English in 1306.

In March 1309 Bruce held his first parliament at St Andrews, and the following year a general meeting of the Scots clergy recognised him as king in defiance of his papal excommunication. He slowly extended his power over the Lowlands as well as the Highlands as the isolated English garrisons were worn down without hope of rescue. Linlithgow fell in 1310, Dumbarton fell in 1311 and Perth fell to Bruce himself in January 1312; in 1313 Bruce was confident enough to turn his attention to Scots overseas possessions seized by Edward and reconquer the Isle of Man. The preoccupation of Edward II and his feuding barons was such that Bruce was able to raid Northern England at will from 1312, levying blackmail from the local communities and exercising more power than their own king; then in March 1314 James

Douglas captured Roxburgh Castle, and Bruce's nephew Sir Thomas Randolph, the rising star among his lieutenants, captured Edinburgh Castle. This left the English with Stirling, thanks to provisioning up the Firth of Forth and the strength of its walls. Edward Bruce now besieged it, and governor Sir Philip Mowbray promised to surrender if he was not relieved by 24 June 1314. This finally stung Edward II, who had regained confidence since his favourite's murder after the birth of his son and heir (Edward III), into personally leading an army to Scotland to relieve Stirling; it is unclear if either Edward or Robert Bruce wanted this decisive resolution to the war and Edward may have acted without his brother's orders.

Bannockburn and after, 1314–18: Victory in Scotland, Defeat in Ireland

The English army which Edward led north was the largest seen since his father's campaigns, with probably around 2,000–3000 cavalry and 16,000 infantry. Joint command under Edward was vested in the earls of Hereford and Gloucester, two major Welsh Marches barons; Hereford, the 'Constable', had served with Bruce earlier and was now the guardian of his interned wife and daughter and Gloucester, Edward's nephew, was a relative of Bruce's (Bruce's grandfather had married Gloucester's aunt). Some of the dispossessed Anglophile lords whom Bruce had deprived of their lands were in the army, such as ex-'Guardian' Sir Gilbert de Umfraville and his relative the Earl of Angus. The Scots army, which mustered in May in the Tor Wood south of Stirling to block the only possible English line of advance on the castle via the old Roman road, was probably about half that size, around 6,000–8,000 men, and was heavily reliant on the defensive infantry 'schiltrons' as under Wallace and Moray. The Scots had fewer landed gentry and fewer horses than their southern neighbour so this was a necessary tactic, but weapons and protective clothing were probably better than assumed by the popular myths of kilt-clad peasantry carrying spears and scythes. Their infantry probably had good-quality pikes and some would have swords plus padded jerkins to wear – some looted in recent campaigns.

The English arrived at Falkirk on 22 June, but a battle was not inevitable. Bruce was more cautious than Wallace and was apparently prepared to consider withdrawing and letting Edward relieve Stirling, but changed his mind after hearing about poor English morale. Bruce had dug pits across the causeway around the line of the Roman road, the inevitable route for the English cavalry as it avoided the marshy farmland on either side, to force the attackers onto a narrow 'front'. But governor Mowbray emerged from the castle and reached the English camp to warn Edward of this; his plea for caution was ignored, as was the argument that Edward had fulfilled his promise by arriving outside Stirling before 24 June and under the terms of the truce with the Scots the castle did not now need to be surrendered. Bruce, meanwhile, moved north out of the Tor Wood to the more densely forested 'New Park', Alexander III's hunting park outside Stirling, on the 22nd; he led the rearguard, his nephew Randolph the vanguard, Edward Bruce the third division and according to one source Douglas led a fourth division on behalf of the underage 'Steward', Walter Stewart. On the 23rd hostilities opened, though the exact site is still disputed and some historians argue that the battlefield monument is in the wrong place and should be a mile or so to the east or north-east. After a quarrel between the cautious Gloucester and Hereford and the impatient Edward, the English moved forward towards Bruce's position, and a memorable opening incident saw Hereford's nephew Sir Henry Bohun charge on his huge warhorse at the isolated King of Scots as if in a 'one-to-one' joust. Bruce, sitting on a smaller Scots horse or pony, carefully dodged to the side as Bohun reached him and delivered a crushing swipe at his challenger's head as his horse carried him past, cleaving

Bohun's skull in two. This was taken in subsequent accounts as symbolic of how the crafty Scots leader made up for lack of brute force against superior opponents throughout the wars. An English attempt to infiltrate round the 'right' (north-east) side of the battlefield, avoiding the pits set around the line of the Roman road, to reach Stirling was driven back by a 'schiltron' under Randolph.

The main battle took place on 24 June on an indefinite site but one which involved the English having to cope with a line of pits that inhibited a cavalry charge, boggy ground to either side of a narrow 'causeway' and solid bodies of bristling spears in the 'schiltrons'. The Bannock Burn had to be crossed, and then served as an obstacle if the English needed to retreat quickly. Given the boggy ground, the smaller Scots force could not be outflanked. The initial English cavalry charge against the 'schiltrons' was a risky tactic, given that the wall of pikes was solid and would not be broken up easily with horses inclined to panic. Infantry could stand against cavalry if it kept its nerve and had no 'chinks' in the wall for the horses to ride through, and the Scots were well aware of what was at stake; they had been devoutly praying on their knees for divine aid as the English advanced and had high morale. Breaking the 'schiltrons' required 'thinning out' the ranks of defenders first, usually by archery, to be surer of success. But Edward's army was short of trained archers to fire a devastating 'hailstorm' of arrows compared to its successors after 1330, particularly in France, when the use of archery became a decisive weapon for the English. The initial charge by the cavalry, possibly a hasty decision by Gloucester after a row with the king, was beaten back by the Scots pikemen and sometime in the resulting struggle the earl was unhorsed and killed. The English infantry 'push' against the 'schiltrons' that followed was held back – and the fact that the two front ranks were intermingled in a hand-to-hand struggle meant that the English archers (mostly Welsh) could not fire at a clear target and were afraid of hitting their own men. The

English were pushed back, and eventually broke; traditionally the Scots camp followers, waiting across the ridge out of sight of the battlefield, heard that their side were winning and eagerly charged into sight to join in, making the enemy think that they were fresh reinforcements (one unlikely modern theory has it that refugee Templar Knights from France, given sanctuary by Robert Bruce after their Order was closed down, led or formed this force). Casualties are unclear, but the Scots' were relatively light whereas possibly 11,000 English infantry (two-thirds of their total?) and 700 men-at-arms were killed; the panic-stricken flight across the Bannock Burn and marshes added to the extent of casualties. Rather than rallying his men Edward II fled on horseback all the way to Dunbar Castle, for which he was mocked in both countries; his military reputation never recovered. Earl Patrick of Dunbar (son of the 'Competitor' earl of the 1292 succession claim) smuggled him back to England on a fishing boat – and defected to the Bruce cause to save his Border estates from ravaging.

The long list of English noble captives at Bannockburn included the Earl of Hereford, whom Bruce was to exchange for his wife and daughter; the latter, his heiress as he had no son yet, was to be married in 1316 to Walter Steward, the 'High Steward', as the lynchpin of the south-western Scottish dynastic alliance of Bruce and Stewart. Other Scots hostages retrieved from years in captivity, logically in exchange for the prisoners taken at Bannockburn, included Bruce's sisters Mary and Christina, the former of whom was married to his Argyll 'strongman' and close friend Sir Neil Campbell. Among Bruce's new coterie of lords set up in the confiscated territories of pro-Comyn, pro-Balliol or Anglophile exiles was his nephew Thomas Randolph, who now became Earl of Moray as his main lieutenant in the north; ravaged Buchan was left without an earl. The Western Highlands and the Hebrides were handed over to the Macdonalds, while in the south-west the main regime stalwarts were the Stewarts (with 'High Steward' Walter married to Marjorie Bruce) and, guarding the Borders, the Douglases. There was a risk, however, that the Comyn and Balliol allies driven into exile would prove an asset to the English Crown and endeavour to return home by force as a 'fifth column', which arguably proved disastrous for the Bruce cause in 1332–33. Bruce preferred to take no risks by allowing these magnates to stay in Scotland; taught by hard experience since 1306, he clearly regarded them as irreconcilable. But they, like himself in similar circumstances of confiscation in 1306, now had nothing to lose in mounting surprise attacks on Scotland when convenient. Bishop Lamberton, clerical stalwart of the regime, appears to have been back in Scotland already, probably in 1312.

In 1315 Bruce turned his attention to the western seaways and thence to Ireland – a necessary diversion from the main war on the Borders as some of the pro-Comyn 'Disinherited' had fled there – and early in that year John MacDougall led a naval expedition to take back the Isle of Man for Edward II. From Man a new attempt could be made on the confiscated Balliol lands in Galloway. A naval force was duly prepared on the Ayrshire coast to 'show the flag' in the Inner Hebrides in late spring 1315, led by King Robert himself. Meanwhile messengers were sent to the Gaelic lords of Ulster offering them support for a rising against the English, which was to be assisted by Scots troops led by Edward Bruce. Domnhall Ua Niall, King of Tir Eoghain (Tyrone), responded positively and invited the Bruces to send an expedition, and Edward Bruce assembled an Irish expedition at Ayr while his brother was preparing his fleet there. A charismatic if somewhat impulsive general and a natural leader for the Irish lords, Edward also had the advantage of the Bruce family's lineal descent from some of the most famous past Gaelic leaders – ironically their descent from the leader of the Anglo-Norman conquest in the 1170s, Richard de Clare, Earl of Pembroke ('Strongbow') meant that they were also descended via his wife Eva from the ancient kings of Leinster and Munster. This gave him a claim to the dormant Irish 'High Kingship', albeit mainly via Norman not Gaelic blood. Edward was also recognised as Robert's heir by an assembly of Scots nobles on 26 April 1315 at Ayr, before he sailed – if Robert were to die, Scotland would need an adult male monarch for wartime rather than Robert's daughter Marjorie.

In June Robert Bruce himself led a naval expedition from Tarbert across the Inner Hebrides, in alliance with Angus Og Macdonald, to ensure that the exiled MacDougall's fleet could not endeavour to move northwards. Meanwhile Edward and around 6,000 men landed around Larne and Glentrim in Ulster on 26 May, and his lieutenant and nephew Thomas Randolph defeated the local English administration and its Irish levies under Sir Thomas Mandeville. Ua Niall and twelve other local kings swore allegiance to Edward as 'High King of Ireland' at Carrickfergus in June, and they marched on to sack Rathmore and (on 29 June) Dundalk. The Scots/rebel army had overrun much of Ulster, and ironically the main loyalist force left to hold out was led by King Robert's father-in-law Richard de Burgh, earl of the province, supported by his kinsman King Fedlimid Ua Concobair of Connacht. While the English 'Justiciar', Edmund Butler, was rallying an Anglo-Irish army in the South, Edward defeated De Burgh and Fedlimid at Connor; but when Butler's army was ready he had to retreat allowing the two forces to link up. Once shortage of supplies forced them to retreat, Edward was able to resume the offensive. Some supportive risings broke out elsewhere and he now raised the serious possibility of driving the Anglo-Normans out of Ireland – in his own mind at least. On 6/7 November, marching south, he defeated another Anglo-Irish 'settler' army under 'Welsh Marches' baron Roger Mortimer, Lord of Ludlow and by marriage (to Joan de Geneville) Lord of Trim in central Ireland, at Trim.

Robert Bruce backed Edward up with enthusiastic letters to the Irish Gaelic lords, reminding them of the two peoples' common cultural/ethnic heritage – the original 'Scots' had come to Argyll from Ulster around AD 500 – and calling them one nation ('nacio') that should now jointly recover its liberty. This line was also taken in appeals to the Papacy for recognition of their cause's validity. The stress on the unity of the Gaelic-speaking peoples was probably genuine as much as a political tactic, arising from King Robert's gratitude to the Gaels of the Hebrides (and the Northern Irish) for their military support in 1307–14. Unlike any other Scots king since Malcolm III and Donald Ban, he had experience of relying on the Gaels as much as the 'Anglicised' south of Scotland – and had lived among them as an exile. But he did not join Edward immediately, returning to the Borders after his expedition to the Hebrides to besiege Carlisle in summer 1315. Its fall would have opened the floodgates to Scots raiding and possible long-term control of Cumberland, but he was unable to take the castle due to the courageous defence of local commander Sir Andrew de Harclay (or Harcla), Edward II's most competent commander. In May 1316 Edward Bruce was optimistically crowned as 'High King' of Ireland, and the surprise death of Robert's daughter Marjorie in childbirth at Paisley on 2 March 1316 (following a fall from her horse) confirmed his heirship to Scotland until Robert had a son. Marjorie's and Walter Stewart's son (Robert) could hardly succeed to a nation in the middle of war as an infant.

Robert Bruce took an army to Ireland to assist Edward in autumn 1316, leaving Sir James Douglas and Walter the 'Steward' as 'Guardians'. The Bruces' joint force outnumbered the English and they penetrated right across the Irish Midlands in a bold march as far as Limerick. But they had little support from the Gaelic lords beyond Ulster, and their specifically 'pan-Gaelic' propaganda alienated semi-autonomous Anglo-Norman settler barons. There was an added problem caused by chronically poor summers from 1315 onwards meaning a serious shortage of food and resultant famine; this was a Continent-wide phenomenon but it meant trouble in finding supplies, half-starved soldiers unwilling or unable to fight, forced seizure of food with less left for the unfortunate locals and rising resentment. The pillaging carried out by their army added to an image of the Bruce expedition as yet another set of self-seeking 'robber barons', worse than the English, and when Robert Bruce returned home his brother had to pull back into safer territory in Ulster. He was killed in battle by the English administration of Dublin's generals, John de Bermingham and Edmund Butler, at Faughart near Dundalk on 14 October 1318, and the Irish expedition had to be abandoned. The Irish 'Annals of Loch Ce' reckoned the killing of Edward Bruce to be the best deed done in the country for ages due to the misery he had brought there – testimony to how the idea of a 'pan-Gaelic' alliance had failed to win local support.

Triumph: From the Declaration of Arbroath to the Peace with England

Robert Stewart now became heir to Scotland aged two, and was recognised by Parliament on 3 December 1318 as the next king if Robert Bruce had no more children. The loss of the planned adult male heir possibly stimulated the sole plot against Bruce's government, which was now uncovered and led to executions (1320). The principal culprit was William de Soulis, grandson of one of the unsuccessful 'Competitors' of 1292. The war had bought time in distracting the shaky government of Edward II from sending another expedition to Southern Scotland and, as Scottish raids into Northern England escalated with impunity, Edward was forced onto the defensive. He could however still count on papal support, not least as Edward Bruce's crowning as King of Ireland had defied the 1155 papal bull 'Laudibiliter' by which the Papacy gave that kingdom to the rulers of England, and as Robert Bruce prepared his army in Lothian to attack Berwick in late 1317 two papal envoys arrived in England. They were supposed to command both Edward II and Bruce to a two-year truce, but Bruce refused to let them cross the frontier as he was not addressed as king in the documents; he pointed out that he had been elected as king by the people and was addressed as such by other sovereigns meaning that his demanding they use that term was reasonable.

In March 1318 Sir James Douglas recaptured Berwick-on-Tweed from the English with the aid of some of its inhabitants – the final loss of all that Edward I had gained since 1296. The humiliation spurred Edward to raise another army in summer 1319 and besiege it, but King Robert marched his army to the defence and with a typical fondness for what would now be termed 'psychological warfare' sent Douglas and his Borders raiders on a swift cavalry thrust southwards from the Solway Firth over the Pennines into Yorkshire to cut Edward's supply route. The real or perceived target was Queen Isabella and her household, waiting at York, and as the Douglases approached she was hastily evacuated by water to Lincolnshire. Archbishop Melton led out the regional levies to block the Douglas advance but at the Battle of Myton-in-Swaledale on 20 September Sir James contemptuously drove this large but unprepared force into the River Swale. After this, Edward had to abandon the northern campaign as he had no troops available to protect Yorkshire and local landowners currently fighting for him at Berwick, led by his cousin Earl Thomas of Lancaster, insisted on going home to save their estates. Lancaster ended up executed by the suspicious king in 1322.

The swift Douglas raiders on their ponies caused chaos across Northern England in these years – in a region already hard-hit by the recent famine. Apart from the humiliation and the useful acquisition of loot and 'blackmail money' from communities desperate not to be sacked, the war within England was hoped to force Edward to give in and recognise Scottish independence in a peace treaty. Lacking that prospect of French military aid or an imminent French attack on Gascony, which had assisted the Balliol regime against Edward I in the mid-1290s, Bruce skilfully used his mobile raiders' experience of guerrilla warfare to carry out 'hit-and-run' raids. The English government agreed to a three-year truce later in 1319, and then tried to use diplomacy to rally international support from the Papacy against their foe (an excommunicated murderer who had violated the sanctity of a church). In reply, the Scots lay and clerical 'political nation' was summoned to Arbroath in 1320 to draw up a dignified but firm response which would show that the defiance of Edward's claims was the united will of an entire people not just the work of a power-seeking excommunicate. The 'masterminds' of this move were presumably King Robert, Bishop Lamberton and the Chancellor of Scotland and host of the meeting, Abbot Bernard of Arbroath. The resulting letter, written by Bernard on behalf of the meeting and sealed by fifty-one magnates and clerics, left the king out of their number so that the current Pope (John XXII) could not refuse to accept a missive involving an excommunicate. But it made clear that the letter's supporters were united in their assertion that Scotland had always been an independent nation; it had been unjustly invaded by Edward I with a long list of atrocities and King Robert had saved the country from tyranny and destruction. If he was judged unworthy of the crown the Scots would accept that, but would choose another king rather than accept the King of England – and the Balliol claim was cancelled out by the fact that John Balliol had been unable to defend his people from invasion.

The letter was taken to the papal court, now at Avignon in Provence (leased by the Pope from King Robert of Naples, a junior branch of the French royal family), and Pope John was impressed enough to write to Edward II urging him to make peace with Scotland – though he was to change his mind again in 1321 after ferocious lobbying (and money?) from the English. The Declaration had little political effect in driving the Papacy to back Scotland rather than England, the latter being more politically important in the 'realpolitik' of international relations. Ultimately, renewed Anglo-French war from 1324 to 1325 and the flight of Edward's queen abroad to plan revolution would be far more useful in driving Edward II's unpopular, favourite-ridden and venal administration to collapse. But the Declaration had long-term significance, not least as a loud expression of national unity and self-confidence for the Scots – with the 'community of the realm', or at least its lay and ecclesiastical leaders, taking the lead rather than waiting on the will of the king. Its expression of popular sovereignty, vested in a people who had removed one king for incompetence and chosen another and who would never accept a foreign invader, seemed to represent the 'democratic' form of monarchy established in Scotland, with kings as removable by popular will. The use of these arguments had their own, contemporary reasons – they made it clear to the international community, as led by the Holy Father, that the Scots would accept neither Balliol nor Edward as their king.

The vicious war of raids and counter-raids resumed unabated on the Borders in 1322, with the more determined and coordinated Scots having the better of it and pressing far southwards. These guerrilla attacks particularly raised the English profile of Sir James Douglas, now known as 'the Black Douglas', as a 'bogeyman' in the region; his family were to assume military leadership on the Scots side of the Border for the next century and a third. Sir Andrew Harclay, commander at Carlisle, was concerned for his pillaged Cumbrians and as no aid was forthcoming from the king he agreed to a local truce with the Scots on 3 January 1323 without seeking the king's permission. This provided for Bruce to pay 40,000 marks to England and to receive one of Edward's daughters to marry his heir. It was judged as trespassing on the royal prerogative of foreign policy – and an alliance between Harclay and King Robert to coerce King Edward. As a result Harclay, too independent-minded for Edward to trust, was arrested and executed.

Left without any effective commanders in the North and in fear that giving any great magnate an army there could lead to the latter turning traitor too, Edward agreed a fourteen-year truce with the Scots on 30 May 1323. Recognition of King Robert was not included, but it gained both sides some breathing space. The catastrophic relationship between the petulant, suspicious and militarily incompetent English king, a sharp contrast to his father, and his magnates was the main reason for the Scots success in finally forcing a truce. But the vagaries of the climate since 1315 also played their part, in that the sequence of famine years in 1315–19 seriously damaged the ability of the English government to raise and supply armies; this and the ravaging of the North added to low morale. The resolution of the war had to wait until after Edward II had been deposed by an invasion launched from France by Isabella, now marginalised by her husband, and Edward Bruce's ex-foe Roger Mortimer in 1326. The populace rallied to the invaders, Edward fled and was captured while his 'favourites' were gruesomely lynched and in January 1327 the abandoned king was forced to abdicate in favour of his fourteen-year-old son Edward III. Isabella and Mortimer effectively took over the regency and used it to enrich themselves, but were in a shaky position despite initial popularity. Edward II was apparently murdered.

In spring 1327 Isabella and the militarily experienced Mortimer went back on a pledge made in exile in 1326 to recognise Scots independence, and made preparations for war. The crucial issue was the land seized from the 'Disinherited' of the Balliol and Comyn factions in Scotland; many of these men came from Northern English families and had relatives and friends eager to insist on at least partial restoration in any treaty. They were backed by Earl Henry of Lancaster, brother and heir to the 'martyred' Earl Thomas and a lynchpin of the new government – and Henry was the guardian of the new King Edward. The regency endeavoured to rally the 'political nation' with a final expedition to fight the ageing and ailing

King Robert, and in July a large army marched north from York with Edward III in titular command under the practical control of the veteran Mortimer. The Scots army, under Sir James Douglas and Thomas Randolph, Earl of Moray, carefully avoided battle as they retreated across County Durham. But 'hit-and-run' raids continued to provoke the English, and when the latter found the Scots drawn up in a formidable position on the banks of the River Wear the new English king wished to attack and show his valour (a sharp contrast to his father's record). Mortimer vetoed it, and an uneasy stand-off continued until the Douglases launched a daring midnight raid on the English camp a few nights later and humiliatingly cut through the ropes of Edward's and others' tents. The teenage King of England was left crawling under the fallen canvas while the raiders killed and looted at will in the chaos-strewn camp. After this Mortimer ordered a retreat to York, the expedition was abandoned and serious negotiations were resumed.

In spring 1328 an English council meeting at York during the festivities for Edward's marriage approved terms whereby Scotland's independence under King Robert would be recognised, all English lordships held within Scotland would be transferred to Scots legal jurisdiction, Scotland's boundaries as of 1286 would be accepted and English lawsuits against the Bruce regime at the papal law courts would be dropped. The 'Disinherited' would be abandoned, and one of Edward's sisters would marry Robert's son David Bruce. This formed the basis of the Treaty of Northampton. The fight for recognition of Scotland's independence was thus achieved fourteen years after Bannockburn. In the fashion of medieval power politics and dynastic reconciliations at an elite level, the marriage of David Bruce (aged four) to Edward II's sister Joan 'of the Tower' (of London, aged seven) was rushed through on 17 July 1328 at Berwick to seal the peace despite the participants' tender ages. Joan was duly despatched to Scotland.

The End of the Reign of Robert I: 1328–29

The weak point of the Treaty of Northampton was the exclusion of the 'Disinherited', some of whom came from cross-Border dynasties which had held lands in Scotland for two centuries and just happened to have backed Balliol or Comyn rather than Bruce in the 1300s. King Robert had needed extensive lands to reward his followers and create new loyalist dynasties, and some of those who had been evicted had little reason to be expected to stay loyal. But the evictees had strong support in England, as seen above, and the weak Mortimer/Isabella regency was to be overthrown by a coup at Nottingham Castle by the vigorous young Edward III in May 1330. In the meantime King Robert was ailing, apparently from some skin disease probably picked up on campaign – which later writers were to call 'leprosy'. It had similar side effects of physical disfigurement and evidently involved physical weakness too, so a series of strokes was possible; it could have been psoriasis (Henry IV of England, Edward III's grandson, was to suffer something similar). The king's foes alleged that it was a punishment for his killing the 'Red' Comyn in a church. In these circumstances King Robert could not be expected to live until his son David, born on 5 March 1324, reached his majority; and on 27 October 1327 his wife Elizabeth died at Cullen Castle, Fife, probably in her late forties. Robert did gain the bonus of papal recognition in 1328, as his excommunication was finally cancelled – ending the main diplomatic weapon that a hostile England could use against him.

The king promised to go on Crusade to atone for his sins in 1328. This was too optimistic, and after a further period of illness he died at Cardross Castle near Dumbarton on 7 June 1329, probably aged fifty-four and ten months. David became king at the age of five, with Randolph as regent. As is well known from its recent discovery, the king's heart was not buried with the rest of him at Dunfermline Abbey but was taken on Crusade to fulfil his promise. Sir James Douglas, in charge of the expedition, took charge of it and hung it in a casket around his neck. The planned Crusade to Palestine was postponed so Douglas joined in the latest expedition of the 'Reconquista' in Castile instead, fighting for King Alfonso XI in the Moslem emirate of Granada in 1330. He was killed at the siege of Teba, memorably taking off the casket and throwing it into a crowd of his foes as he was overwhelmed. It was later found and returned to Scotland to be buried at Melrose Abbey as the king had requested; the site was lost but it was rediscovered in 1996. The saviour of Scotland's independence, an indomitable fighter, a skilled guerrilla leader and strategist but a great statesman too and a shrewd chooser of first-class subordinates, Robert was among Scotland's greatest rulers. Given the practicalities of ruling two kingdoms at once, one as an absentee king represented by his own countrymen in a land seething with humiliation, it is unlikely that Edward I's 'solution' of 1299–1307 would have lasted long once he was dead even if Robert Bruce had never revolted or had been quickly killed. The various inter-state 'unions' of the Middle Ages that did last were by consent and involved far more autonomy or an alliance of dynasties. The fact that independence was preserved as it was, in a 'head-on' clash commencing in Edward I's lifetime, was down to King Robert. But his lack of an adult male heir left the chance of the Balliol family later regaining the throne – which would have been less of a threat had he taken the risk of being more generous to those nobles who had backed the 'wrong side' in the recent wars. Two of these men, Henry de Beaumont (married to the heiress of the defunct Earldom of Buchan) and David of Strathbogie (son and heir of the exiled Earl of Atholl) were competent military commanders – were they safer in exile as totally irreconcilable, or unfairly treated?

In Bruce's ravaging in Buchan, Lorn and Ireland he showed a callous if practical streak resembling Edward I's – though it was common for aristocratic medieval commanders to care more about fellow knights than to protect the less politically important casualties of war. Destroying men and munitions undermined foes' ability to sustain future rebel campaigns. But his relative generosity to the prisoners taken at Bannockburn contrasted sharply with Edward I's brutality and he seems to have had greater ability as a strategist than any other medieval Scots king. The contrast with the quality of Scots 'command decisions' in 1332–34 is notable.

Bruce *Versus* Balliol, Round Two: The Troubled Early Years of David II

David II was crowned at Scone on 24 November 1331, with the first anointing of a Scottish king (by the Bishop of St Andrews) added to the usual ceremonies. The ever-careful King Robert had secured a papal bull for this purpose (13 June 1329) so that it could not still be said that a Scots coronation was not complete or legally valid. The accession of a five-year-old king would not have given a serious chance to the Balliol cause had Robert Bruce's feared lieutenants remained active in defending the realm, at least until Edward III (as eager to assert his rights as his grandfather) had disposed of Mortimer and trained and funded an adequate army. It was probably the death of the 'Black Douglas' in Spain in 1330 that first gave ideas to the most aggressive of the 'Disinherited', former Buchan lord Sir Henry Beaumont, and then he had to convince John Balliol's son Edward, who was living on the family estates in Picardy. In 1332 Beaumont persuaded Edward Balliol to come to England. Balliol personally appealed to Edward III for aid in regaining his ancestral crown and estates; however the king had to agree that English troops should not cross the Tweed in the Treaty of Northampton so he told them to go north by sea. They raised an army of adventurers, estimated at 500 men-at-arms and 1,000 on foot by one source (the Bridlington Chronicle) and at 1,500–1,800 men in all by another (the

Lanercost Chronicle). They were buoyed up in the desperate venture by the fortuitous death of the Scottish regent, Bruce's nephew Thomas Randolph, on 20 July at Musselburgh; he was a highly capable general who would not have made his successors' mistakes. He was replaced as regent by Earl Donald of Mar, son of Bruce's sister Christina and probably lacking much military experience. Beaumont, by contrast, was a veteran of the English army from the Battle of Falkirk in 1298 and so had experience of defeating the Scots.

On 31 July the invaders sailed, landing at Kinghorn in Fife and marching overland via Dunfermline to the River Earn where a traitor showed them a ford to cross. Mar had drawn up his army on the ridge of Dupplin Moor, west of Perth, and had a useful position, but failed to send out adequate scouts; the Scots seemed to have forgotten the lessons of sudden attacks taught them by Bruce and Douglas. While he was inactive, Beaumont, the real leader of the invaders, sent Sir Alexander Mowbray and his advance guard across the ford un-intercepted to attack the Scots camp by surprise on the night of 10/11 August, though in the event they mistook a collection of civilian 'camp-followers' at Gask for the main army. Beaumont and Balliol arrived at dawn to reinforce them, and they climbed up onto the moorland above to secure a defensible position at the head of a valley – again, without interception. When the Scots army heard of their arrival the boldest of their senior officers, the late king's illegitimate son Sir Robert Bruce accused Mar of being a Balliol sympathiser who had let the invaders take a strategic position. The Battle of Dupplin Moor on 11 August duly saw a display of incredible Scot incompetence matched by English discipline. The result was a general slaughter, in which both Scots commanders and 2,000–10,000 Scots were killed. The disaster was entirely avoidable, and suggests Scots overconfidence and an inadequate appreciation of what archers could do to a packed force.

While Sir Andrew Murray/Moray, son of Wallace's

co-leader of 1306 and Lord of Avoch Castle in Ross, assumed the vacant regency and 'Guardianship', Edward Balliol was crowned King of Scots at nearby Scone. However, he did not have the men to keep hold of the Angus-Fife region in winter when no reinforcements could be expected, so his army marched southwards to the Balliol lands in Galloway where a friendlier welcome might be expected. The remnants of the Scots army hung on their flanks, harassing them but not daring to fight – which tactic could have been pursued by Mar in August to greater usefulness. Balliol settled down in southern Galloway for the winter, within reach of the English in Carlisle, but was tackled by the best strategist of the current Douglas line, Sir William the 'Knight of Liddesdale' (son of a cousin of Sir James). Backed up by the arrival of regency troops under the Steward's son Robert – King David's nephew and heir – and the new Earl of Moray, John Randolph, he defeated Balliol at the Battle of Annan on 16 December 1332. Balliol was forced to flee to England, having shown that he had overestimated the amount of support he could call on in Scotland. With English help he was able to besiege Berwick in spring 1333, but it held out and he had to retreat again. But the Scots had their own problems, as the militarily capable Murray was captured in a skirmish on the Borders and carried off for ransom and a new 'Guardian' had to be appointed. This was Archibald Douglas, brother of Sir James and uncle of the new Lord (William) Douglas.

On 23 April the main English army arrived at Berwick to commence a full siege, and the king followed to Tweedmouth on 9 May. Justifying his attack to the envoys sent by King Philip VI of France by saying that the Scots had invaded England first, he took time off the siege for his usual knightly pursuits and went sightseeing to Lindisfarne with his family. Pageantry and pleasure were always part of war for this Arthurian enthusiast, but he was to show himself more realistic than his grandfather and his acts of cruelty were more sporadic and calculated. Governor Sir Alexander

Seton could not have halted the imminent land attack due to the English starting fires so he appealed successfully for a truce. He was given fifteen days' grace to wait for relief, and would surrender if none arrived – giving the Scots army time to reach Berwick and the impatient Edward a chance to fight them. Twelve children of prominent townsmen were sent out as hostages. On the final day of the truce a large Scots force under 'Guardian' Sir Archibald Douglas arrived, crossed the Tweed to cut off Edward's army (on the north bank) from Northumberland and occupied Tweedmouth. Sir William Keith entered the town with a small contingent over the half-wrecked bridge to announce that he was taking over as commander. He cancelled the promise to surrender, so Edward spitefully hung Seton's hostage son Thomas from a gallows within full view of the defenders and announced that he would kill two more of the boys every day that Berwick resisted him. In practical terms the atrocity shocked Keith into reopening negotiations, Douglas having moved off to raid towards Queen Philippa's base at Bamburgh Castle. He agreed to surrender on the evening of the 19th if Douglas had not arrived and relieved the town by then. He was permitted to leave the town and go to inform Douglas, and on the morning of the 19th they arrived within reach of Berwick and crossed the Tweed to find that Edward had drawn up his army on the high ridge of Halidon Hill between them and the town.

To attack Edward, the Scots would have to descend from their own position, cross a marsh and then climb up the hill, giving the English the advantage – and Edward had brought along a large force of archers to shower them with arrows as they did so. The first European ruler to make use of the concentrated 'fire-power' of archers against a conventional 'feudal' host of cavalry and infantry, Edward may have been advised by veterans of Boroughbridge in 1322 (when Harclay had used this tactic on a smaller scale against Thomas of Lancaster) and had certainly sought the advice of Sir Henry Beaumont about his tactics at Dupplin Moor in 1332. The

Scots seem to have been unaware of the danger of archers – a sharp contrast to the caution and flexibility of Robert Bruce and Sir James Douglas. Edward's army was blocking the only safe route to Berwick, but their army was larger and they were overconfident and seem to have hoped to use weight of numbers to push the English (on foot) back into the Tweed. The Scots charged downhill and over the marsh, but the slope up Halidon Hill slowed their advance and a hail of arrows met them; then the Balliol infantry charged them. Those who hesitated or retreated were run into by those still advancing behind them, and when Edward Balliol's men on the English 'left' eventually broke the first line of the Scots, flight began. Edward ordered 'no quarter' (though Douglas had done so first) and thousands were killed in the slaughter that followed – Douglas himself, and the earls of Ross, Lennox and Menteith also fell; Edward celebrated his triumph by executing large numbers of prisoners. Berwick was stormed on the same day. The only senior Scots lord to escape was Robert Stewart, who took refuge at Dumbarton Castle and soon crossed the sea to the safer haven of Bute, part of the ancestral Stewart lands that Balliol had handed over to Alan Lisle. Balliol gave the Stewart mainland territories to David of Strathearn. Subsequently Robert was able to recover his mainland lands by a guerrilla war aided by the Campbells.

Unlike the English the Scots could not afford to lose many senior figures without a serious effect on military capability; the majority of the Scots aristocratic military elite fell at Dupplin Moor and Halidon Hill. The 'Guardianship' passed to John Randolph and Robert Stewart, both young and inexperienced. With the Bruce regime left without the means to resist, Edward was able to reimpose Balliol as his client king on Scotland and thus returned Anglo-Scottish relations to the pattern of indirect rule via a vassal, which his grandfather had chosen in 1292–96. Despite his shattering victory he kept his word to Balliol and did not seek to take the Scots throne himself, showing his realism and probably the small role that

Scotland played in his vision of himself as a great European warrior king. Edward III left it to Balliol to restore himself to the throne with his force of 'Disinherited' and adventurers. It may have been due to a desire to let Balliol seem less of an English puppet or overconfidence in the depth of his support – or distaste for a long campaign?

As events turned out, the Balliol expedition secured the Lowlands, and Beaumont and Strathbogie marched on north-eastwards to regain their ancestral lands. Bruce having devastated them thoroughly and pulled down the castles, Beaumont was kept busy rebuilding his castle of Dundarg on the Aberdeenshire coast. The Bruce forces pulled back to evade open battle with the dreaded English archers and returned to Bruce's and Douglas's tactic of guerrilla warfare, in which Sir William Douglas of Liddesdale and his rival Sir Andrew Ramsay made their names. Meanwhile Edward III forced Balliol to hand over Lothian, whose principal castles were garrisoned by the English (July 1334). In May 1334 King David and his wife Joan (Edward's sister) left for France; they became useful pawns for King Philip in his stand-off with England.

Lacking the resources to stand up to the English army in an open battle, the 'resistance' fell back on their main ally and sought to draw Edward away to a war over his diminished lands in Gascony, which his French overlord coveted. The ransomed Sir Andrew Murray, as husband of David Bruce's aunt Christina, was to resume the 'Guardianship' at a council meeting their leaders held at Dumbarton Castle in September 1335. It was autumn 1334 before Edward was ready and willing to lead a major army into Scotland, boldly choosing to fight in winter when the Scots would not be expecting him. The lesson learnt at Halidon Hill meant that the Scots within his reach in the South were extremely unlikely to venture to engage his army, and it was too far to march all the way to Dundarg where Balliol's lieutenant Beaumont was now being besieged by the main northern 'Bruce' army under Sir Andrew

Murray. Worse, Beaumont and Strathbogie took one side in a legal dispute and Balliol another; they kept away from Balliol's court. In 1334 Strathbogie revolted, joining the Bruce cause – though he was to defect again the following summer as the Balliol cause revived and turned harshly on his ex-allies.

The winter of 1334/5 turned out to be extremely harsh, which inhibited movement, and Edward proceeded no further than Roxburgh. A second, impressively sized expedition of around 13,000 men mustered at Newcastle in June 1335 to march to Berwick and was joined by Balliol and some of his lieutenants, along with Edward's brother Prince John (Earl of Cornwall), his brother-in-law Count William of Julich, Germany, and rather more of the English nobility than had turned out for most of Edward II's campaigns. Edward divided his army into two, giving one contingent to Balliol, and marched across Southern Scotland via Nithsdale and Carrick en route to Glasgow. He did not waste time with sieges of those local castles still in Bruce hands, but concentrated on destroying their cause's resources – and his lieutenants were allowed to burn abbeys (e.g. Newbattle) too. Balliol joined Edward in Glasgow after crossing Lothian, having committed his own excesses to try to assert himself as a warrior king to be feared rather than part of the English army's baggage. The ravaging was designed to punish the small Scots freeholders who formed the backbone of the Scots army and had played the pivotal role in Wallace's and Bruce's 'schiltrons', ruining their economic resources and killing as many of them as possible.

The invaders then moved on to Perth where Edward held an assembly of his Scots collaborators to show the alleged strength of support for Balliol (not least to outside observers such as papal envoys). On 18 August an assembly of previously pro-Bruce nobles, allegedly with the permission of their leaders Robert Stewart and David of Strathbogie, agreed to recognise Balliol as their king; Edward III then made Strathbogie his 'Lieutenant' in Scotland. Unlike his grandfather he would use

Scots, not English, viceroys to minimise resentment. A naval descent from England sacked Dundee, while in the north-east David of Strathbogie deserted back to the Balliol cause and started terrorising the smallholders of Mar and Buchan in another campaign of burning and pillaging. The only bright moment for the Bruce cause was a successful ambush of a smaller English force by 'Guardian' John Randolph on the Borough Muir outside Edinburgh on 30 July.

However at this juncture King Philip finally intervened, securing funds from his nobles to pay for an army of 6,000 men to aid King David – though this was a threat more than a definite commitment and this chivalrous international knightly enthusiast was more interested in the Mediterranean than in Scotland. Philip, after all, had not been born to rule France – until 1328 he had been Count of Valois, nephew of the late King Philip IV with three of the latter's sons ahead in the line of succession. Married to the heiress to the defunct 'Latin' Crusader claim to the Byzantine Empire, he wanted to be the leader of a Crusade which the Pope was planning in Asia Minor rather than to send valuable men to Scotland, and the Pope wanted the successful and allegedly pious King Edward to stop his futile war in the North and join Philip. Philip's envoys visited the king and asked Edward to submit his claim to Scotland to the joint arbitration of him and the Pope. To complicate matters, Philip's own enemies as King of France were asking Edward to press his own claim to France and invade that country, promising a revolt there.

The Bruce cause was best served by lying low or temporarily surrendering and waiting for Edward to return home and leave Balliol exposed to rebellion – a repeat of the 'rebel' tactics of 1299–1302. An Anglo-Irish expedition also intervened on Edward's behalf, besieging the Stewarts' Rothesay Castle. As John Randolph, Earl of Moray, was captured attacking Roxburgh, halting the Bruces' campaign in the Southern Uplands, Robert Stewart, the Earl of Fife and many other great nobles made their submission to Edward. He was able to inform the French envoys that Scotland was submissive to his control and there was no cause for France to interfere, set up large and costly garrisons at Edinburgh and other Lowlands strongpoints and retired to Roxburgh for Christmas. Andrew Murray's army at Dumbarton found it prudent to secure a three-month truce from early October, though this excluded Edward Balliol so his lands could still be attacked. In these propitious circumstances the defeat and death of senior Balliol commander David of Strathbogie, his army destroyed by Sir Andrew Murray at Culblean on 30 November 1335 as he was besieging Murray's wife's garrison in Kildrummy Castle, seemed a minor setback. Murray had been hastening to relieve Kildrummy and draw off Strathbogie's army; aided by locals sent from Kildrummy to guide him through the woods, Murray was able to take the pursuing Strathbogie by surprise and destroy his men (who do not seem to have had archers). Strathbogie was cut down. The destruction of his army heralded the collapse of the Balliol cause's Scots support in the north-east, undermining the possibility that the 'Disinherited' and assorted turncoats could hold out without regular English expeditions to rescue them.

The papal mediators finally persuaded Edward to agree to a three-month truce in January 1336, and urged him to make up his differences with Philip and join the Crusade. Even if Edward was unwilling to let Philip lead the latter, he could not refuse outright without arousing Church wrath. The basis of a settlement was to be that Edward Balliol was recognised as King of Scots for his lifetime, and as he had no son David Bruce was his heir. Balliol was probably over fifty and David not yet twelve so this was logical; and David would be susceptible to English pressure once he was king as his wife was Edward's sister. Andrew Murray and the other Bruce commanders in Scotland agreed to it. But David, now residing at Château Gaillard near Rouen in Normandy (built by Edward III's ancestor Richard I), refused. Possibly Philip put him up to it to keep the war going and bleed Edward slowly of his military resources. With the danger of a French expeditionary force landing in Scotland in 1336 Edward sent his cousin Earl Henry of Lancaster, commanding in Scotland in his absence, to deal with Bruce attacks in the north-east and rebuild the vital coastal fortress at Dunnottar. As soon as possible the king hurried north to Perth (June 1336) to start destroying the east coast countryside, removing resources before the French could use them. He relieved the Bruce forces' siege of Lochindorb Castle in Moray, where David of Strathbogie's widow was holed up, so asserting his military supremacy as far north as his grandfather had done, and burnt Aberdeen to the ground in September. In the meantime his younger brother John of Eltham, Earl of Cornwall, ravaged Carrick and the Clyde valley. The Scots chroniclers' hatred for the king was shown in their story that the sudden death of John at Perth was due to the homicidal Edward stabbing him during an argument, which is unlikely. But he was taking a gamble in concentrating his main army so far north, as Philip's fleet – allegedly assembled for the Crusade – was cruising the English Channel and an invasion of England could not be ruled out. Luckily the gamble paid off and in October Edward hurried south again. He then wintered on the Clyde, while in the north-east Murray's army destroyed Dunnottar and undid his recent achievements.

As England and France drifted into war during 1337–8 Edward's vital ability to devote time to marching large armies to Scotland every year diminished. In this situation, the Bruce forces could slowly regain the upper hand and wear down his garrisons – and without the imminent threat of confiscation or English ravagers Scots landowners could contemplate defecting more safely. Philip's aggression thus speeded up the revival of Bruce fortunes, and he sent supplies via Dunbar Castle, now held against the Balliols by Earl Patrick's Countess, 'Black' Agnes (sister of John Randolph and daughter of the late regent Thomas Randolph). Murray and his allies could move in to besiege the vital strongpoint of Stirling Castle in spring 1337. Edward concentrated on building up a European coalition against Philip, centred on assorted princes of the Low Countries and Rhineland, and while he was on a brief expedition to relieve Stirling Castle in May Philip announced his legal confiscation of Gascony, the lands held by Edward from the French Crown in Aquitaine. Edward now had to concentrate on his Continental war; Scotland was a side issue. The main English force in the region was now led by his most trusted and capable commander, William Montague/Montacute, the new Earl of Salisbury.

Their 'set-piece' action of 1337–38 was the prolonged and unsuccessful siege of Dunbar Castle, which was set on isolated 'stacks' of rock on a cliff so the English could not wheel their siege-towers up to the walls or dig under them and resorted to bombardment. The militant 'Black Agnes' personally led the defence, assisted by Alexander Ramsay, and shouted defiance at the attackers from the walls. Reportedly when Montague threatened to have her captured brother, John Randolph the co-'Guardian', executed if she did not surrender she quipped that that did not bother her as then she could inherit his Earldom of Moray. Edward visited the siege in spring 1338 to no effect, and after the French war drew him south again Montague had to give up the siege in June. Meanwhile Sir Andrew Murray died sometime in 1338, and Robert Stewart succeeded as sole 'Guardian'. The Balliol position collapsed in Galloway thanks to the guerrilla war waged by Sir William Douglas, who took over Liddesdale in 1337 by conquest and in 1338 took the crucial strongpoint of Hermitage Castle.

In July 1338 Edward sailed for the Low Countries, and with no major English army available for the Scots war Balliol's position in Scotland declined irreversibly. As the military balance tipped, the last of his 'Disinherited' allies restored to the North, led by de Beaumont, had to flee again. 1339 saw Balliol's power restricted to a dwindling area around Perth, and with the region blockaded by sea the English could not send reinforcements; King Edward was in Flanders. Sir

William Douglas visited King David in France and brought a force of French crossbowmen and men-at-arms back to the Lowlands to aid the Bruce cause. Finally, in August, Robert Stewart's army besieged Perth; a churchman with a knowledge of siege warfare called William Bullock aided Stewart to build siege engines and the English surrendered on the 17th. Balliol and his remaining adherents had to flee to England. Edward III, like Edward II in 1312–14, was left with a precarious hold on Edinburgh and Roxburgh castles, and in April 1341 the former was retaken by Sir William Douglas by a trick. A party of Highlanders, shaved and dressed in Lowlands clothes to resemble civilian carters, crossed the Firth of Forth with a load of coal and commandeered a waggon to 'bring supplies' up from the city to Edinburgh Castle. They arrived at dawn to haggle with the porter, and the waggon 'accidentally' broke down underneath the gateway portcullis so it could not be lowered. Then the ambushers produced weapons, killed the porter and set on the few guards awake, and as Douglas blew a horn more men sprinted up the road to help them seize the gate and storm the castle. This news seems to have persuaded King David that it was safe to come home.

David II in Power and in Captivity, 1341–71: An Underestimated King?

On 2 June 1341 King David and Queen Joan landed from France at Inverbervie near Aberdeen, the country now being safe for them to return. The teenage king was totally inexperienced in the type of warfare that would be of use for a nation usually outnumbered by its neighbour's army, though King Philip had taken him on his campaign against Edward III in 1339. From his military actions as an adult king he seems to have been impatient to show his mettle. For the moment, he chiefly resided at Kildrummy (his aunt Christina's castle) and Aberdeen in the north-east for the summer of 1341, before coming south to Lothian to raid into England. Aided by French troops, David was now able to launch a raid into Northumberland to open a new front in the Anglo-French war; however he had no experience of war and his attack on Newcastle was badly organised. In a mirror image of English overconfidence and Scots resourcefulness from the 1320s, his besiegers failed to set adequate guards and the besieged raided his camp to kidnap one of his senior commanders, John Randolph, Earl of Moray. A frontal attack on the walls failed, and David retreated as Edward sent an army north under the Earl of Derby. The English king joined in the campaign in an attempt to catch his brother-in-law, but the Scots evaded him in Ettrick Forest.

A temporary truce saw a series of chivalric jousts between the Scots and English knights at Roxburgh, with the international 'camaraderie' of knights seeing Douglas arriving there with twelve Scots jousters to issue challenges for a tournament while twelve more Scots jousted at Berwick. Unfortunately Douglas was injured in the hand in his joust against the enemy commander Derby and had to be taken home in a litter; he was replaced as 'team captain' for a second tournament by Alexander Ramsay who had more success. This seems to have worsened his dislike of the latter. It was Ramsay who led the successful Scots attempt to retake Roxburgh Castle in 1342, and as a reward he was granted its custodianship and the sheriffdom of Teviotdale by King David. The titular governor of Roxburgh until now had been Douglas, who retaliated by kidnapping Ramsay, dragging him off to isolated Hermitage Castle and starving him to death. This sordid feud thus removed one of the Scots' best commanders, but luckily King Edward was by now distracted by his 1342 expedition to intervene in Brittany. In February 1343 an Anglo-French truce at Esplechin included Scotland in its terms. Edward could not afford the time or resources to launch another invasion – and Balliol was never to return; in any case he had no male heir to keep his cause going. It is unclear whether the marriage of King David's sole full sister, Margaret, to Earl William of Sutherland was aimed at providing a new line of succession to 'cut out' Robert Stewart, or at any rate the latter's children. Robert's (first) marriage, to Elizabeth Mure of Rowallan (a Stewart retainer's daughter) in around 1335, does not appear to have been recognised by the Church and Robert obtained their children's specific legitimation only in 1347 once King David was a prisoner abroad. One source has it that David's choice of heir in these years was Margaret and William's son, John Sutherland, who died in 1361 aged fourteen.

In 1346 King David accepted Philip VI's pleas to open a new front in the Anglo-French war, which had resumed in 1345 with an English expedition to Aquitaine and had now seen Edward III invade Normandy. With Edward and his army absent in France, the north of England was vulnerable, but Philip only sent urgent envoys to David after he had been routed humiliatingly at Crécy (26 August) and Edward had besieged Calais. David held a rendezvous of his levies at Perth, though this was disrupted by the Earl of Ross, principal commander of the north-western levies, using the occasion to kill his rival Ranald of the Isles and then returning home to avert retaliation. The authority of the king was ignored by both sides, though this was not unusual for the North. David took his diminished army on to Liddesdale to take Liddel Castle and execute its governor, then pressed on into England. He only had around 2,000 men-at-arms and 13,000 lightly armed infantry, but he ignored Sir William Douglas's request to call off the raid and headed to the Tyne to cross and start ravaging the County Palatine of Durham. Archbishop William Zouche of York, Sir Thomas Rokeby and Sir Henry Percy led out a well-equipped army of around 12,000 men. The Scots clearly did not expect to find such a force waiting – when the English caught a Douglas raiding party in the fog near Durham on 14 October and the Scots fled to inform their king of the size of the opposition he claimed that there were not that number of armed men in the whole of Northern England. On the 17th, at Neville's Cross, he came face to face with the Archbishop's army and realised his mistake too late. The Scots charged, but were decimated by the English archers as at Halidon Hill; two of their three battalions broke and fled and the third, the king's, was left exposed and overrun. David was shot with an arrow in the nose and captured by an English squire after a personal tussle in which he knocked out two of his captor's teeth. The earls of Moray and Strathearn and the royal chancellor, chamberlain and marshal were all killed, and Sir William Douglas and the earls of Fife, Menteith and Wigtown captured; Robert Stewart and the Earl of March escaped.

Edward III now had both claimants to the Scots throne in his hands, and David was paraded through the streets of London on a black charger and lodged in the Tower. He spent most of the next eleven years in captivity, mostly at royal estates around London or in Hampshire, while Robert Stewart acted as regent in Scotland. In 1347 Queen Joan arrived to join her husband in England. After the fall of Calais in 1347 a truce was arranged between England and France to last until April 1354, with the devastation of resources and evidence of seemingly divine wrath from the 'Black Death' adding to the reasons for a lull in the fighting, and from 1348 tentative negotiations for David's ransom were underway. Edward could threaten to replace him with Balliol again to achieve better terms from the Scots, and indeed while David was in captivity English official documents once more referred to Balliol as 'King of Scots' though this time he did not possess any territory in his realm. Negotiations with the Stewart regency were entrusted to the captive Sir William Douglas, who was allowed to return to Scotland with a secret mission to deal with certain nobles in 1352. The following year he was released permanently, and may have come under suspicion of double-dealing and selling out to Edward III as a few months later he was suddenly murdered by his cousin William, Lord Douglas, while they were hunting at Galswood in Ettrick Forest (August 1353). It would appear from King David's actions after his return home that he may have now turned against Robert Stewart – did he suspect the Stewart family of plotting?

Edward III came to a private agreement with King David in November 1352 without waiting to hold formal negotiations with the regent and his council, who would have to put any treaty to a meeting of their parliament. The terms included one of Edward III's sons – who were descendants of Malcolm III's daughter Queen Edith/Matilda of England – succeeding David in Scotland, and in return for agreeing this the Scots nobility were to regain various estates in England that had been confiscated. David was to be released and sent home with a body of English commissioners in order to win over his magnates to the 'deal' (at Parliament in Perth, February 1352). If he failed to do so in the prescribed time, the commissioners were to decide whether to let him stay in Scotland to continue to argue the English case or to move him back to Newcastle or Berwick. He probably agreed to do homage to Edward in exchange for this, and Sir William Douglas certainly did so; Edward was clearly trying to build up a powerful party of allies among the Bruce government elite to replace the now-useless Balliol. But the said parliament turned down the deal indignantly, probably led by the Stewart family who would lose their succession to David's throne, and in March 1352 David returned to London. The breakdown of Anglo-French negotiations in 1354–55 led to the new King John II of France resuming the war, with Scotland bound to help them by David's previous alliance with Philip VI. While Edward was campaigning in France again, Stewart's regency allowed a French mercenary to lead a successful assault on Berwick on 6 November 1355.

The English king returned home from France, troops were immediately summoned to Newcastle in December and in January 1356 his army arrived at Berwick to retake it – much sooner than expected. The French commander there fled, and the townsmen were left with no chance of rescue and had to surrender and beg Edward's mercy. He moved on into Lothian in a pitiless campaign of midwinter destructions that became known as the 'Burnt Candlemass', and on 25 January, at Roxburgh, Edward Balliol was forced to abdicate his rights to Scotland in return for a pension and the payment of his debts. The ex-king retired into such obscurity that we cannot be certain of the date or place of his death or his age, though it was probably around January 1364 near Doncaster in Yorkshire and he was presumably well over seventy. Next day Edward began his advance on Edinburgh with his army burning a swathe of countryside 20 miles across as they advanced. Edinburgh's lower town was burnt on Candlemass Day (2 February) in the climax of the punishment, and then Edward moved back via Haddington to cross Ettrick Forest en route to Carlisle. The English as well as their victims suffered from famine on the return march in the icy weather as supply ships failed to reach the Forth. However, the raid achieved its objective of reminding Stewart's council of what awaited them if they failed to cooperate with Edward's proposed settlement.

Edward's eldest son's attack on central France from Aquitaine that summer was spectacularly successful. King John was taken prisoner and deported to England. Edward now had the unique boost of the kings of both Scotland and France as his captives, and while the French regency government faced popular revolt and near anarchy the Scots regency had to give up hope of France rescuing them. On 17 January 1357 the Scots Parliament appointed commissioners to treat with Edward, and in August 1357 the preliminaries were agreed at Berwick. The terms were taken back to the Scots Parliament, which agreed them on 26 September, and on 3 October the Treaty of Berwick was signed. The Scots Parliament at Scone then ratified it on 6 November. David was to be released in exchange for a ransom of 100,000 marks, a huge sum that was to be paid in ten equal instalments – and was not all paid (the same happened to the huge sum Edward demanded for King John's ransom). On Christmas Day, Queen Joan, the Bishop of St Andrews and the Earl of March received safe conducts to go to England and arrange the handover of the first instalment, and indeed the queen was never to return to Scotland, which may show her low opinion of her husband's homeland. Possibly suffering from poor health or annoyed at her husband's liaison with his future wife Margaret Drummond, widow of Sir John Logie, she died in Kent on 14 August 1362.

David now returned to Scotland, but he clearly had no ill feeling towards Edward as he continued to visit the English court most years during the late 1350s and 1360s. Indeed, the friendliness he showed towards his ex-captor has been taken by modern nationalist historians as a sign of lack of patriotism and a desire to put his personal welfare above his country's. More generously, he was suspicious of the intentions of certain of his great nobles – above all, Robert Stewart – and called on Edward's power as a counterbalance to them. Certainly, his intentions towards England were suspected by the Stewart faction, although Robert Stewart received the vacant Earldom of Strathearn in November 1357. In spring 1363 William Douglas seized the royal castle of Dirleton, and Stewart, Douglas and veteran negotiator the Earl of March formed a 'band' (written bond of alliance) to force David to change his councillors. These three great lords together controlled much of the south of Scotland. But David moved swiftly to attack Douglas's estates, defeating him at Lanark, and after this show of royal power the other two surrendered. On 4 May Stewart renewed his oath of fealty to the king at Inch Murdach, and he and his older sons were probably taken into custody.

David now proceeded with his alliance with England openly, with another visit to London, and on 24 November 1363 a treaty of alliance was signed. Edward, with a large family of active and competent sons to provide for, pushed for David to recognise one of them as his heir as in 1351, and David's dislike of Stewart was such that he went along with this and may even have thought up the idea. To modern eyes it seems the ultimate snub to the Bruces' struggle for Scots independence for David to accept or even plan the succession of an English prince, but it should be remembered that he had spent much of his life in France and then in England, had an Anglo-Irish mother from Ulster and would have regarded himself as one of an international 'freemasonry' of European sovereigns rather than as an exclusively Scots figure. There was also possibly potential Church legal opposition to Robert Stewart's succession as his eldest three sons were all by a dubious marriage. An English prince ruling Scotland should bring an end to the danger and misery of constant wars with England; and David clearly did not regard his subjects' likely reaction as barring such a scheme. Edward's initial candidate was his third surviving son, John 'of Gaunt' (Ghent), but in November 1363 the Scots Parliament voted against accepting John or any other son of Edward's.

In November 1363 David and Edward now agreed that Edward should be named as David's heir, passing on the Scots crown to one of his sons; the English king's second son Lionel, Duke of Clarence and currently Lord Lieutenant/governor of Ireland, was now suggested instead of John. Lionel was married to Elizabeth de Burgh, David's cousin and heiress of the Earldom of Ulster. Despite Scots hostility the plan to name Edward III as formal heir and one of his sons to succeed was in fact put to the Scots Parliament at Scone in March 1364. The reaction was as hostile as could have been expected. It was never passed, and Lionel died in Italy in 1368. Robert Stewart remained heir presumptive. It would appear from the equivocal references to Stewart's current reputation in the 1360s by the chronicler John of Fordun that there was contemporary criticism of past mistakes that he had made as regent in the 1330s and 1340s and his alleged cowardice in fleeing at Neville's Cross; he was not universally backed as a 'nationalist' champion.

David's surprise second marriage – to Margaret Drummond in February 1364 at Inchmahone Priory, Aberfoyle – can be read as a desire to produce children and to remove Stewart from the line of succession. Margaret was not as 'low-born' as supposed by hostile Stewart dynasty writers, but her family provided a new faction in Scottish politics, a possible 'King's

Party' to set against the Stewarts and their allies. They were showered with profitable marriage alliances and land grants, the queen's son by her first marriage (John Logie) became a royal favourite and David even drew the Stewarts into the new Drummond-Bruce network by backing the marriage of Robert Stewart's eldest son John to the queen's kinswoman Annabella Drummond. John Stewart (the future King Robert III) now became Earl of Atholl in 1367. At some point, probably in 1367/8, Robert Stewart and his third son Alexander of Badenoch were arrested and imprisoned at 'high-security' Loch Leven Castle, marooned in a loch in Fife, and other Stewart sons may have been arrested too as some chroniclers claim. This was presumably to head off a revolt, and was apparently at the queen's request, but by 1369/70 all the Stewart menfolk had been released and restored to favour in a wary *modus vivendi*; instead it was Queen Margaret who fell from favour as she had been divorced and disgraced by March 1370. This is traditionally seen as a 'Stewart triumph' but was more probably masterminded by the king's courtiers, led by administrator Sir Robert Erskine and the family of the king's new mistress Agnes, sister of George Dunbar, Earl of March. Agnes, like Margaret, already had children – so was David (only forty-six) still looking for a new heir? The likelihood is that David was planning to marry Agnes, but this was forestalled by his unexpected death at Edinburgh Castle on 22 February 1371. Only forty-seven, David and his allies would have expected him to reign for many more years; instead the Stewart dynasty took the throne. Possibly his head injury at Neville's Cross (an arrow barb had not been removed) flared up again. Given the extreme instability and frequent humiliations of his reign and his plan to allow an English prince to succeed him, David's reputation is still much lower than that of his father. He cannot be called gifted or successful, but he was determined; his reputation may have stood higher had he reigned longer and left children. Contemporaries paid tribute to his bravery and his tenacious pursuit of his rights.

5

The Stewarts: 1371–1542

Robert II, 1371–90: Head of the Family 'Firm'?

Scotland now entered a less fraught period of development, with no more attempt to overthrow its reigning dynasty by the English who were preoccupied with their kings' claim to France. The war there had resumed in 1369 as Charles V, the formidable son of the unlucky John II, endeavoured to regain the swollen Duchy of Aquitaine from England. However it was not until 26 March 1371 that Stewart was crowned, due to an armed hosting at Linlithgow by William, Earl of Douglas – possibly following his failed anti-Stewart appeal to an estates meeting there. This meeting is otherwise unknown. The 'Scotichronicon' suggests that Douglas claimed the throne for himself as heir to the Balliol-Comyn claim, but there is no record of his having any genealogical connection with that dynasty.

A series of complex 'pay-offs' can be seen in the lands and offices distributed by Robert II in the early 1370s, often to potential foes, and this adds to the impression that the Stewart family were in a weak position and needed to shore up support. The stress placed by historical writings in the next few decades on the glories of the reign of Robert Bruce, the new king's grandfather, would suggest a conscious attempt at propaganda to link the two men in the public mind and add to Robert II's dynastic legitimacy. Luckily Robert's daughter

Margaret was married to John Macdonald, 'Lord of the Isles', so he could count on the Macdonalds' loyalty. Robert also had a large and mostly capable brood of sons, most of them already adult in 1371, and could use them as senior earls. The eldest, Earl John of Carrick (born 1337?), was recognised as heir to the throne by the inaugural parliament, and the entail of the crown created in 1373 placed his sons (when he had any, which was not until 1378) as heirs after him. The second son, the ambitious and ruthless Earl Robert of Menteith (born 1340), already had a son – Murdach – and they were to be heirs after John and his sons. Robert of Menteith secured the Earldom of Fife (which carried with it the rights to crown each new king) from Countess Isabella, daughter of that Earl Duncan who had been unable to crown Robert I in 1306. Married to John Dunbar, Earl *de iure uxoris* – equivocal enough about Robert II to fail to do his duty as crowner in 1371 – Isabella now transferred the earldom to Robert of Menteith under a complicated early fourteenth-century succession entail, which had named firstly Robert I and then the earls of Menteith as its heirs. The king's third son Alexander (b. *c.* 1342) was now made Lord of Badenoch (adjoining Moray to the south) and became the regime's strongman in the Highlands, his ruthless acquisitiveness and brutality earning him the nickname of the 'Wolf of Badenoch'. Alexander also acquired the king's Lieutenancy of the North as far as the Pentland Firth, excepting Moray, in 1372. The Earldom of Caithness was disputed between several claimants, and the most powerful, Alexander de Ard, resigned his claim (*c.* 1376) in favour of a Stewart claimant – David, Robert II's elder son by his second marriage (to Euphemia, sister of the late Earl Hugh of Ross) and probably still in his teens. Meanwhile the new king also confirmed the transfer of lands inherited from the Mac Ruaris of Garmoran by the senior line of Macdonalds, the 'Lords of the Isles', to his son-in-law 'Lord' John's eldest son, Ranald (March 1372). This was the central act in 'buying off' John's children by his first marriage so that his son by his second marriage, to Robert II's daughter, would inherit the main Macdonald lands and lordship. This young man, Donald, now secured the rights to inherit the lands of Lochaber and Kintyre/Knapdale, rounding off Stewart allies' control of the western flanks of the Highlands.

As many of the principal earldoms as possible were thus concentrated in Stewart hands, aided by Robert II's luck in having a larger family than any king since the days of Malcolm III. But, like the similarly placed Edward III of England, his large family of aggressive sons and feuding grandsons was to damage his dynasty's stability long-term, as the ability and ambitions of the junior princes threatened their seniors. The Stewarts' build-up of resources was necessary to strengthen their power but led to much negative 'spin' about their 'misgovernment', particularly aimed at Alexander of Badenoch who apparently had a large army of mercenaries ready to be unleashed on his local landed rivals (lay and ecclesiastical). The two foci for resistance were likely to be the other landed affinities who had prospered under David II – the Douglases in the South and the Leslies/Lindsays in the North. Both were bought off with marriages and grants.

The dotage and death (June 1377) of Edward III of England and accession of his ten-year-old grandson Richard II ended any latent threat from England to the new dynasty, though the occupation of Roxburgh and Annandale by the English continued to damage relations and, once King Edward was dead, Earl George of March sacked Roxburgh with impunity before withdrawing again. Payment of the remnant of King David's ransom was also abandoned in 1377. The early 1380s saw a reassertion of Scots landed and ecclesiastical power within the disputed Eastern Borders, apparently coordinated by John of Carrick, the king's heir, who became Warden of the Marches in 1381. Two of John's daughters were married to the heirs of senior Douglases (those of Archibald 'the Grim', Lord of Galloway and illegitimate son of the 'Black Douglas', and Sir James of Dalkeith). It seems that, despite his subsequent reputation as an ineffective semi-invalid, John was a capable and aggressive asserter of royal rights at this point, and that he rather than his father (usually resident in Perthshire not Edinburgh) was the Stewart most concerned with the Borders.

In August 1383 the Scots government concluded a treaty with the regency for Charles VI in France providing for French military aid in the event of an Anglo-Scots war within a year, which was evidently seen as likely. As the Anglo-Scots truce expired in January 1384 the Scots (probably unaware of the simultaneous Anglo-French truce) assaulted the Scots lands still in English hands, Archibald Douglas recapturing Lochmaben Castle and the Earl of Douglas reconquering Teviotdale. The earl died shortly afterwards, being succeeded by his son Earl James, and in April John 'of Gaunt' raided Edinburgh (which paid him off) and Haddington. French envoys arrived encouraging the Scots to enter their truce with England, not ready to fulfil the promise of aid made earlier, and according to the chronicler Jean de Froissart some Scots lords were annoyed at King Robert's preference for a truce. In November 1384 a council meeting chose to appoint John of Carrick as 'Guardian' of the kingdom with full powers over control of administration of justice. The sixty-eight-year-old king seemed to have been pushed aside by his heir, and with him the policy of peace with England. It is probable that the Douglases and a 'war party' were heavily involved. The decision to join in the unexpectedly renewed Anglo-French war brought a French expeditionary force in 1385 to Scotland under their veteran admiral Jean de Vienne. Douglas and Moray, leaders of the 'war party', greeted them in Edinburgh and both Carrick and the king arrived to meet them later, and the French eyewitness Froissart later gave an unflattering account of King Robert's deteriorating eyesight and general sluggishness. The joint army crossed the Borders (without the king) to attack Wark, Ford and Cornhill castles and then moved back to the more useful siege of Roxburgh

Castle. The advance of a large English army, led for the only time by Richard II in person as well as by John 'of Gaunt', led to the commanders deciding not to engage them in battle but raid Cumberland instead before pulling back. In the east, the unchallenged English sacked Dryburgh, Melrose and Newbattle abbeys and then burnt down Edinburgh, and soon afterwards De Vienne's expedition went home.

No major action followed until 1388, and when war resumed that spring the Douglases again took the lead – but by this date estrangement was apparent between John of Carrick and his next brother Robert of Fife/Menteith. In August 1388 Fife joined Archibald Douglas, Lord of Galloway, in leading the western 'prong' of a double invasion of England in a siege of Carlisle, while the Earl of Douglas led the eastern expedition to attack Newcastle; there was also Scots involvement in an anti-English rising in Ulster. The French contemporary writer Froissart plays up Douglas's chivalric heroism in the campaign and does not mention him disobeying orders as Scots writers working under Douglas's foe, Fife's regency, do – an interpretation continued by the pro-Douglas ballad composed (in the next century?) to commemorate the battle which followed. This then formed the basis for the English ballad *Chevy Chase*. Douglas's army of around 7,000 reached Newcastle at the end of July to find the Earl of Northumberland's sons, Henry (the famous 'Hotspur') and Ralph, in command and could not penetrate the town. The earl himself was in command at Alnwick to the north. Retreating to the Border with the Percy force in pursuit, Douglas halted to besiege Otterburn Tower – and a chronicle account alleged that he disobeyed orders to join Fife in the siege of Carlisle. The Douglases were taken by surprise by 'Hotspur' (according to the Wyntoun version) while encamped at Otterburn around 5 August, but the Percys mistook an encampment of Douglas retainers for the main army and while they were sacking its tents the main Scots body attacked them. The resultant battle lasted into the night, leaving Douglas victorious but mortally wounded and 'Hotspur' among the many English prisoners. The Scots only had light casualties.

The loss of Douglas prevented the Scots exploiting the victory – Archibald 'the Grim' of Galloway, aged sixty to sixty-five, successfully claimed the earldom but other Douglas lands were taken by Sir James Douglas of Dalkeith and Sir Malcolm Drummond (husband of Earl James's sister Isabella). It left John, Earl of Carrick, without a major ally in the current tussle for power in Scotland. On 1 December Robert II and Earl Robert of Fife secured a council agreement at Edinburgh to require John to hand over the 'Guardianship', apparently due to the lax administration of justice in the North and his physical incapacity to lead the army if the English invaded. This presumably refers to his lameness following a kick by a (Douglas?) horse, which had probably occurred recently. Fife took over the 'Guardianship', and was to hold it until 1393. The effort of a royal progress to Buchan to assert his rights in 1390 may have been too much for Robert II's health, as on 19 April he died at his ancestral castle of Dundonald in Ayrshire aged seventy-four. Not having become king until he was over fifty and then being eclipsed by his sons, Robert II had an ambiguous reputation in his lifetime with the chronicler John of Fordun notably dismissive of his abilities. His reign began with a series of compromises with the political elite, and the political history of Scotland from 1371 to 1406 gives the impression of two successive monarchs being overshadowed by their most vigorous relatives and of a vicious struggle for power. Both Robert II and Robert III ended at the mercy of the Earl of Fife, whose family were to govern the realm until the bloodbath of 1425. The new king in 1371 was short of reliable support and needed his capable and ambitious sons' help, although the resulting impression is of a 'mafia state' run by a feuding clan, dominated not by the king but by ruthless operatives such as Robert of Fife and the 'Wolf of Badenoch'.

Robert III: 'The Unluckiest of Men'?

The accession of John of Carrick as king posed the danger that he would remove his brother Robert of Fife from power; the latter had been 'Guardian' for their father so his office supposedly lapsed. There was a long gap until John was crowned on 14 August, and some time in between the late king's death and the coronation, Fife was confirmed as 'Guardian' though John was not obviously incapable of ruling. Also, John chose to take the regnal name of 'Robert III', linking himself for propaganda purposes to his great-grandfather Robert I and implicitly challenging Robert of Fife for the role of custodian of the family's most charismatic name ('King John' also brought to mind John Balliol, deposed and humiliated, and John II of France, defeated and captured by Edward III). The likelihood is of a 'deal' between the two brothers – at the expense of Alexander of Buchan, who now led his wild Highland 'caterans' to sack and burn the town and cathedral of Elgin on 17 June. This most notorious of the Wolf's actions was then and later seen as the epitome of his gangster-like tendencies and the breakdown of order in the North, but the Bishop of Elgin was involved in legal disputes with Alexander and had been helping the Countess of Ross to open divorce proceedings against him. The sack served to warn Alexander's enemies – led by Fife and his son, the new Justiciar Murdach – that he was not to be trifled with.

In autumn 1391 a royal constable was installed in Urquhart Castle in the Great Glen, to hem in Alexander's lands from the west, and in 1392 the separation of Alexander and Countess Euphemia proceeded at the papal court at Avignon. By 1394 Euphemia and her son by her first marriage, Alexander Leslie, had regained control of their lands in Ross from Alexander and were installed, free of his control, at Dingwall blocking Alexander from the far north. In 1392 the Earldom of Lennox was entailed to the fiancé of Earl Duncan's daughter, Fife's eldest son Murdach (born *c.* 1362), while the latter's sister

Marjorie was married off to the heir of Campbell of Loch Awe as the lynchpin of an alliance between Fife and the Campbells (who now became hereditary lieutenants of Argyll, inheriting the former power of the MacDougalls). Yet the grip on power exercised by Robert of Fife and his family was clearly not complete, and in February 1393 there was enough support in the council for a proposal to terminate the 'Governorship' to succeed. The underlying reason seems to have been the growth in status and ambition of the new king's elder son David, Earl of Carrick from his father's accession and now aged fifteen, whose own affinity had been extending with royal grants since 1390.

The family struggle between Fife and David continued through the mid–late 1390s and centred on dominance of the north-east. David was backed by his maternal uncle, Sir Malcolm Drummond, and sought to marry the daughter of George Dunbar, Earl of March. The king, who presumably accepted the match at first as the Church did not block the parties' request for a papal dispensation, changed his mind and – after they appear to have married – led an army on Dunbar's town of Haddington sometime in 1396/7 to force him to oppose it. There appears to have been some irregularity in the legality of the union. Dunbar found it prudent to retire to England, and in March 1397 the Papacy ruled that the young couple should live apart for the moment but could remarry later; in the event they did not resume their relationship.

Behind the seeming picture of near anarchy under a 'weak king' overshadowed by his brothers and son it can be seen that Robert III was building up an 'affinity' of family connections of his 1384–88 faction to back him and Prince David. In 1397 one of Robert's daughters was engaged to George Douglas, Lord and later Earl of Angus, son of the Countess of Mar and the late William, first Earl of Douglas (d. 1384). George was built up as a Douglas challenger to Fife's ally, Earl Archibald in Lothian. Clashes between George's affinity and that of Archibald's ally, Douglas of Dalkeith, followed. David joined the royal council and on 28 April 1398 became the 1st Duke of Rothesay, though on the same day Robert of Fife acquired the Dukedom of Albany to balance this. The chosen titles implied that David was to be built up as the Stewart viceroy for their hereditary lands around the Firth of Clyde and into Argyll and that Fife/Albany would operate in the old Pictish lands, north of the Forth – Alba. David later also acquired the Earldom of Atholl. In January 1399 the council appointed David as 'Lieutenant' of the realm for a three-year period, seemingly replacing Fife/Albany with David as the real power in the realm. In any event, King Robert was eclipsed again by his more vigorous relatives.

The replacement of the relatively pacific Richard II by his vigorous cousin Henry IV, son of John 'of Gaunt', in England in September 1399 opened up a risk of attack. Unlike Richard, Henry was a champion jouster and an experienced general who had fought on Crusade in Lithuania and been on pilgrimage to Jerusalem, and a foreign war could shore up his usurping regime. Moreover, his accession was disputed – he had been exiled and unjustly deprived of his father's Dukedom of Lancaster and on invading England was reliably supposed to have sworn that he was only returning for his lands and titles, not to depose King Richard. He was not the closest heir of the childless Richard, and faced conspiracy from the opening of his reign; his most powerful followers in the North, the Percy family – 'Hotspur' and his father Northumberland and uncle Worcester – were now virtual viceroys of the region after helping Henry to the throne. To this toxic mixture was added a quarrel between Prince David and Earl George of March, because early in 1400 David decided not to remarry the earl's daughter. Instead he was betrothed to Mary Douglas, daughter of the heir to the Earl of Douglas (Archibald) who would shortly succeed his father Archibald 'the Grim'. March unsuccessfully asked the king to see that David carried out his responsibilities to marry his daughter instead, and in retaliation started negotiating with the English Borders magnate Ralph, Earl of Westmorland, on behalf of Henry IV. In reply David's new brother-in-law Archibald Douglas seized Dunbar Castle from its earl so he could not assist the invasion. The earl and his family fled to England, while Henry IV sent letters to King Robert and his nobles informing them that he expected them to meet him at Edinburgh to do homage to him according to 'ancient tradition' (citing the legendary history of Geoffrey of Monmouth where the first King of Scotland was a dependant younger son of the King of Britain). The Scots took no notice, and English troops advanced unopposed to Leith in August. The English king reminded the Scots in his official declarations that he was partly of Scots – Comyn – blood, which posed a latent threat as he could claim his ancestral lands back from their Bruce/Stewart confiscators. Albany kept the main Scots army safe at Calder Moor and reportedly refused David's wishes to fight, while David and his brother-in-law Douglas held out in Edinburgh Castle and unsuccessfully challenged Henry to a combat of 100–300 champions to decide the issue of homage without more bloodshed. After a few days' stalemate, Henry accepted that no Scots would turn up to do homage and marched back to the Border.

The death of Queen Annabella in autumn 1401 is cited by the chronicler Bower as leading to the destabilising of relations between David and his ambitious uncle Albany. David exploited his rights as 'Lieutenant' more aggressively by armed force, such as in his activities around St Andrews while the see was vacant pending the papal approval of new Bishop Thomas Stewart (his half-uncle) – he attempted to seize the episcopal castle and dispense the see's revenues himself. He aggressively interpreted the Lieutenant's right to take possession of custom revenues by collecting them from east coast burghs personally with an armed entourage. The impression given is of David as 'out of control' and behaving like a brigand – but was this exaggerated by Albany? The royal council was probably ignored by an increasingly headstrong and confident young prince who could expect to be king soon, but some time in winter 1401/2 David was seized by two of Albany's adherents en route to St Andrews to receive the episcopal castle's surrender. David was then imprisoned in the castle, while his ally Sir Malcolm Drummond was captured around the same time and removed to Kildrummy Castle where he died a few months later (probably due to foul play). The king was absent in Ayrshire and at most sent some documentary authorisation. The seizure and imprisonment of a legally appointed royal 'Lieutenant' should have required the council's prior approval. It is highly probable that Albany induced the Douglases to abandon the king's heir in return for recognition of their virtual control of Southern Scotland plus a more aggressive policy towards England. David was moved to Albany's castle of Falkland and died there on 25/27 March 1402 – due to dysentery according to Bower, though even this pro-Albany chronicler conceded that it was commonly believed that the prince had been deliberately starved to death. The twenty-four-year-old prince was a threat to Albany and Douglas and if he was released they could expect vengeance, so his removal was logical. Pro-Albany writers were to claim that the prince had been headstrong, dangerously rash and personally immoral and his uncle had only sought to lock him up until he learnt self-discipline. But it left only Prince James, the king's second son, aged seven in the way of Albany succeeding to the throne.

The second 'Guardianship' of the Duke of Albany was to last until 1420, and his sub-dynasty was to control Scotland until 1424. But the new regime had a shaky start, as the regime gave sanctuary to a mysterious pretender to the identity of the murdered Richard II, the so-called 'Mammet', and Douglas-led raids penetrated the north of England. Douglas and Albany planned a major invasion while King Henry was preoccupied fighting the Welsh. Albany's son Murdach joined Douglas for an invasion of Northumberland and, while the Earl of Northumberland waited at Alnwick to catch them on their return march, they raided south into Durham. On 14 September, heading back for the Border, they clashed with the combined armies of Henry 'Hotspur' Percy (who had been following them), Northumberland (from Alnwick) and the exiled George Dunbar at Homildon (now Humbledon) Hill. The Scots were apparently taken by surprise that Northumberland had arrived in time, and on Dunbar's advice the Percys avoided a hand-to-hand clash and showered the Scots with arrows from a distance. A body of archers on nearby Harehope Hill, protected by a ravine from the Scots cavalry, rained arrows on the enemy, while the archers in the main Percy army directly in front of the Scots did so too. Douglas failed to charge the English and was then shot in the eye with an arrow, and the Scots panicked. The result was a catastrophic rout for the Scots, with both their leaders – Douglas and Murdach Stewart – captured along with three more earls, eighty senior knights, and a number of French mercenaries.

Homildon Hill shattered the Douglas threat to the English Borders for years, and the Albany regime was lucky that it also led to a military showdown between Henry IV and the Percys as the king demanded that the victors hand over their prisoners to him rather than taking all the ransom money for themselves. 'Hotspur' refused to hand over the injured Earl of Douglas. The main Scots beneficiary from the bloodbath was Henry Sinclar, Lord of Roslin and Earl of Orkney, who was captured but quickly ransomed and was able to build up his landed power while the Douglases were crippled. Hotspur's defiance of Henry IV led to an exchange of insults, with the Percys bringing up the charge that Henry had sworn to them that he would not depose Richard II when they helped him to invade. In July 1403 Henry narrowly survived a rebellion by the Percys, luckily arriving at Shrewsbury in time to link up with his son Prince Henry before the Percys attacked him. The Percys' prisoner Archibald, Earl of Douglas, was fighting for them and was now captured by the king.

The Albany regency had other problems, not least the lack of reliable lieutenants in the North arising from the death of Alexander Leslie, Earl of Ross, in May 1402. This was challenged by the husband of the girl's aunt Mariota, Donald 'Lord of the Isles'. This would lead to Donald seizing Dingwall and eventually to his attack on Buchan in 1411, culminating in the Battle of Harlaw. Already in 1402 Donald's brother Alexander, Lord of Lochaber, raided east to sack Elgin. In August 1404 Countess Isabella of Mar, widow of Sir Malcolm Drummond, agreed to marry and transferred the control of the Mar lordships to Alexander, illegitimate son of the 'Wolf of Badenoch' (considerably her junior), who thus became one of the principal magnates of the north-east. This latest landed coup for the acquisitive Stewart menfolk was at the expense of the pro-Albany local lords who had been controlling the Mar estates with Isabella since Drummond's suspicious death, and the resulting confrontation between Alexander and his uncle Albany brought the ageing king himself to Perth to give authority to the negotiations that ensued. A ceremony at Kildrummy in December 1404 duly ratified the legality of the marriage and the appointment of Alexander as Earl of Mar.

The acquisition of Mar by the Wolf's son may represent a latent challenge by the elder Alexander to his brother Albany; the Wolf is now believed to have died as late as 1405 rather than in the 1390s as earlier suggested. In 1404 the hereditary Stewart lands in Renfrew, Lennox, Carrick and Clydesdale were turned into a fief for Prince James – as a base to challenge Albany? The king seems to have been building up the obscure Sir David Fleming as a new favourite in the Borders, to the fury of rival Douglas claimants. But in October 1405 the king returned permanently to Ayrshire, and in February 1406 his courtiers made a botched attempt to send Prince James to France, apparently a sudden decision (according to chronicler Bowers) intended for his personal safety. Given the question of who would have benefited if the prince had been killed, the answer has to be 'Albany'– at least in the fears of the king's advisers. In February 1406, James was brought by the Earl of Orkney and Sir David Fleming, at the head of a small army, from his residence with Bishop Wardlaw in St

Andrews to East Lothian, to act as the royalist leader for some confrontation between the Fleming/Orkney faction and their Douglas foes in their land dispute. Instead, as the prince was being rowed out from North Berwick to the Bass Rock (presumably for his safety), a Douglas force from Edinburgh Castle under Sir James Douglas of Balvenie attacked and overwhelmed Fleming's party on shore at Hermiston Moor. This was treason, attacking a royal expedition commanded on behalf of the king's heir, but realpolitik trumped legality and nobody was ever punished; the royal force was dispersed. James had to wait for around a month on the Rock before a ship returning to Danzig, the *Maryenknight*, picked him up there. This does not suggest any coherent plan to smuggle him out of the country, with a ship ready.

James was apparently supposed to stay in France for his own safety until he was an adult – an echo of David II's position there in 1334–41. Instead, on 22 March 1406, his ship was intercepted by English vessels off Flamborough Head and the prince ended up as an unexpected 'guest' at the English court. King Henry promised to bring him up as his ward as Charles VI of France had been meant to do, but in practice James was now a political pawn of the English monarchy. The threat of returning him to Scotland was to be held over the heads of the Albany regime for the next eighteen years to induce their cooperation. More immediately, the shock of this news was supposed to have caused Robert III to have had a fatal seizure and he died at Rothesay Castle on Bute on 4 April, probably aged around sixty-nine. He was later supposed to have called himself 'the worst of kings and the most miserable of men' and asked to be buried in a midden, a verdict accepted for centuries as summing up the career of an unfortunate and frequently sidelined ruler whose reign ended in powerless ignominy. One son was probably murdered by the king's power-hungry brother and the other son was captured by the national enemy while apparently fleeing the realm in fear of his life. On four occasions the royal council agreed to someone else (brother or son) superseding Robert as head of the government. He was overshadowed by two strong and ruthless brothers and an equally forceful elder son, though his personal qualities (e.g. humility) were probably more admirable than this formidable trio's. But part of this was the result of bad luck in 1388 – his own physical impairment (lameness) and the death in battle of his principal supporter, the 2nd Earl of Douglas. The combined power of king and heir did hold Albany in check to a degree between 1399 and 1402, and moves may have been underway to do so again as Prince James entered his teens, but were aborted by the crises of 1406. The weak nature of governmental control over the localities in the kingdom had long encouraged the growth of power blocs of magnates, making the king no more than 'first among equals' in the harsh realities of power, and an ailing or underage king scarcely that. Robert III was in an impossible position.

James I: Prisoner to Autocrat, 1406–37

The new king was in the Tower of London as a 'high-security' prisoner of the English by July 1406. He seems to have been well educated as a royal ward (as Henry IV had promised) though kept under strict surveillance. He was taken around the kingdom to other secure castles from time to time; at some point he was in the custody of the Treasurer, Sir John Pelham, at Pevensey Castle in Sussex. As with the Bruce hostages in the 1300s, he was kept well away from the Border and any potential rescuers. It was probably Henry V who moved him back to the Tower at his accession in March 1413, keeping him there as a valuable hostage who could be used to pressurise his kinsmen in Scotland to carry out the English king's wishes in vital military matters (e.g. by not sending troops to France when Henry invaded it in 1415). His fellow hostages included Murdach Stewart, eldest son of Albany, who was also kept as a prisoner for years after Homildon Hill by Henry IV and Henry V to blackmail his father.

James was to stay in the Tower until he was more useful in the king's campaign in France (July 1420). According to his subsequent poetic account of his first sight of his future wife, Joan Beaufort (daughter of the late John, Earl of Somerset, eldest illegitimate son of John 'of Gaunt' by Chaucer's sister-in-law Katherine Swynford), *The Kingis Quair* – 'The King's Book' – the Scots king spotted her one day when he was looking out of his window (presumably in the Tower) and fell in love with her. The fact of a Scots sovereign writing a love poem in the current Chaucerian style, referencing chivalric and courtly poetry and classical myth, shows his intellect and range of abilities, and he also referred in this work to reading *Consolation of Philosophy*, by the arrested sixth-century Roman aristocratic philosopher Boethius, and comparing their plights. Boethius was unjustly suspected of treason and was eventually executed by the Gothic 'barbarian' King Theodoric, a military tyrant – so this comparison was not very flattering to Henry V.

While James languished in captivity there was no noticeable Scottish effort to achieve his release, though the embattled Henry IV had other priorities. The suspicion arose at the time, and has been played on since, that the devious and power-hungry Albany had no desire to see James back at home usurping his power and was more concerned to achieve the return of his own heir Murdach (who was eventually exchanged in August 1415 as part of the Anglo-Scots truce while Henry V invaded France). The Earl of Douglas had been ransomed earlier, in June 1408, and showed his gratitude to the regime by agreeing to a 'bond' of alliance with Albany and marrying his daughter Elizabeth to the duke's second son John, Earl of Buchan. Albany maintained a wary policy towards England, allowing the fugitive Earl of Northumberland to invade the North again in 1408 to keep the fuel of Percy's rebellion burning but doing nothing to aid him. Northumberland was probably lured back by Henry

The Stewarts: 1371–1542

IV's agents with false stories that the area was ripe for revolt, and was quickly killed. In 1416 Albany finally got round to sending his second son John to London to negotiate James's release but the talks broke down (possibly due to the size of the ransom that cash-strapped Henry V wanted).

The domestic affairs of the Albany regime in 1406–20 were largely uneventful, a sharp contrast to the years before and after this and a testimony to the stability that the alliance of Albany and Douglas had secured. James was to play up the misrule, inter-clan disorder, favouritism of the courts and partisanship of the regime after he replaced it in 1424 but, whether through fear or genuine acquiescence, the government was not challenged except in 1411 by the Macdonalds. That clash was centred on the claims of Donald, 'Lord of the Isles', to control the Earldom of Ross after Alexander Leslie died in 1402, and his forcible acquisition of Dingwall and concurrent eastward expansion of his brother Alexander of Lochaber. The latter was contained by Albany loyalists in the north-east, and was forced to do penance for his sacking of Elgin in 1402. But Donald was a more serious challenge as head of the Macdonald kindred and leader of an army of thousands of Highland and Hebridean 'kern', and he claimed Ross via his wife Mariota, sister of the late Alexander Leslie. In the absence of titular 'Justiciar of the North' Murdach in England, Albany built up his son by his second marriage, John (born c. 1381), Earl of Buchan, to hold the north-east along with the Wolf of Badenoch's son Alexander, Earl of Mar. John proved an able military commander. In July 1411 he and Mar held back the Macdonald army of Donald of the Isles as it invaded Buchan, its furthest-ever eastern penetration, at the Battle of Harlaw; the heavily armed, protectively clothed and well-disciplined north-eastern and Lowlands troops halted a typical Highland charge by larger numbers of enthusiastic but less disciplined and probably poorly armed warriors from Lochaber and the Isles. This later became emblematic of how the 'civilised' Lowlanders were to keep the 'wild Islesmen' at bay; the Albany troops held the field of battle and next morning they found that the Macdonalds had retired to their homeland overnight. A subsequent campaign by Albany to Inverness in 1412 secured the surrender of Dingwall and the submission of the Macdonald leader, who abandoned his claims to Ross. In 1416 the current holder of the Ross lands, Countess Euphemia, died and Buchan (her uncle) succeeded as Earl of Ross to confirm Albany control of the region.

Having failed to persuade Henry V to release the king, Albany now sent Buchan as his ambassador to the French court to offer military support to Charles VI, whose army had been routed at Agincourt in October 1415 and who was now facing Henry V invading Normandy from 1417. The sporadically insane French king and his promiscuous wife and feuding courtiers could not count on the loyalty of their great feudal lords; a force of loyal and well-trained Scots would be invaluable, and so the 'Auld Alliance' entered a new phase with Charles's son and heir, the Dauphin Charles, sending envoys to Scotland in 1418. A picked body of 6,000–7000 Scots mercenaries, under Buchan and the Earl of Douglas's heir Archibald (Lord Wigtown), was sent to France in October 1418. John Stewart of Darnley led a regiment of Scotsmen to protect the Dauphin's person, not least from assassins sent by the English or the Duke of Burgundy. From October 1422 the Dauphin, excluded from the French throne in Henry V's favour by the Anglo-French Treaty of Troyes but holding out south of the Loire, was King Charles VII, leader of the 'resistance'. Buchan won a spectacular victory over Henry V's brother Thomas, Duke of Clarence, at Bauge on 23 March 1421. Clarence's invasion of Maine from English-held Normandy was routed and he was killed, the first French victory since the invasion.

By this date Albany was dead, having expired on 3 September 1420 at Stirling Castle probably at the age of eighty. His reputation has been blotted by the number of coups and murders with which he was associated and his undeniable lust for power, but in political terms he was among

1. Ruins of Iona Abbey, Scotland. (Philip Nixon)

2. Ruins of Dumbarton Castle, the principal fortress of Strathclyde. (Stephen Sweeney)

3. Ruins of Caerlaverock Castle, the site of a famous siege by Edward I in 1300. (Chris Andrews)

4. Ruins of Roxburgh Castle, Kelso, Scotland. (Amberley Archive)

5. Holyrood Palace, Edinburgh, Scotland. (Amberley Archive)

Left: 6. Full-length statue by Daniel Chester French of Edward I, King of England, standing, facing slightly right. (Amberley Archive)

Below: 7. Ruins of Linlithgow Palace. The palace was built by James I in 1424–37, then extended by James IV and James V, who was born here in 1512. (Steve Brown)

Opposite: 8. A portrait of John Balliol with his wife. (National Library of Scotland)

Johan Baliol Treg

9. Edward II, King of England, half-length portrait, facing slightly left, above inset of joust between Henry de Bohun and Robert Bruce. (Amberley Archive)

Right: 10. Robert I, King of Scotland 1274–1329, bust portrait, facing right. (Amberley Archive)

Below: 11. Site of the Battle of Strathfillan. This is where Robert Bruce was ambushed by his Comyn rivals and Edward I's partisans after his Coronation in 1306 and forced to flee Scotland (Richard Kermode)

12. Ruins of Melrose Abbey, Scotland. (Philip Nixon)

13. Hermitage Castle. Mary Queen of Scots and the castle's owner Bothwell were besieged here by rebel lords in 1567. (Chris Andrews)

Robert the second
and his second
wyff
Elizabeth Moore
dochter of ye L: Rowallan

14. A portrait of Robert II with his wife. (National Library of Scotland)

15. A portrait of Margaret Tudor, Henry VII's daughter, who was married to James IV. (Jonathan Reeve, JR982b20p83715001600)

16. Pocahontas at the court of King James. (Amberley Archive)

IACOBVS.QVINTVS.SCOTTORVM.REX ANNO.ÆTATIS.SVE. Z 5

MARIA.LOTHORINGIA.ILLIVS.IN.SECVNDIS.NVP TIIS.VXOR.ANNO.ÆTATIS.SVE. Z 4

17. James V of Scotland and Queen Mary of Guise. (Amberley Archive)

JAMES the FIFTH.

Pub.May 10, 1806 by J. Scott, 442 Strand.

18. James V. (Amberley Archive)

19. Site of the 1513 Battle of Flodden, in which James IV was killed. (Andrew Curtis)

20. Mary, Queen of Scots, is kneeling next to George (?) Douglas, who was mortally wounded during the Battle of Langside. A priest administers last rites, a bishop stands to the left behind the fallen soldier; several soldiers wearing armour stand nearby, some with horses. (Amberley Archive)

21. Mary, Queen of Scots. (Amberley Archive)

22. Photograph of portrait painting shows Mary, Queen of Scots, half-length portrait, facing left. (Amberley Archive)

Right: 23. Charles I, King of Great Britain, 1600–1649. (Amberley Archive)

Below: 24. Charles I and Henrietta Maria with their children, afterwards Charles II and James II. (Amberley Archive)

Above left: 25. Charles II, King of Great Britain, three-quarter-length portrait, facing left, in garter robes. (Amberley Archive)

Above right: 26. Charles II, King of Great Britain, 1660–1685. (Amberley Archive)

27. Site of the Battle of Carbisdale, which saw Montrose's final defeat by the Covenanters in 1650. (Donald Bain)

the ablest and most successful of the Stewarts as well as being the longest-lived. He was succeeded as 'Guardian' and regent by his eldest son Murdach, who was already in his late fifties, and efforts to retrieve King James were speeded up. Henry had summoned James to France that July, in order to parade him at the siege of Melun, where Scots troops were in the defending French garrison, and Henry required the Scots king to ride up to the walls and order them to surrender. The Scots excused their refusal on the grounds that James was not a free agent. When the town fell, Henry had them all hanged for treason. James was taken around with Henry's court, along with the equally powerless Charles VI of France, and participated in the English king's entry to Paris in December 1420; then on 23 February 1421 he was back in England with Henry for the Coronation of the new Queen Catherine, Charles VI's daughter. Back in France, James was allowed to hold titular command at the siege of Dreux in Normandy. In May 1421 English and Scots negotiators agreed on the basis for the terms of his release, involving the surrender of a large group of highly born Scots hostages as sureties for the payment of a large ransom. But it was not until after Henry's death in August 1422 that the English regency government opened the final negotiations, and in August 1423 Murdach summoned a general council to agree the terms. Bishop William Lauder of Glasgow, Chancellor of Scotland from 1420, appears to have been the prime mover in speeding up matters. The two nations' commissioners met at Pontefract in autumn 1423, and the ransom was set at the high price of 60,000 marks – 10,000 to be paid each year. The Scots would leave France, and James would receive a noble English bride – Joan Beaufort whose uncle, Bishop Henry of Winchester, was now a senior figure on the English regency council so she could act as a 'bridge' from her fiancé to the English government. The agreement was signed on 10 September 1423 in York Minster.

James's marriage to Joan Beaufort took place at the church of St Mary Overy, Southwark, on 12 February 1424. Now

Southwark Cathedral, the church was under the authority of Bishop Beaufort. A seven-year truce was signed, to commence on 1 May 1424, and twenty-eight Scots peers or their eldest sons were arranged as hostages. James began his journey north, and on 28 March the terms of ransom were signed at Durham. On 5 April the King of Scots affixed his seal to the treaty in Melrose Abbey and was released into the company of his countrymen; Murdach handed over his seal of regency. On 21 May James was finally crowned King of Scots at Scone by Bishop Wardlaw of St Andrews, the prelate who had been his guardian before he left the country eighteen years before. The Crown was hopelessly short of revenue, the regency having alienated lands and offices to the nobility to buy support, and the fierce power struggles of the 1380s, 1390s and early 1400s having seen each successive regime needing to shore up its power base for fear of disappointed supporters defecting to plotters. As a result it was perhaps inevitable that the first parliament of the reign, opening on 24 May, saw a reaction. James resorted to cancelling all acts of patronage (giving away lands and offices) by his predecessors since the reign of Robert I, thus restoring his financial position and control of Crown lands, and those seriously affected included the earls of Douglas and Mar who had acquired large concessions in grants of tax revenues. But the king's power depended on the acquiescence of his senior peers – governors of the far-flung regions and raisers of armies from their tenants – who unlike in England owned estates in compact regional 'blocs'. Asserting the rule of the king's law over all his subjects – especially regional magnates – and vigorously administering justice was one way of impressing the need for loyalty to the sovereign, and James was to be tireless in this for the next twelve years. Historians differ over whether he created a new system of hierarchic justice or just reimposed one that had been dormant under his weak father and grandfather. But he was to find that the Scottish polity did not react smoothly to his orders and not all his subjects were to be intimidated easily. His government's formal assertion in parliament in 1426 that from now on the country would be governed solely by the laws of the King of Scots was asserting both centralism and the levelling effect of the law – there would be one law for rich and poor alike, with no private hereditary customary jurisdictions. But was James's view of his role's importance touched with megalomania?

James was helped in his centralisation of power by the deaths in battle of two of his most powerful subjects within months of his taking power. Buchan had returned to Scotland to seek reinforcements in 1423, and his father-in-law the Earl of Douglas led out this expedition. Both were killed in battle at Verneuil in northern France on 17 August 1424, as the English regent of France for Henry VI, the king's uncle Bedford, destroyed the Franco-Scottish army in Maine in the most crushing English victory since Agincourt. Douglas lost his third successive major battle, an unenviable record for which he was later nicknamed 'The Tyneman' ('The Loser') to distinguish him from the other Douglas earls. Within weeks, in October, the king asserted his power over the Douglases by using a meeting with the new Earl Archibald to require him to hand over more of his offices. The junior Douglas clan – the 'Red Douglases', earls of Angus – became James's clients.

In spring 1425 it was the turn of the Albany Stewarts, with Murdach's father-in-law, the Earl of Lennox, already in custody but the family obediently turning up to parliament as summoned. James did not strike until the ninth day of the meeting, probably careful to check that the other peers would not intervene. On 25 March Murdach was arrested and was sent to Dunbar Castle; his younger son Alexander, his wife Isabella (sent to Tantallon Castle in Lothian) and twenty senior lords were all arrested too in a clear and emphatic purge of the Albany faction. The charges the Albany menfolk faced are uncertain, but may have included the allegation that as no parliament had ever ratified Murdach's appointment as regent this had been usurpation. Unofficially the fact that James had not been ransomed for eighteen years was behind the king's assault on the entire family. In a no doubt deliberately shocking act of royal punitive justice Murdach's eldest son Walter was tried at Stirling Castle on 24 May 1425, found guilty, taken outside onto the 'Heading Hill' and executed, and next day Murdach, Alexander and Murdach's father-in-law, Lennox, faced the same fate. The only male of the family to escape was a fugitive younger son, James 'the Fat', who had fled to the Highlands; he led a force of 'caterans' to sack Dumbarton and then fled to Ireland. Murdach was probably a scapegoat for his late father's treatment of James.

The purge of the Albany menfolk and the deaths at Verneuil left the Dukedom of Albany and the earldoms of Fife, Menteith and Lennox in the king's hands, a useful addition to royal revenues. Mar remained with Earl Alexander, the regime's strongman in the Highlands, as James needed his services as a general against the Macdonalds. The king's power was reasserted and James has duly been praised by pro-centralisation historians as a 'new monarch' who put the feuding nobility in their place. It is arguable that the means that the king used were counterproductive in building up resentment as well as respect from the peerage. His extensive expenditure on new royal building projects, such as at Linlithgow Palace, served to project his image and that of the monarchy as a fitting partner for his Continental rivals. He was active in extending the kingdom's commercial links, having learnt more about the dynamics of the outside world in his years abroad than his predecessors had. In 1425 he agreed to a request from a Flemish embassy to restore the 'staple' (entrepôt for Scottish wool) to Bruges from Middleburg and in 1429 a hundred-year commercial treaty was signed with Duke Philip of Burgundy/Flanders. In his relations with the Church, James showed a determination to assert royal rights and to deny the Papacy any role of legal supremacy over his legal system. Personally he was conventionally pious and interested in the latest manifestations of Christian spirituality, as he and Queen Joan invited the zealous new religious Order of the Carthusian monks to set up their first monastery in Scotland (at Perth, opened in 1429). But he banned churchmen from travelling to Rome to seek new sees without royal leave, endeavouring to keep the distribution of Church patronage in his own hands, and unilaterally reformed Church legal procedures. The concerned 'reformist' Pope Martin V summoned the Bishop of Glasgow and Chancellor (1426), John Cameron, to Rome but James refused to let him go and sent an embassy to protest that this would be prejudicial to the smooth running of the government. To James, as to the later Henry VIII of England, the Crown's rights had supremacy over those of the international Church; luckily the Papacy was too weak to confront him and in 1435 the humanist diplomat Aeneas Sylvius Piccolomini (later Pope Pius II) was sent to Scotland to patch up relations.

A poet and an accomplished lute player, whom the chronicler Abbot Walter Bower of Inchcolm flatteringly referred to as Orpheus for his musical skill, James was a civilised monarch in the European courtly tradition. But his relentless pursuit of extra taxation to fund all this (and his sporadic Highlands campaigns) were to lead to accusations of greed and – unusually – resistance to his taxes in Parliament. In 1431 the parliament summoned to fund his second Highlands campaign only granted the required taxes in return for their commissioners controlling how it was levied and spent. This and the next protests in Parliament in 1437 suggest that James could not persuade his subjects of his need for so much money, and reinforces the appearance of the king as a hot-tempered autocrat who expected obedience and sought to change how the realm was normally governed. James was more akin to Henry V than to his own father and grandfather in his concept of how to be a monarch.

By 1429 James had ceased to keep up his annual £10,000 payments of instalments of his ransom, though this could be due to shrewd assessment that England was too bogged down in an unwinnable war in France to attack him as well as parsimony. The 1424 truce lasted until 1430 as planned, though in 1428 Charles VII sent the Archbishop of Rheims with an embassy to James asking for aid and for the king's eldest daughter, Princess Margaret (born December 1424), to marry Charles's son Dauphin Louis. James was to receive the County of Saintogne in France – another welcome source of revenue. A treaty was signed promising both the princess and troops for France, but was not carried out until the war swung decisively in France's favour in 1435.

James sought to round off his restoration of royal power with a demonstration of his authority in the Highlands and Hebrides. The Lord of the Isles, now Donald's son Alexander, and his mother Countess Mariota of Ross needed to be taught that the king's writ ran in their lands too. In July 1428 a general council was called at Perth to fund a campaign in the Highlands, though there was significant opposition to the cost from some of the nobility, and the earls of Mar (Alexander, the king's cousin) and Atholl (Walter Stewart, the king's youngest and only surviving uncle) talked them round as to its necessity. It was a warning sign that James ignored. The local lords across the Highlands and into Ross and Lochaber were summoned to meet the king for a parliament at Inverness, and when they had arrived Alexander Macdonald, Countess Mariota and around fifty others were arrested. Most were speedily released, but were deemed to have needed a lesson that the king's authority was to be obeyed unquestioningly – and probably regarded the king as an untrustworthy despot who ignored the 'sacred' custom of safe conduct. Alexander and Mariota were kept in custody for an uncertain period while James sought and failed to find adequate substitutes to rule their domains on his behalf; he approached Alexander's uncle John 'Mor' Macdonald with an offer of the leadership of Clan Donald as a royal lieutenant but was ignored. Alexander was later released and reinstated, but in spring 1429 revolted against the king and attacked Inverness – and sent envoys to

Ireland to recall the exiled James 'the Fat', Albany's grandson, as a Stewart rival of the king who could be set up against James. Unfortunately for the rebels, James 'the Fat' died later in 1429, aborting any invasion. Alexander's army in Lochaber was defeated on 21 June by the royal army, in a clash where clans Chattan and (?) Cameron defected to the king's men when the royal banner was raised sooner than commit treason against their overlord, and he fled to the Hebrides; in July the king took Dingwall and Urquhart castles to regain control of the Great Glen. Alexander was required to surrender unconditionally and was replaced as royal lieutenant of the north-western regions by the Earl of Mar. He had not the resources to supervise the entire region, and in September 1431 he was defeated by Alexander at Inverlochy. The royal army in Caithness was also defeated and the Macdonalds and their allies remained autonomous of the Crown. Worse, the parliament called to Perth in October 1431 saw the king's wishes for heavy taxation resisted and he only secured it by accepting his leading subjects' insistence on their setting up a committee to supervise its disbursement – a clear sign of mistrust. James could not afford a large-scale war and grudgingly pardoned Alexander.

The truce with England was kept up while James was preoccupied with the North, and in February 1429 the king met Bishop (now Cardinal) Beaufort at Berwick to discuss an extension after 1430. The possibility of Princess Margaret marrying the young Henry VI instead of the Dauphin was raised. In 1433 another Beaufort, the queen's brother Edmund, visited Scotland to offer a permanent treaty involving the return of Berwick and Roxburgh and King James advised the 'Three Estates' to accept this but they voted against it. Borders hostility was complicated in January 1435 by the forfeiture of the Earl of Dunbar, who fled to England. His kin and tenants were a potential 'fifth column' within Scotland, and months later his son Patrick returned from exile with a small force of English troops to cause trouble in Lothian, but they were intercepted.

1435 saw the death of Bedford and the realignment of French politics to the ruin of the English cause, as Duke Philip of Burgundy abandoned his long-term alliance with the English to support Charles VII (whose men had murdered Philip's father in front of Charles in 1419). The English position in France collapsed, and James finally implemented the 1428 French treaty as a new French request for troops arrived. Princess Margaret was despatched to the Loire valley to marry the Dauphin in spring 1436, though the lack of money at Charles VII's court meant that the wedding at Tours was unceremonious and the Scots delegation were annoyed at the disrespect shown to them. In August 1436 James finally invaded English-held territory to besiege Roxburgh Castle, his army strengthened by the first significant siege guns seen in Scots Border warfare – expensive but a potential way of shortening sieges. But his appointment of his cousin Robert Stewart of Atholl rather than the higher-ranked earls of Douglas or Atholl as his 'Constable' rankled with the status-conscious nobility, and the siege was unsuccessful. As an English army arrived James beat a swift retreat, which may have been advisable due to magnate disaffection but was subsequently mocked.

In retrospect this was seen as the point at which his regime lost the respect or fear of some of its leading citizens, and in October a meeting of the general council called to raise more taxes saw open resistance. Sir Robert Graham, a royal opponent with a family grudge over the confiscation of the Earldom of Strathearn from his nephew, was elected as 'Speaker' and denounced James's demands to loud approval from the audience. The taxes were refused, and Graham boldly even attempted to make a 'citizen's arrest' of the king for misgovernment (apparently expecting some magnates to back him as they had promised) but was arrested by the royal guards. The meeting ended in stalemate, and Graham was imprisoned but escaped to the Highlands and was banished. The subsequent political manoeuvres are clouded by hindsight and the 'official version' of the resulting act of regicide, but in early 1437 Graham linked up with Robert Stewart, grandson of the Earl of Atholl, in a plot to murder the king, and Stewart is supposed to have drawn in his grandfather. Allegedly Earl Walter, surviving son of Robert II by his second wife, was still brooding over the fact that that king's first marriage had been of dubious legality and so its offspring could be reckoned as illegitimate – making him the rightful king. Probably his grandson Robert was the prime mover in the plot.

James had become dangerously politically isolated, and on the night of 20/21 February 1437 Robert Stewart opened a door of the king's current lodgings at the Dominican friary at Perth to Graham and his band of murderers. Robert and his grandfather were both in the royal party staying at the friary, and Robert had removed the door-bar of the king's bedroom door beforehand. As the murderers noisily approached, the king and queen were caught defenceless. The queen's maid Catherine Douglas thrust her arm through the latch and used it as an impromptu bar while the king levered up some floorboards and dropped into the drain below, hoping to squeeze out through the exit into the courtyard. But as well as his having put on weight, the exit from the drain had been blocked up from outside to stop tennis balls rolling in – the first mention of tennis at a British royal court. The murderers had forced the door open, breaking Catherine Douglas's arm; one threatened to kill the queen until he was reprimanded by a more scrupulous colleague, and the raiders spotted the hole in the floor. They then dropped into the drain to pursue the king and caught him. The most powerful King of Scots to date ended trapped like a rat in a sordid hand-to-hand knife fight in a drain, aged forty-two.

The coup was apparently without any clear plans for seizing power once the king had been killed, and Atholl and his grandson made no attempt to proclaim a new king. As the murderers fled the scene the queen had the presence of mind to send a message to Edinburgh Castle to have the new king, her son James II, kept safe from kidnap. The shocked court moved to Edinburgh where he was crowned king on 25

March at Holyrood Abbey (the younger and survivor of twin sons, he had been born on 16 October 1430). The murderers do not seem to have proclaimed Earl Walter as king, but their faction rallied in the Perth region to challenge the new regency and as far as the inadequate sources admit they held out for a few weeks in a stand-off against the queen's backers in Edinburgh. The majority of great nobles swung over to the regency's side rather than backing Walter and his grandson; if either of the latter had hoped for James I's detractors to back a coup they were disappointed. The Earl of Douglas and others marched on Perth, and the plotters were hunted down in Perthshire, tried for treason and gruesomely executed in early May in the usual manner for regicides. The death of James I, like his reign, can be interpreted in differing ways, but it is clear that his ambitions, willingness to alienate people and lack of tact had made his regime dangerously fragile even if its active enemies were few. A talented and determined ruler with a cultural hinterland of music and poetry, he stands out from among the shadowy early Stewart rulers and the chronicler Bower could even give him a definitive physical description as stocky, of medium height and a keen wrestler. Aeneas Sylvius Piccolomini says that he had become seriously overweight by 1436. His harshness was counterproductive, and his demise left Scotland in a position of a long regency which was to be repeated all too frequently over the next century and a half.

James II, 1437–60: King *Versus* Douglases?

Scotland had seen a long regency racked by struggles for power before, in the 1240s, and the instability that marked James II's minority was not the inevitable result of a regency in a 'weak' central state overshadowed by its nobility or a new problem for the early Stewart polity. A regent was always at a disadvantage in that they lacked full royal power and they could be overthrown by a coup and/or their royal ward kidnapped. On this occasion, power for the six-year-old king was initially exercised by the Queen Mother Joan, but she could not lead armies – one of the great nobles was needed for that role. Given the destruction or natural extinction of so many aristocratic dynasties under James I, the obvious remaining candidate for this role was Archibald Douglas, 5th Earl of Douglas, head of the greatest landed family in the south, and he duly became 'Lieutenant-General' of the realm and co-regent. But the regency council soon fell into faction, with the ambitious Sir William Crichton, royal household intimate of James I, and his kinsmen opposed by another rising family – the Livingstons, headed by Sir Alexander the keeper of Stirling Castle. Crichton now became Chancellor. The death of the Earl of Douglas, at Restalrig in Lothian on 26 June 1439, brought their rivalry into the open as they struggled for control of the regency, and the Queen Mother chose the side of Livingston and moved herself and her son the king to Stirling. Reportedly James was smuggled out of Edinburgh Castle in a trunk to avoid Crichton's guards stopping him leaving. Crichton and his allies, left behind at Edinburgh, refused to give way, and Livingston besieged them in Edinburgh Castle to no avail. Crichton came to terms with Livingston, and surrendered the castle in return for a guarantee of a large share of Crown offices and lands.

Queen Mother Joan now proceeded to alarm Livingston by marrying Sir James Stewart, the 'Black Knight of Lorn' – a Douglas ally, younger brother of Lord Lorn and a descendant of the 'Steward' Alexander Stewart (died 1283, great-grandfather of Robert II). Livingston ruthlessly neutralised him by throwing him and his brother in the dungeons at Stirling Castle and arresting the Queen Mother too (3 August 1439); all three were released once Joan had resigned as regent and played no further role in politics. Under this agreement, the king was to remain at Stirling Castle under Livingston's control. Livingston and Crichton now shared out the benefits of power between themselves as uneasy allies and co-regents, neither being strong enough to destroy the other, although Crichton attempted a coup by kidnapping the king (still at Stirling Castle) while he was out hunting and carrying him off to Edinburgh Castle. Livingston followed him with his forces and forced him to hand the boy over. After this the senior clergy had to patch up another truce, and on 24 November 1440 they infamously removed the young Earl William of Douglas (aged only sixteen?) and his brother David from the political arena by inviting them to dinner with them and the young king at Edinburgh Castle and murdering them. The Douglases were dragged outside into the courtyard and executed – and King James was supposed to have pleaded for their lives in vain. The 'Black Dinner' left the senior line of Douglases extinct in the male line, though the brothers' sister Margaret, the 'Fair Maid of Galloway', inherited the lands of Galloway and Wigtown. The earldom and the main Douglas lands passed to the siblings' great-uncle Sir James 'the Gross' (d. 1443), younger brother of the fourth earl who fell at Verneuil; he was suspected of an unsavoury alliance with the regents to remove his rivals.

The triumvirate of Crichton, Livingston and Sir James Douglas now ruled until the latter died in March 1443, and the former two then quarrelled over power. With the help of the new Earl of Douglas, James's son William (born 1425?), an anti-Crichton faction used a council meeting at Stirling in November 1443 to depose the Chancellor, but he refused to accept this and held out at Edinburgh Castle. Finally in 1445 Douglas, by now having acquired a papal dispensation to marry his cousin Margaret of Galloway and so acquire her section of the Douglas inheritance, blockaded Edinburgh Castle until Crichton came to terms. The Chancellor was allowed to keep his office and lands, but in effect gave up much of his power. The following years duly saw the young king starting to assert himself, and Crichton and Livingston fading from power. The Queen Mother died on 15 July 1445 at Dunbar Castle, where she had taken refuge in an apparent abortive attempt to rally armed support against the regency; she was not much over forty. Her husband seems to have fled to England and mostly lived there; summer 1445 was also the probable date of the Crichtons seizing Edinburgh Castle in a further dispute with the Livingstons and being besieged there by the royal army until another truce was patched up.

The Anglo-Scots wars resumed in 1448, with the nine-year truce of 1438 having expired the previous year. The restless English 'Warden of the East Marches' from 1440, Lord Poynings, burnt Dunbar and Dumfries. In retaliation the Earl of Douglas (as Warden of the West Marches), the Earl of Orkney and the Earl of Angus, the three main landowners of the Borders region, led an army across the Tweed and sacked Alnwick on 3 June and Warkworth on 18 July. An embassy led by Crichton and Bishop James Ralston of Dunkeld proceeded to the Low Countries to search for a bride for the king among the vassals of Scotland's commercial ally, Duke Philip of Burgundy. The duke's great-niece Mary of Guelders (born 1433), daughter of Duke Arnold of Guelders, was eventually chosen and negotiations were entrusted to Crichton; once the treaty was signed he escorted her to Scotland, landing at Leith on 18 June 1449. She married James on 3 July at Holyrood Abbey, and from then on the king took on more of the duties of government. The marriage preceded a showdown with the Livingston faction, whose large collection of offices were sought by their rivals, and in September 1449 Sir Alexander Livingston and most of his male kin were arrested at Parliament in Edinburgh and indicted for misgovernment. Sir Alexander escaped with his life, but one of his sons and his nephew Robin, the royal comptroller of finance, were forfeited and executed in January 1450; Sir Alexander's eldest son James was forfeited *in absentia* but had escaped and in 1454 was pardoned and restored as Chamberlain. The January 1450 Parliament saw a determined effort to restore law and order and good government after the factionalism of the 1440s, with the interests of a vigorous king and disgruntled subjects coinciding. Eighteen statutes were passed, announcing a general peace and introducing measures against rebellion, brigandage, spoliation of farmers' crops and cattle by roving brigands and defiance of the king's laws. Illegal castle-building was banned and those erected without licence during the regency were to be pulled down – a repeated measure to undo the free-for-all actions of autonomous local lords during a time of weak government.

Most of the Livingston lands went to the already well-endowed Earl of Douglas, whose estates stretched across Southern Scotland and whose affinity was now so strong that it was seen by the young king as a potential danger. In the bloc of Douglas estates, it was the earl rather than the king who was the focus of loyalty for his tenants and he possessed a substantial 'private army' whose loyalty to the king could not be counted on. Douglas and his brothers – James of Ormonde, Hugh, John of Balveny and Archibald (who had acquired the Earldom of Moray in defiance of genealogically closer heirs) – were to be the next targets for the expansion of royal power, and he was suspected of seeking support from other potentially threatened nobles (e.g. the Livingstons) at the king's expense. In autumn 1450 the earl and a large entourage went on pilgrimage to Rome to celebrate the papal jubilee, with their lavish spending a sign to all (James in particular) of his power and political potential. Douglas's private negotiations with great lords in London in January 1451 on his return journey were also seen as suspicious, and while he was absent the Earl of Orkney was sent round Galloway to collect royal rents on the king's estates and repress disorders, showing the locals that the king not the 'Black' Douglas was their ultimate overlord. He was allegedly treated with scorn by local Douglas retainers, so the king followed with an armed force to occupy Lochmaben Castle and some Douglas estates were confiscated.

On the earl's return he was summoned to the king, obeyed and was officially pardoned and restored to his position as

'Warden of the West Marches' and most of his estates. The king had made his point that the earl was a subject like any other, but the mutual tension and suspicion between the two men almost inevitably continued. Some Douglas vassals defied royal officials and continued to show where their loyalties lay, and among 'crimes' which were subsequently cited to justify the royal crackdown the earl's personal contempt for royal authority was the most serious affront to the king. In one incident, it was said that he arrested the head of the McLellan kin, the 'tutor' (guardian of an underage lord) of Bomby, and when the accused's uncle Sir Patrick Gray turned up at his castle with a legal order for his release William kept him busy with dinner while his men executed the prisoner. He then offered Gray his nephew's headless body to take away, and Gray fled in fear of his life. William formed a 'bond' with Alexander Lindsay, the aggressive 'Tiger' Earl of Crawford (a major lord in the north-east), the head of the Macdonald lordship Earl John of Ross (the principal lord in the north-west) and the Earl of Moray – all major landed powers in the north of Scotland – for their mutual defence against all foes, the king included. The implicit threat was that if James threatened one of them the rest would march on his power base in central Scotland from two separate directions. In February 1452 William accepted a safe conduct to come to Stirling Castle and explain himself to the king, and arrived on the 21st to be greeted by James and invited to dinner the next day. That evening, at a private audience with the king in one of his chambers, a quarrel broke out between them and James apparently produced a copy of the recent 'bond' as evidence of illegal conduct and ordered Douglas to abandon it. The earl refused and James, losing his temper, called him a 'false traitor', shouted something to the effect of, 'If you won't, this will!', produced a knife and stabbed him in the neck. Some royal hangers-on, including Crichton's son Sir William, Lord Boyd and Douglas's enemy Gray, then rushed in and finished the earl off, leaving him with twenty-six wounds.

The likelihood is that this murder was unpremeditated, even though James and his followers all had weapons handy, and that Douglas's arrest was the original intention and things went wrong. The new Earl James, William's brother, reacted as violently as might have been anticipated. While the king was marching north to Perth to defeat the treacherous Earl of Crawford, Earl James led a posse of Douglas and allied cavalry to Stirling and they rode through the town dragging a copy of the king's safe conduct for Earl William at the tail of a horse in public contempt. But the other two principal Douglas families, the earls of Angus and the Douglases of Dalkeith, backed the king with an eye to a share of their disgraced relatives' estates and were duly rewarded. Crawford was defeated by the main royal ally in the north-east, the Earl of Huntly (chief of the Gordons), at Brechin and while the 'Black' Douglases held out in the south their allies Crawford and Lord Lindsay had their lands forfeited by Parliament on 12 June. Parliament then voted a motion that Earl James had defied the king's law by refusing a safe conduct to come and explain himself so he should be outlawed as a traitor too. All the Douglas rebels' titles were forfeited, and the Earldom of Moray was given to a rival contender – conveniently, Lord Crichton's son Sir James. The Edinburgh populace and local lords showed their loyalty with an impressive general levy of volunteers for the war, said to be around 30,000 strong, and the king led them into Dumfriesshire to lay rebel lands waste and occupy or demolish Douglas castles. Outnumbered and with his northern allies defeated, Earl James surrendered in return for a promise of pardon at Douglas Castle, the ancestral family stronghold, on 28 August, and was allowed to keep his earldom and receive his brother's 'Wardenship of the West Marches'.

The fact that Douglas was prepared to abandon the war and that the king forgave him marked a truce rather than a final settlement – with neither side clearly trusting the other. Whether deliberately flouting the king or merely protecting himself against another attack, Douglas chose to visit the

Lord of the Isles and Earl of Ross in Knapdale to sign another 'bond' of alliance before his next visit to England. This could be interpreted as presaging a Macdonald invasion to aid the Douglases, and in March 1455 James duly attacked the earldom's 'core' lands, sacking Inveravon Castle in Linlithgowshire and marching on Glasgow. Having collected a south-western Highland army there to outnumber the Douglas tenants, he marched via Lanark into Ettrick Forest, requiring all Douglas castles to surrender or be sacked. While he was besieging Douglas's ally Lord Hamilton at Abercorn, the earl attempted to collect an army to the south in Galloway to intervene but it broke up, his vassals clearly despairing of victory. He gave up and fled to England, and his brother Moray was killed and his brother Hugh captured and executed by the 'Red Douglas' (Earl of Angus) at the Battle of Arkinholm on the River Esk. The last Douglas stronghold in Galloway, Threave Castle, was forced to surrender. As a reward for their aid, the earls of Angus now gained their cousins' forfeited title of 'Lord Douglas' as well as a share of their estates; the Douglases of Dalkeith gained the Earldom of Morton.

The fall of the 'Black' Douglases was complete, though Earl James lived in exile in England as a court pensioner until 1488. James II seemed to have completed his father's work of reasserting royal authority across the kingdom. With the kingdom's premier dynasty broken up and no adult male Stewarts to require earldoms and estates, the young king was more powerful than any of his predecessors since Robert I. The year 1454 had seen the death of the ex-regent and Chancellor, William Crichton, and James was now fully master in his own house. His chief adviser was now his cousin Bishop James Kennedy of St Andrews (*c.* 1406–65), son of Sir James Kennedy of Dunure and Robert III's daughter Mary Stewart, a cultivated and well-travelled cleric who had represented Scotland at the Council of Florence in 1439–40 and been promoted in his absence to succeed Bishop Wardlaw at St Andrews. He was a capable and conscientious administrator, and even resigned after a short period as Chancellor in 1444 alleging that the work interfered with his episcopal duties and the latter had to be his priority.

The aggressive young king now sought to resume the wars with England, the protector of the exiled Earl of Douglas, with the added factor of the assumption of power by his mother's Beaufort kin's foe the Duke of York after the First Battle of St Albans in 1455. James's uncle, Duke Edmund of Somerset, York's arch-enemy, had been among the casualties there and York was now governing, and James sent envoys to France in November to propose that Charles VII attack Calais while he attacked Northumberland. Charles did not respond, but York's government sent insulting 'reminders' that James was failing to pay homage to his liege lord King Henry as per the legal requirements set out in Edward I's reign. However the Beaufort faction and Queen Margaret were able to reassert themselves at York's expense during 1456–58.

In July 1457 James agreed to a two-year truce with England and used his troops and money for an impressive expedition to the Highlands instead, showing his presence and administering rigorous justice to impress the local lords. Inverness Castle, the centre of royal power, was extensively rebuilt. Loyal officials were put in place at the main castles to act in his name when he was busy elsewhere and prevent any new rising such as that of the Crawfords in 1452. In March 1458 the king held another parliament at Edinburgh to assert royal power via the administration of justice, centralising the latter with a supreme court for civil justice, which was to meet annually at Edinburgh, Perth and Aberdeen. Local courts were reformed and the justiciary court was ordered to go on annual circuits to deliver justice in the localities, and among other acts the coinage and weights and measures systems were reformed.

James's dynasty was by now assured by the births of three sons – the heir, Prince James, probably born in May 1452 at St Andrews; Alexander, born around 1454/5; and John, born around 1457. But, as with James I, the strong position of the monarchy depended heavily on the life of the king in his heir's infancy, and with the potential rebels among the nobility under control it was international affairs that were to end James's rule. The truce with England was extended for another nine years in February 1459, but the revival of strife among English court factions emboldened James to intervene. It is unclear if, as alleged much later by historian Bishop Leslie, King Henry's shaky government offered James the return of David I's lands of Northumberland, Cumberland and Durham in return for aid against the exiled Duke of York in 1459–60. But James's family links to the Beauforts made his choice of Queen Margaret's faction as his ally logical, and after York's nephew Warwick and son Edward returned from exile to overthrow the queen's regime in summer 1459 Henry VI was captured at the battle of Northampton. His queen and her son Prince Edward fled to Scotland, and an alliance was arranged as a result of which Margaret was able to raise an army of Scots and anti-York Englishmen and invade Northern England. James led his own army and a large Highland contingent to besiege Roxburgh Castle, which had been in English hands for decades. His army was equipped with the latest expensive artillery to batter down the walls, probably including the still-extant cannon 'Mons Meg' (now at Edinburgh Castle). Roxburgh town surrendered, and the castle was on the verge of falling when James was unexpectedly killed in a misfire of one of his cannons – either a cannon blowing up or a wedge shooting out of it. He had been standing incautiously close to it to watch it being fired, ignoring the danger. He was mortally wounded and died at the town's friary shortly afterwards, aged twenty-nine. The queen, Mary of Guelders, bravely assumed command of the expedition and continued the siege, keeping up morale, and the castle quickly surrendered. The army then returned home, via Kelso Abbey where the new King James III was crowned on 10 August, and the late king was buried at Holyrood

Abbey. As vigorous and capable a ruler as his father, like James I his reign came to an unexpectedly early end at least partly due to his personal carelessness. Like his father he left a somewhat violent reputation, but he had not alienated his nobles so widely and his main target was the undoubtedly over-resourced and arrogant 'Black' Douglas dynasty. It would be anachronistic to claim that he was seeking to curb the aristocracy as a body, rather than one 'over-mighty' family, and compared to his father and his son he operated through, rather than in defiance of, the established power structure, making good use of Parliament to secure agreement for his legislation. His most notable personal characteristic was a livid red birthmark on his face, from which he was nicknamed 'Fiery Face', and his murderous attack on Earl William of Douglas while the latter was under safe conduct in his presence shows his temper. Probably this one incident has given a distorted impression of his character and methods; the 1452 crisis shows that as a ruler he was more acceptable to his leading subjects than his son was to be.

James III, 1460–88: The Wrong Sort of Man to Triumph as a Scots Ruler?

Unlike in 1437–39, the regency was initially stable and the Queen Mother, a European princess and niece of Duke Philip of Burgundy, made no unwise marital alliances with members of the Scots nobility. The latter undid the pretensions to power of both Joan Beaufort in 1437 and Margaret Tudor in 1513, but Mary of Guelders – a cool-headed woman, as shown by her continuing the siege of Roxburgh after her husband's death – survived. Possibly the absence of one noble dynasty with resources outweighing the others added to stability; the Douglases were now manageable. There was a regency council of seven, among whom the outstanding members were Bishop Kennedy and the Lord Privy Seal,

James Lindsay, Provost of Lincluden. The previous regime's policies continued, as did work on the new royal residence at Falkland Palace – influenced by the Queen Mother's family's primarily non-defensive homes in Flanders – and royal-held Ravenscraig Castle. So did aid to the family of Henry VI, and Queen Margaret's allies in Yorkshire attacked and killed the Duke of York; her own army defeated the Yorkists and recaptured King Henry at the Second Battle of St Albans, but York's eldest son Edward destroyed the queen's allies in the Welsh Marches, hurried to London ahead of the queen and was acclaimed King Edward IV (March 1461). The queen's army, holding out in Yorkshire, was destroyed at the bloody Battle of Towton Moor (Palm Sunday, 29 March) and she, her increasingly confused husband and their son Prince Edward arrived in Scotland as refugees. Margaret was the niece of James II's unreliable ally Charles VII of France, and the regency government negotiated an alliance whereby she handed over Berwick to Scotland in return for aid. The Lancastrian exiles had enough loyalists in Northumberland to hold onto the castles of Alnwick, Bamburgh and Dunstanburgh, which formed a precarious foothold in England with Scottish help into 1462. Unfortunately King Charles VII died as the Scots appealed for aid and his devious son Louis XI, widower of James III's late aunt Margaret Stewart, had other priorities; in spring 1462 Queen Margaret also sailed to France leaving her husband in Scotland. In October she returned with French admiral Pierre de Breze and an expeditionary force, with which she marched south to retake Alnwick. But they could not progress further, and as they sailed back to Scotland many of their ships were wrecked. In retaliation for the Scots aid to the Lancastrians, the young Edward IV sent the arch-foe of the Stewarts, the exiled Earl of Douglas, to the Hebrides to persuade John Macdonald, Lord of the Isles, to defect to the English and attack the regency government from the north. In the Treaty of Ardtornish (February 1462) he transferred his allegiance to England in return for a – wildly optimistic

– promise of all Scotland north of the Forth. Luckily for the regency, the Macdonald levies lacked the military capability to proceed further than Inverness, which John's illegitimate son Angus 'Og' seized; some time in 1462/63 a Scots army drove them back and regained control of the Great Glen area, leading to John returning to his allegiance to James III.

Henry and his family were installed by their allies at Bamburgh until Margaret and her son sailed for the Low Countries in July 1463. Henry was taken back to Scotland, but on 1 December the Queen Mother died, still barely thirty, and Bishop Kennedy assumed the regency. Effective aid to the declining Lancastrian cause ceased, and the Scots government agreed a truce with Edward in December 1464; it was extended for fifteen years in June 1464 after Alnwick, Bamburgh and Dunstanburgh had surrendered. Ex-King Henry could not return to Scotland for fear of extradition and took refuge in Lancashire instead; he was captured and put in the Tower of London in 1465. But the Scots still had possession of Berwick, and relations with Edward IV's regime remained uneasy.

The regency government of Bishop Kennedy lasted until he died on 10 May 1465, and was then succeeded by a triumvirate of his brother Gilbert, Lord Kennedy (keeper of Stirling Castle), Robert Fleming of Cumbernauld (James II's Steward of the Household) and Sir Alexander Boyd (keeper of Edinburgh Castle and supervisor of the king's military training). The truce with England was extended for fifty-four years, and a marriage between James III and a noble English lady was to be arranged. On 9 July 1466 Boyd staged a coup with the backing of Kennedy and a faction of nobles, seizing the king (who was normally kept safe at Stirling Castle) while he was at Linlithgow presiding at an audit of the Exchequer. The king was taken to Edinburgh Castle, and was required to preside at a parliament called there for 9 October where Boyd officially begged pardon and was then legally pardoned and made the king's personal 'governor'. The offices of state were shared out among the attendant Boyd allies, and Boyd's eldest son Thomas was made Earl of Arran (26 April 1467). Some time before then he married the king's eldest sister Mary; he also became the Lord Chamberlain in the manner of Crichton's son in the previous regency.

The main policy initiative of the new government was to arrange an alliance with King Christian of Denmark and Norway, overlord of the Hebrides, as proposed at the January 1468 parliament at Stirling following a suggestion made by Christian's ally Charles VII some years earlier. James would marry Margaret, Christian's daughter. The new Earl of Arran, as the king's brother-in-law, was sent to Copenhagen to negotiate and a treaty was drawn up and signed on 8 September 1468. Under this, the Orkneys and Shetlands would be handed over to Scotland as security for the full payment of Margaret's dowry – which the impecunious Christian, originally the Duke of Oldenburg and now the first sovereign of a new Danish/Norse dynasty struggling to deal with a double realm plus a breakaway Sweden, was unlikely to afford. In retrospect, this treaty was to set the seal on the full unification of the Scots lands under one dynasty and extend Scotland to its final boundaries; and the government duly sought to impose its full central control on the islands by buying out the claims of the Earl of Orkney, William Sinclair. Arran returned home to obtain ratification of the treaty, and was back in Denmark to collect Princess Margaret in June 1469. The party sailed to Leith, where Arran received the unwelcome news from his wife that in his absence there had been a coup by the Boyds' enemies. The Boyds both fled, Arran returning to Denmark with Mary and his father fleeing to England; in their absence Parliament attainted them for treason and confiscated all their lands and offices. Meanwhile Margaret of Denmark, aged probably thirteen, was married to James III at Holyrood Abbey in July 1469. The king, now seventeen, assumed more of the government. His sister was to return to Scotland later to intercede for her husband, but was held captive until her marriage had been annulled by a complaisant Church in 1472. She was then married off in 1474 to a leading regime loyalist, James, Lord Hamilton, over thirty years her senior. From this marriage would descend the senior line of claimants to the Scots throne after the Stewart dynasty, the ducal Hamiltons.

The new regime annexed the confiscated Boyd lands to the Crown, and the 1470s saw comparative political stability with no one faction dominant. In the absence of any overly powerful aristocratic dynasty, the comparatively centralised and autocratic monarchy of James I and II was resumed under an adult king. The sources indicate that the king was not as interested in governing or in warfare as his predecessors, though he and his queen showed themselves on tour in the North to Inverness in autumn 1470. The principal noble dynast north of the Great Glen, John Macdonald, who was defying summonses to appear before the king's courts for assorted crimes and had never been punished for his 1462 rebellion, was forfeited for treason *in absentia* by Parliament in December 1475, which was in practice more of a political 'shot across the bows' to make him cooperate. He was restored to most of his lands when he finally appeared to explain and beg for pardon at the next parliament at Edinburgh in July 1476, though he lost Knapdale and Kintyre. This asserted royal judicial supremacy without the need for war. He was confirmed as Lord of the Isles – a useful legal assertion that the Macdonald lands ultimately belonged to the king and could be confiscated.

The king was said by later writers to be more interested in unusual pursuits such as literature, music and architecture than in war or governance, and certainly had close relationships with men outside the usual power structures such as the physician and astrologer William Scheves/Schaw, whom he made Archbishop of St Andrews in 1478, and the architect Robert Cochrane – allegedly venal and corrupt. How much of this was subsequent propaganda by discontented senior nobles involved in later plots, who feared for their loss of land and offices at the hands of these low-born outsiders, is unclear. Indeed, in modern times sympathetic historians have commended James for having relationships with men outside the usual inner circle – of nobility – and perhaps the cultivated influence of his Flemish mother and her circle of courtiers inspired this development. The malign nature of his 'favourites' may also have been exaggerated – the king usually gave land and office to his intimates, only the latter had until now been of high birth so those who were now cut off from this patronage resented it. James III evidently had an enquiring mind and was ready to seek friendships outside the usual group of aristocrats or court-connected gentry – who were to be targeted as scheming social climbers by their enemies in the 1480s (and by sixteenth-century chroniclers remote from the events).

James suggested unsuccessfully to Edward IV in 1474 that his next brother Alexander marry the widowed Duchess Margaret of Burgundy, Edward's sister. A marriage was arranged between the Scots king's infant eldest son James (born March 1473) and one of Edward IV's younger daughters, Cecily, with a dowry of 20,000 marks plus an extra 5,000 as compensation for the late Bishop Kennedy's plundered barge. The English invasion of France in 1475 led to a treaty between Edward and Louis XI, and as a result the English king, secure from French aid to a belligerent Scotland, abandoned the plan to marry his sister Margaret to Alexander and stopped payments on Princess Cecily's dowry. England and Scotland drifted apart again, despite an attempt by James to interest Edward in marrying his increasingly estranged and now (1476) widowed brother, the Duke of Clarence, to James's sister Margaret. Clarence was interested in the far richer Duchess Mary of Burgundy, and James offered Margaret as a bride to Edward's brother-in-law Lord Rivers instead.

James seems to have been living apart from his queen, who was usually to be found at Stirling while he resided at Edinburgh, and also to have avoided the usual royal peregrinations around the Lowlands administering justice. The latter may have added to grumbling that he was not carrying out his duties adequately. The meetings of Parliament in 1472, 1473 and in the 1480s were used for royal demands for extraordinary taxation, not usually required in peacetime, which aroused resistance and were not fully granted; the king already seems to have been intent on building up a full treasury. The Scots senior nobility seems to have been shaken by the sudden arrest of James's youngest brother John, Earl of Mar, for unspecified reasons in 1479 or 1480. Imprisoned at Craigmillar Castle with royal favourite Thomas Preston in charge of him, John died some time later and was rumoured to have been murdered on the king's orders; it is possible that he was feared to be plotting a revolt or that he was seen as a threat by the king's advisers. Mar's plans (if any) cannot be known, but it is more certain that the king's other brother Alexander, now Warden of the East Marches, was an ambitious and warlike young man who was frustrated with the policy of peace with England. He had been raiding across the Borders in defiance of the treaty, trying to disrupt the king's pro-English policy by irritating Edward IV. At some point in 1479 Alexander either was arrested, imprisoned in Edinburgh Castle and escaped or fled to avoid arrest; he ended up holding Dunbar Castle in armed defiance of the king.

The castle held out during a siege of around a month despite bombardment by the king's cannons, and Alexander then fled to France – the obvious refuge for anyone seeking to overturn the Anglo-Scottish alliance by force. Louis XI, now at odds with Edward IV, welcomed him and in January 1480 Alexander married a noble French bride, Anne de la Tour. The Anglo-Scots treaty now collapsed, war resuming in April 1480 and the Earl of Angus burning Bamburgh, but Louis did not join in. Luckily for James III, whose pro-English efforts had collapsed humiliatingly, Edward IV failed to launch his expected attack on Scotland in 1481. Alexander moved on to England at the request of Edward's agents and signed up to a one-sided treaty with Edward at Fotheringhay Castle on 11 June 1482. Under this alliance he would be assisted by England to take his brother's throne, but would become Edward's vassal and would hand over Berwick, Liddesdale, Eskdale and Annandale to England. He would marry Edward's daughter Cecily, who had been engaged to his nephew Prince James – provided that he could free himself from his French marriage. The expedition to install Alexander was left to Edward's viceroy in the North, his brother Duke Richard of Gloucester (later Richard III). In mid-July around 20,000 men duly besieged Berwick, where the town surrendered but the castle held out, and the invasion of Lothian followed. But in the interim James III suffered a catastrophic blow, as it became apparent that he could not rely on the support of a substantial part of the nobility – the crucial figures who had the task of raising their tenants to form his army to resist Edward. The royal army was to muster at Lauder. Seeing a chance to be rid of the king's unpopular favourites, his half-uncles John Stewart, Earl of Atholl, and James Stewart, Earl of Buchan – the sons of Queen Joan Beaufort by her second husband the 'Black Knight' of Lorn – and the 5th Earl of Angus, head of the Red Douglases, led a group of nobles to arrest the king at Lauder on 22 July. Those of his favourites who were in the camp were seized and hanged from the town's bridge; the most prominent victim was Robert Cochrane (Angus was to be nicknamed 'Bell-the-Cat' from this episode, referring to his brave offer to be the person to undertake a dangerous task for the benefit of his allies like the mice putting a bell on the cat in the Aesop fable). The king was then taken as a prisoner back to Edinburgh Castle. Queen Margaret, estranged from her husband, and her sons were at Stirling Castle, and an impasse followed as Duke Richard and Alexander arrived in Edinburgh – the English army only had pay and supplies available for a short period, but the rebel nobles in the castle were not ready to negotiate and it was unclear if they wanted to depose James (and if so in whose favour, his son or his brother?).

The Scots king's government, represented by Archbishop Scheves, Avandale and Argyll, did negotiate and on 2 August agreed with the invaders to restore Alexander to all his confiscated lands and offices and pardon him for his treason; but they did not have possession of the king to ratify this and Atholl and Buchan, who did, would not cooperate. Alexander, not trusting their ability to carry out their promises, secretly agreed with Richard to continue to work for his own assumption of the crown. With 8,000 marks from Edinburgh's civic leaders as an inducement Richard began to withdraw on 4 August. He left it to Alexander to attempt to break the impasse in the role of an independent actor, not the ally of an occupation force, and moved back to besiege Berwick Castle, which surrendered to Richard on 24 August. Berwick thus changed hands for the final time in the long run of sieges since 1296.

Alexander, accompanied by his uncertain allies Scheves, Avandale and Argyll, proceeded to Stirling Castle to negotiate with the queen and agreed to help the government restore the king – in return for assurances of his full return to all his former powers. The accord he seems to have reached with Margaret and his friendly encounters with her eldest son James, the Duke of Rothesay (now nine), seem to have aroused the king's suspicions; did Alexander promise to respect the prince's rights and/or seem a more stable guardian of them than the king? Alexander now marched on Edinburgh Castle to besiege Atholl and the captive king there; the castle was legally in the hands of the queen and her deputy as castellan, Lord Darnley (John Stewart), and his garrison remained in the castle throughout the king's captivity there so presumably Atholl trusted them. Did this arouse the king's fear of his wife's intentions? The king was released around 29 September and handed over to Alexander. Darnley and his men were pardoned by the king for their actions during the crisis in terms which imply that the latter had been in some fear of being killed earlier. In the new government Alexander was to be 'Lieutenant General' of the realm (i.e. in charge of military affairs) and the 'governor' of Prince James so his role was enhanced.

Parliament duly met at Edinburgh on 2 December to

ratify these agreements, but for some reason – a rearguard action by the king? – Alexander's appointment as Lieutenant General and restoration to other offices was delayed. The impatient duke could not muster sufficient support to force his appointment, and resorted to an attempt to seize Edinburgh Castle to force the issue in January 1483. His abortive coup alienated crucial figures, and the king was able to return some of his allies to office and summon sympathetic nobles and some time that winter admitted an English garrison into his Dunbar Castle. He ended up fleeing to England, and on 9 July he and his supporters had their lands declared forfeit by the Scots Parliament. The surprise death of King Edward on 9 April deprived him of his patron and led to another bout of civil strife in England in which Duke Richard was to seize power.

The new King Richard III faced revolt from the loyalists of his deposed nephew Edward V and had no time for Scots affairs, and James III was eager for peace. In November 1483 the latter sent an embassy to England to negotiate. Richard delayed a reply, but his exiled ally Alexander had to make do with a role as an instrument of pressure on the Scots. He led an unsuccessful raid on Annandale with the exiled Earl James of Douglas in February 1484, but neither attracted much local backing. A second raid, on Lochmaben Castle in August, only led to Douglas being captured, and on his return to England Alexander gave up and moved on to France where King Louis had now died and the regency for his son Charles VIII was not interested. He was killed in a tournament at Paris in June 1485 by Charles's cousin and heir, Duke Louis of Orleans (later Louis XII). Richard finally agreed to open serious negotiations with James's envoys at Nottingham in September 1484, and a three-year truce was agreed. Princess Cecily having been bastardised by her uncle along with her disappeared brothers, Richard now promised James's son the hand of his niece, Anne de la Pole.

The next English government of Henry VII, son of Margaret Beaufort who was the niece of James III's late grandmother

Queen Joan, could be expected to be less hostile to the Scots than its predecessor. Henry raised no objections to James besieging and recovering Dunbar Castle in winter 1485/6, and on 3 July 1486 a three-year truce was signed, with James's second son, Prince James, being promised the hand of Princess Cecily's sister Katherine of York, also sister of Henry's Queen Elizabeth. In January 1488 the king's second son also received the Dukedom of Ross, designed to build him up once he was adult as the main bastion of royal power in the North. Queen Margaret had died in July 1486, aged barely thirty – the fourth Scots queen to die relatively young, following queens Annabella Drummond (in her forties), Joan Beaufort (around forty-three) and Mary of Guelders (around thirty). Her Italian biographer of 1491, Giovanni Sabadino, was to claim that she had been a better ruler than her husband – and that she and Alexander of Albany had imprisoned him in 1482 for the good of the realm.

James III had been recovering his confidence after the disasters of 1482, with Parliament obligingly passing a new Treasons Act in 1484 to punish future plotters and assorted minor allies of Duke Alexander being judicially hounded. Most of his successes were in international diplomacy, where he secured the honour of the grant of a 'Golden Rose' as a favoured son of the Papacy in 1486. In the January 1488 Parliament he made a point of insisting on his rights to take over the priory of Coldingham in the East March for his Chapel Royal despite the claims of the local Home family (one of whom was its prior) as its patrons. The Homes had backed him in 1482–83, but Prior John Home refused to vacate his office as the king ruled, backed by his nephew the Master (heir) of Home, and their defiance of royal orders led the king to set up a special committee to deal with all those who had defied his orders over the Coldingham business. The meeting was also concerned with other special measures to bring more rigour and royal control to the administration of justice, but the threat to forfeit the Homes was its main political impact; it brought in the Homes' dynastic allies, the Hepburns of Hailes, the Huntlys of Buchan, the Montgomeries and ultimately the Campbells of Argyll. The head of the latter, the Earl of Argyll, was now sacked as Chancellor; he was replaced by Bishop William Elphinstone of Aberdeen, one of the outstanding royal administrators of the era.

The complex bonds of familial politics landed the insistent king with a coalition of landed families backing the Homes in armed defiance of him, though his half-uncles remained loyal this time. James Shaw of Sauchie, castellan of Stirling Castle and thus in control of its resident Prince James (the heir), handed the prince over to the rebels in early February. According to Lindsay of Pitscottie (a century later), the rebels persuaded the prince and issued statements to the effect that the king suspected his loyalty and was coming with an army to Stirling to deal with him as he had dealt with John of Mar in around 1479, i.e. by murder (one story had it that a royal henchman had poisoned the late Queen Margaret). It is surprising that James III had taken no steps to secure his heir from a Home marital connection after what had happened to him in 1482. He was taken by surprise by the outbreak of revolt and by the prince's part in it, and the latter's flight followed his younger brother's elevation to the Dukedom of Ross so the prince could have feared for his safety. A struggle between king (at Edinburgh) and prince (at Linlithgow?) to win adherents followed, with the Earl of Angus – head of the Red Douglases and a prime mover in the 1482 revolt – among those who deserted King James while his half-uncles and the Crawfords remained loyal. The king – rarely seen outside the south – moved to Aberdeen to seek lordly support during the consecration of Elphinstone as bishop there, but few of his recruits would venture south with him and he seems to have initially accepted but then abandoned a proposal for a negotiated settlement. This so-called 'Pacification of Blackness', which required that he choose 'wise' councillors and give more prominence to his eldest son, was abandoned, and the 'war party' induced the king to march south to the Forth and seek aid from Henry VII. But the rebels had the upper hand in winning over support with the reasonable claim that they were only helping the heir to protect his position from his vindictive father. James III, in Fife, faced them as they held Stirling Castle. Buoyed up by success in an initial clash near the site of Wallace's 1297 victory, he attacked the rebels on the 'field of Stirling' close to the castle on 11 June 1488. This battle, normally called 'Sauchieburn' as the site was between the Sauchie and Bannock burns, was close to the site of Robert I's victory of 1314 – an ironic location for the type of internal Scots power struggle which the Bruce victory was supposed to have ended. Little is known about the battle, where there were few notable casualties (mainly royalist), and the prince was supposed to have ordered that his father not be harmed but to have used a royal standard at the battle and so proclaimed his intention to depose him. The defeated king abandoned his most treasured possessions, Robert I's sword and a box of gold coins, and headed for the royal naval captain Sir Andrew Wood's ships in the Forth, but was overtaken and stabbed to death by a 'mystery man' (later supposed to be disguised as a priest), probably at the Bannock Burn mill. Aged probably thirty-six, James was the first Scots king to die in battle at the hands of his subjects since 1058, and at that to be stabbed by a lowly citizen rather than to be killed in combat by a relative claiming the crown. It was an end which has been seen as fitting for a reign dominated by his political mismanagement and failure as a leader. Certainly he was not as capable or skilful a statesman as his equally autocratic father and grandfather, and he failed to 'bond' with his most important subjects or to compensate for this with a degree of skill in politics. He did have some achievements – a large treasure hoard amassed during his reign, which the new regime carefully recovered from assorted locations, was estimated in value at £24,517 10s, the equivalent of two years' annual revenue. But his tactics can be seen to have aroused deep suspicion – though he may have suffered from successful spin by his enemies, who asserted that he murdered his brother and wife. The desertions in 1482 and 1488 were not exclusively his fault, and James I and James II had not faced adult brothers as a focus for resistance as he did. His Anglophile policy was bold for his position and era, and he had favourable personal qualities that his predecessor had lacked. But did James III make his own bad luck? Was it the king's unpredictability that ruined him as much as his autocratic nature? His modern biographer Norman Macdougall rates him as being as autocratic (and tyrannical) as any of the dynasty.

James IV, 1488–1513: 'Renaissance Monarch' – With a Fatal Overconfidence?

The new king, now fifteen, was old enough in the hard political/military world of medieval Scotland to have been less of a 'puppet' of the rebel coalition than his defenders could claim. The likelihood is that he knew full well what he was doing when he fled, or was taken, to join the Homes in February 1488, that he felt his position as heir under threat from his younger brother and that he was openly seeking to depose his father at Sauchieburn. Like the similar case of Czar Alexander I of Russia in 1801, political reality made it likely that the son's deposition of his father would be followed by the murder of the ex-ruler – but publicly the son had to distance himself from a possible charge of parricide. The sordid death of the late king at the hands of an unknown assassin rather than in the heat of battle was also a blot on the new regime, and Pitscottie's 1570s history had it that the new king promised the Dean of the Chapel Royal to wear an iron chain for life like a self-mortifying holy hermit to repent for the unfortunate circumstances of his accession. He was crowned at Scone on 24 June, the anniversary of Bannockburn. The leading figure of the government was Border magnate Patrick

Hepburn, Lord Hailes and now Earl of Bothwell, who became 'Master of the Royal Household' and whose family proceeded to scoop up important offices in the manner of the Crichtons and Livingstones in the 1440s and the Boyds in the mid-1460s.

The overthrow of the pro-English James III led to greater tension with the new and unstable Tudor regime in England. But both regimes needed peace, and a three-year truce was quickly agreed; meanwhile the first parliament of the reign in October 1488 saw some of James III's leading adherents being forfeited as expected but within a few years they were allowed home and pardoned. Local offices were carefully taken from James III's loyalists for redistribution, and extortionate terms of financial penalty were imposed on several of the 1488 loyalist lords – or held over them as a threat should they step out of line. In spring 1489 Alexander Gordon, Master (i.e. heir) of Huntly, led a revolt in the north-east against the clique dominating governance and appealed to Henry VII for aid. Meanwhile John Stewart, recently confirmed as Earl of Lennox, and Lord Lyle led a rising in Lennox against the Hepburn-dominated government, and these rebels were joined by the exiled (3rd) Lord Crichton whom James III had had forfeited in 1484. The king was despatched to the campaign in the south-west. But with the Huntly rising in the north-east now distracting the government the royal army had to move back to Stirling and a major clash followed between the king's and Lennox's armies at the 'field of Moss' or Gartloaning (probably near the Touch Hills, west of Stirling) on 11–12 October. Lennox was defeated, though not decisively as his party remained in the field, in possession of Dumbarton which seems to have surrendered to the king before Christmas.

The rising of 1489 had luckily had no royal personnel involved to benefit from any coup and had been held in check, but it had showed substantial magnate discontent and rebel lords Lennox and Lyle were pardoned by the February 1490 parliament. All grants of royal land since the coronation were annulled – the rebels' terms for their surrender? In winter

1492/3 a number of prominent Hepburn allies, including his uncle (Keeper of the Privy Seal) and the Earl of Argyll (Chancellor), resigned from office; the former office went to Bishop Elphinstone, who was to keep it for twenty-two years, and the latter to Angus despite his recent dealings with England. Evidently a 'deal' saw the potentially dangerous Douglas leader brought into government.

The young king was in the far north for the first time in 1493 to make a pilgrimage to Tain, with royal power needing to be asserted as the declining Lordship of the Isles fell into chaos and semi-autonomous Macdonald cadets attacked each other and royal lands without any respect for their distant king. Alexander Macdonald of Lochalsh, the ageing 'Lord' John's nephew, had sacked Inverness but later been defeated and eclipsed as a threat in 1491, and John – who had accepted the king as his overlord in 1476 – was a spent force. Accordingly in May–June 1493 the Lordship of the Isles was declared forfeit to the Crown, and in August the king and most of his senior court lords made an expedition to Dunstaffnage, ancient mainland seat of the lordship, to 'show the flag' and probably to receive homage from local vassals. Following a subsequent pilgrimage to Whithorn in Galloway the royal entourage travelled north to Dingwall, the seat of the Dukedom of Ross, which the king's brother James technically held (but with little real power over his local vassals). Alexander of Lochalsh, who had probably submitted to the king at Dunstaffnage, was then involved in new disturbances of the peace and was murdered in obscure circumstances on Oronsay in 1494 by a distant cousin and local rival, John McIan of Ardnamurchan – whose subsequent reward with local Crown office may indicate that he acted with official approval. In July 1494 James was at Tarbert Castle on lower Loch Fyne to 'show the flag' with an armed host and repair its fortifications, and his naval expedition then took charge of and repaired Dunaverty Castle at the southern tip of Kintyre – evidently aimed at increasing the Crown's military control of the seaways. In May 1495 the king returned by sea again, this time further north to Mingary Castle on Ardnamurchan to receive the homage of the local Hebridean lords.

The formal end of James's minority occurred in March 1494 at his twenty-first birthday, though there were few changes of personnel in government, which indicates relative contentment with the latter years of the Hepburn faction's regime. Elphinstone made an arduous journey to Rome – now in the middle of a French invasion by Charles VIII – to acquire the 'Bull of Foundation' for his new Aberdeen University from Pope Alexander VI, the notorious Rodrigo Borgia. The king's main new interest appears to have been his latest mistress Margaret Drummond; they had a daughter and by 1498 James had moved on to Janet Kennedy.

James began to assert himself in foreign policy for the first time in summer 1495, taking an anti-English line by inviting the rebellious Ulster lord, Hugh O'Donnell of Tir Connaill, to meet him in Glasgow. O'Donnell recommended that James take charge of the latest pretender to Henry's throne, the enigmatic 'Perkin Warbeck'. Currently involved in a failed attack on Kent in July 1495, the plausible and princely seeming Warbeck was a Flemish youth who laid claim to the persona of the disappeared Duke Richard of York, younger son of Edward IV and one of the 'Princes in the Tower'. According to Henry's propaganda he was the son of a Flemish boatman who had been trained by Yorkist agents, and he had attracted the patronage of Charles VIII of France and the new Holy Roman Emperor Maximilian when they fell out with Henry. James initially sent to Maximilian in summer 1495 to suggest a joint alliance to assist Warbeck, but failed to secure a Habsburg princess as his wife either; hence his approach to Ferdinand and Isabella of Spain for an alliance. When Warbeck fled to Southern Ireland in autumn 1495 James made contact with him via his Irish allies. Initially James put more weight on an alliance against Henry with Ferdinand and Isabella, to whom he despatched Archbishop

Blackadder of Glasgow, but they would not abandon their English alliance. So he invited Warbeck to Scotland as a weapon to use against Henry, and on his arrival late in 1495 received him at Stirling as the rightful 'Prince Richard' with a bodyguard in Yorkist colours assigned to him. In January 1496 Warbeck was married to James's distant cousin Lady Katherine Gordon, daughter of the 2nd Earl of Huntly, and the royal army mustered at Restalrig ready for the invasion of England – Warbeck having promised that when he was 'Richard IV' he would hand over Berwick.

The delay in the expedition setting off is a pointer to the probability that James was using the threat of Warbeck as a political 'counter' rather than seriously intending a major invasion to restore 'Richard IV'; it was aimed at both Henry VII and the Spanish sovereigns to impress them with his disruptive potential. The main army crossed the Tweed with the artillery on 20 September, and James proceeded to lay waste to the countryside to the distress of the pretender who protested at his 'subjects' being despoiled to Scots observers' contempt. James told Warbeck sarcastically that despite his promises none of his countrymen had come to help the invaders, and next day Warbeck recrossed the Tweed; James laid siege to Heton Tower with his cannons but called it off and returned to Scotland on the 25th as he heard that the English army had left Newcastle. The short war achieved nothing for Warbeck but enabled James to use more diplomatic leverage on England. An unexpected Cornish peasant revolt against their king's taxes saved James from invasion. James sent Warbeck packing, and the pretender proceeded back to Ireland and then on to Cornwall to stage the region's second rebellion of the year. It ended with his army failing to take Exeter, and Warbeck, outnumbered and outgunned, panicking and fleeing to sanctuary whence he was taken before Henry as a prisoner; Lady Katherine was captured too. Meanwhile James crossed the Border again in July 1497 with his artillery to besiege Norham Castle, stronghold of the English king's senior adviser

Bishop Fox of Durham. His artillery could not cause enough damage in the short time for which he had paid his cannoneers and after a fortnight or so he abandoned the siege.

The war petered out as in September 1497 Bishop Fox's English commissioners met Elphinstone's Scots commissioners at Ayton and agreed a seven-year truce. In 1502 a 'Treaty of Perpetual Peace' was agreed, which arranged for James to marry Henry's eldest daughter Margaret Tudor (born November 1489), sixteen years his junior, and set up mechanisms to resolve the inevitable Border clashes and legal disputes between English and Scots nationals. In the long term the marriage of the '(Scots) Thistle and the (Tudor) Rose' was to bring a Scots king to the English throne but, at the time it was arranged, Henry had two sons and the possibility of Margaret or her offspring succeeding to England would have seemed minor. She arrived in Scotland and was married to James at Holyrood (8 August 1503).

James might have decided to avoid further clashes with England, but he continued to build up Scotland's military capabilities and turned his attention to his navy as well as to his expensive, partly foreign-staffed artillery train. During the course of his reign James was to acquire, build, hire or capture thirty-eight ships, a substantial increase on the naval activity of his predecessors. James, like his grandfather James II, clearly saw himself as an important actor on the European stage, and part of the drive to improve his profile was to acquire Continental links via his shipping. By 1502 James was able to launch an expedition by sea under Lord Hamilton to assist his brother-in-law, King Hans of Denmark, against Swedish rebels, though it only had 200 volunteers and was not very successful. In the following years he brought a number of foreign shipwrights to Scotland to extend old, and create new, dockyards. These were in the Forth rather than the traditional Clyde, with Leith replacing Dumbarton as the king's main base and the focus of warfare thus shifting from the Hebridean seas (implicitly against local rebels) to the North Sea (implicitly against the English). Naval expenditure rocketed from around

£500 to around £7,000 per annum between 1500 and 1508, and high-status ships of considerable size were built as 'prestige projects' to match those of the English kings. The most notable of these were the *Margaret*, named after James's new queen, launched in 1506, and the *Great Michael*, launched in 1511 – the latter, loaded with cannons, was clearly built in competition with the huge warships of James's brother-in-law, Henry VIII, being the largest ship ever built in Scotland.

James, however, only had four 'great ships' fit to vie with the English navy, and was never going to win in a naval 'race' against the better-funded Henry VIII – a man stung by any competition into aggressive response. James relied for much of his aggressive naval activity (privateering in particular) on the three skilled and enterprising Barton brothers (Andrew, Robert and John) whom he loaded with honours. They were issued with royal 'letters of marque' to act as James's privateers and attack shipping belonging to 'unfriendly' states, with him receiving a share of the loot. Their growing reputation for daring and ruthlessness added to Scotland's international prestige while their plundering ships of states with which Scotland had commercial disputes (e.g. Portugal) served to acquire treasure for the king and to intimidate potential enemies. The Bartons did much to sour Anglo-Scots diplomatic relations in the 1500s, and arguably undermined attempts to build closer relations with England – and James's willingness to let them take English ships implied that he was not serious in his protestations of goodwill. Andrew Barton was killed in a famous 'unofficial' naval clash with Sir Edward Howard, son of the Earl of Surrey, in the North Sea in summer 1511, and despite protests at the alleged English aggression James did not break the treaty. James riskily used his flamboyant captains to channel anti-English feeling into a lucrative and containable channel.

James's political control via close associates involved the Church, as he took the unprecedented step of raising his brother, James, Duke of Ross, to the Archbishopric of St

Andrews when James III's favourite, Scheves, died (January 1497) and made him Chancellor as well (1502). As a cleric Ross was invalidated from becoming king so this move was politically useful, but it gave the impression of James treating the Church as a department of State. It also meant that Ross had to hand over his ducal estates to the king – and as Ross was some years short of the canonical age for consecration (twenty-seven, in this case 1503) the king could use the archbishopric's revenues until then. When Ross died in January 1504 the king replaced him with his own illegitimate son Alexander (born 1493), though the boy – already being educated for a clerical career – did not take on the duties of Archbishop until 1510 at the end of his education. Alexander also became Chancellor at an unusually young age, though Elphinstone carried out the office's duties until 1510. Use of Church estates and offices for lay appointees was an established practice of the time, but James practised it more widely than most of his dynasty – a skilful use of patronage helped to ward off rebellion.

But despite this and his many mistresses he was conventionally pious to the extent that he patronised the most zealously austere current monastic order, the Observant Friars (introduced to Scotland by his grandmother Mary of Guelders), and talked of monastic reform – which was used as a reason to suppress several abbeys and hand their lands to rival religious houses run by his clients. John Knox later claimed that he had presided at a rare trial of suspected 'Lollard' heretics in person. He also went on pilgrimage within his kingdom, going to Tain in Ross during his regular northern tours – though this served a political reason: to show himself to his northern subjects. Other pilgrimages seem to have had more exclusively religious reasons, such as when he walked to the shrine of St Ninian at Whithorn in 1507 when his wife and newborn son were ill (the king and queen's first three children all died young). The militant Pope Julius was impressed enough by the devotion (and political value) of the eventual heir, James V, to send him a papal sword and hat as marks of his esteem at Easter 1507, the first such honour for Scotland since the reign of William I. James also talked of going on pilgrimage to the Holy Land. Approaches were made to Venice regarding hire of naval transport, Archbishop Blackadder went there during his own pilgrimage to the Holy Land in 1508 (but inopportunely died) and the king's Northern Irish ally, Hugh O'Donnell, wrote to ask James not to leave his kingdom unless it was safe to do so. But in the event a war broke out between Venice and the papal-led 'Holy League' in 1508–09 as the Pope endeavoured to dismember Venice's land-based domain in Northern Italy, so the project was abandoned. James's wide-ranging interests extended to poetry – his reign saw the first works of Gavin Douglas and William Dunbar – and music, and Spanish ambassador De Ayala wrote in his eulogistic account of the king that he spoke Latin, French, German, Flemish, Spanish and Gaelic. In terms of architecture James built a new royal castle at Kilkerran, a hall at Edinburgh Castle and the oldest extant part of Holyrood Palace (a tower) next to the abbey, and he also remodelled Linlithgow Palace – though his works were minor compared to his wealthier fellow-monarchs' in England and France. He also brought in the first printing presses to Scotland – to print government legislation and nationalistic chronicles.

In the field of royal government James used his twenty-fifth birthday, his legal 'majority', in 1498 to issue an order of 'resumption' as his predecessors had done at a similar age; this cancelled all earlier land grants made during his reign. This added to his capacity for patronage and punishment to his vassals. Once peace was agreed with England there would be no more opportunities for raising 'war' taxes, national defence being the accepted rationale for special grants of taxation, so the truce of 1497 and peace of 1502 reduced James's excuses for raising extra revenue. There was apparently resistance to the large financial demands made of his subjects for funding the embassy to England for arranging the king's marriage in 1502 and to those for the 1502 expedition to Denmark, though not on the scale of resistance which James I had faced. No more taxes were imposed until James's next war with England in 1512 – and then only on the clergy.

James's resources remained substantially smaller than those of England and a head-on clash between the two powers as a result of international European power politics was to bring him down. Indeed, he has been harshly criticised for allowing himself to be drawn into a conflict with the young and aggressive Henry VIII that he could not realistically expect to win. Should he have concentrated on protecting his own interests and ignored the appeals of Louis XII's France for aid as another Anglo-French war loomed? In practical Border affairs James had shown unprecedented cooperation with the English in suppressing the endemic disorder by out-of-control raiders on both sides, the famous 'reivers' for whom cross-Borders cattle thieving and sporadic tit-for-tat murders were part of normal life. The situation was altered when the young, belligerent Henry VIII ascended the English throne in April 1509 as, after an initial hesitation, Henry decided to ally with Ferdinand, the father of his wife Catherine, and attack France to regain parts of the English 'empire' of Edward III and Henry V. As a contrast to the cautious Henry VII's manoeuvrings, England joined the anti-French 'Holy League' in autumn 1511 and Louis put out requests to Scotland for an offensive and defensive alliance, tying each country to assist the other should it be attacked. Given Henry's ambitions this meant that Scotland was likelier to be called on to assist France than vice versa, and James (still smarting over the deaths of 'March Warden' Robert Kerr and Andrew Barton at English hands?) went along with this. The decision of Henry to withhold his father's legacy to Queen Margaret added to estrangement. In July 1512 James signed up to an offensive and defensive alliance with France, and the failure of Henry's expedition to Spain that year to recover Aquitaine meant that in 1513 Henry would be invading French Flanders as his father had done in 1492 and his grandfather had done in 1475. James's attack on the Pope's

English allies led his ex-patron Julius II to excommunicate him (February 1513), a decision confirmed by the next Pope, Leo X.

The invasion of England ended in catastrophe, and with that in mind it has led to historians condemning James for either arrogant overconfidence or quixotic chivalrous folly. But although his resources were far inferior to Henry's there was no certainty that his invasion would end in disaster as David II's similar adventure had done in 1346. Later stories of portents of doom, some relating to divine punishment for James's lechery, are less likely to be accurate than the one about Queen Margaret asking her husband not to risk his life while he had only one living son, a year old (she was pregnant with another child, Alexander, who was born posthumously and died at a year old). The king, with probably the largest Scots army seen yet in England (30,000–35,000?) plus seventeen massive siege cannons, crossed the Tweed around 22–24 August to repeat his attack of 1497 on Norham Castle, which fell to assault within a week – testimony to the effectiveness of his artillery. He then moved on up the Till valley to take Etal and Ford, and set up his camp on the high ridge of Flodden Edge, the main Cheviot escarpment overlooking the Tweed valley. He had the advantage of an unassailable position but a dilemma – what if the English were too wise to try to climb the ridge? The Earl of Surrey was too slow in assembling his army to clash with the Scots before they gained this position, and had to lure them down instead; a week or so of provocative challenges between the two armies followed. Finally on 8 September Surrey moved off north to cross the Till to cut through James's line of supply into Scotland, within sight of the Scots despite the rain. James decided not to attack him despite the chances of disrupting his march, possibly expecting him to march on into the Merse, not to swing round and come at the Scots. The latter was what happened on the morning of the 9th, and as the English headed for the intervening Branxholm Hill James ordered his army down from Flodden Edge to try to take that strategic position first. They made it, dragging the artillery, but despite the two armies being approximately equal in size the Scots attack downhill on the English ended in carnage. The sources are confused and much was added later by legend, but it appears that James's tactic of a charge by infantry pikemen carrying long spears in a 'phalanx' formation of five squares – a contemporary Swiss adaptation of the ancient Scots 'schiltrons' – went spectacularly wrong. The Swiss had succeeded in destroying the Burgundian army this way in 1477, but the combination of an uneven, boggy battlefield and heavy rain plus long, unwieldy pikes caused great problems. Should the army have been held back at the rendezvous for a few days to practise with their new pikes? James gave no obvious directions, the attack ran out of steam, and English halberdiers with lighter, shorter spears, plus the usual archers, gradually wore the Scots down. The massive casualty list was surprising – the Scots king; his illegitimate son, the Archbishop of St Andrews; one bishop; two abbots; nine earls; fourteen lords of Parliament and thousands of soldiers were killed. James became the fourth Stewart king in a row to die violently – the first Scots king to die at English hands.

As a final humiliation, when the English recovered the king's body (Lord Dacre identified it) and it was carried south to the Carthusian monastery at Sheen, near his widow's childhood home at Richmond, the Church refused to bury it as he had died excommunicate. Eventually Henry VIII secured permission from Pope Leo to have it buried at St Paul's Cathedral. In Scotland legends persisted that the king had escaped the battlefield and one of a number of 'decoys' wearing duplicates of his armour had been killed instead, and the ever-colourful Pitscottie was to write that four mysterious horsemen (i.e. of the Apocalypse?) had carried him off. The catastrophe at Flodden has undermined his reputation ever since and added to the enigma of a seemingly successful and multi-talented statesman who died in a futile charge in an unnecessary war undertaken at the behest of the French. The question of his military competence has to be raised as he allowed himself to be outmanoeuvred by Surrey (thirty years his senior and a veteran of the battles of Barnet and Bosworth) and missed his best chance to attack him as he was crossing the Till; at Flodden he fought like a knight rather than directing like a commander. But until that fatal misjudgement he had been the most successful of his line, and his generosity, abilities as a ruler and concern for justice were commended by one of his junior courtiers, the poet Sir David Lindsay of the Mount, who had been entrusted with his son's education, in his *Testament of the Papyngo* (Parrot) around 1530.

James V: People's Prince or Brutal Political Failure?

With the forty-year-old king dead, his surviving son James succeeded to the throne aged seventeen months, the youngest king to date. A council of regents assumed power, headed by the octogenarian Bishop Elphinstone (who died in 1514), and the only surviving male Stewart – Duke John, the half-French son of Duke Alexander of Albany – was invited to come to his father's homeland and assume the 'Governorship', which would hopefully bring French aid to a kingdom shorn of its manpower and leadership for war. The queen was placed in charge of her son, raising the possibility that she would prefer the aid of her brother Henry to that of France. The nearest adult heir in Scotland was the Earl of Arran, son of James III's sister Mary and head of the Hamiltons, who did not challenge this yet. However the Red Douglases did, with their emergence at the head of an anti-French faction of nobles which was to look to England for aid. The aged Bell-the-Cat's eldest son and heir had been killed at Flodden, but the latter's son Archibald (born 1489?), who became Earl of Angus after his grandfather in January 1514, married Queen Margaret on 6 August 1514 and thus assumed the position of royal stepfather and potential regent. The possibility of a Margaret-Douglas-Henry VIII alliance taking charge of Scotland was resisted by the regency council, who voted that the queen had forfeited her right to keep control of her son and urged Albany to return quickly to assume his governorship. However, the queen (and her son) held out with Douglas aid in Stirling Castle.

The two factions summoned rival parliaments, and when Bishop Elphinstone died in October 1514 Angus's uncle Gavin Douglas laid claim to the vacant Archbishopric of St Andrews, backed by the queen and Angus (and England), and seized the town's castle. He was driven out by the regency council's forces led by John Hepburn, the cathedral's prior and the choice of the cathedral chapter to be archbishop. Hepburn was installed as Archbishop, and the council's envoys, Arran and chamberlain Lord Home, induced the queen to go to Edinburgh and patch up a truce with their party. Arran, Home and Archbishop Beaton led the government at Edinburgh until Albany arrived at Dumbarton in May 1515 to assume power.

Backed by the new King Francis I of France, Albany and his allies could negotiate from a stronger position, but the queen refused to hand over her son to four lords sent by them. Albany now advanced on Stirling with a military force and drove the queen to flee into England before taking custody of the infant king. Margaret sought aid from Henry VIII, while Angus returned home to protect his lands from confiscation. However, Albany had problems; he could not even speak Scottish, was the son of a notorious rebel who had had designs on the Crown and he asserted his right to his father's Earldom of March, which meant his lands and authority impinging on that of the Homes in the East March. Lord Home was arrested and was handed over to Arran, next heir to the Crown after Albany, but then formed a 'bond' of alliance with him and the earls of Lennox (from a junior Stewart line), Glencairn and Eglinton, along with Highland allies. The rebel coalition was not strong enough to defeat Albany, a general trained in European warfare, and had the worse of an armed clash near Glasgow, after which the rebellion fizzled out and most of the participants were lured into acquiescence by pardons; Home and his brother were the only persons executed, after a suspected further plot (8 and

9 October 1516). Albany, sailing back to France on 6 June 1517 to gain aid against Henry, now signed up to an offensive/defensive alliance with France in the Treaty of Rouen.

From June 1517 to late 1521 Albany was in France, doing valuable international diplomatic work in shoring up Scotland's position with Francis's aid while at home a commission – Arran, Angus, Huntly, Argyll, the two archbishops and Albany's French military aide Antoine, Seigneur de la Bastie – ruled. De la Bastie was active on the Borders as lieutenant for the Merse and Lothian, but this aroused the ire of the Homes and later in 1517 Home of Wedderburn murdered him in revenge for Lord Home's execution. Dacre and Angus were suspected of involvement, the suspected killers fled to England and the government's appointment of Arran, not the local Angus, as the new lieutenant of the East Marches infuriated Angus. The period of Albany's absence also saw sporadic feuding between Arran and Angus and their followers, culminating in the clash in Edinburgh known as 'Cleanse the Causeway' on 30 April 1520 when the Douglases drove the Hamiltons out of the city by force. Albany returned late in 1521 to reassert his authority, accompanied by 4,000 French troops, and called a Parliament which removed all Angus's allies from office. Parliament agreed to war with England, and in September Albany led a large army on Carlisle but halted in the 'Debateable Land' on the Solway frontier to negotiate, called off the attack and went home, annoying his more belligerent lieutenants. His popularity now waned; later in 1522 he returned to France, where he became involved with Francis's bold plan to use the exiled Yorkist pretender, Richard de la Pole, to invade England. He did not return until September 1523, when he landed with 4,000 French troops at Dumbarton. The resulting autumn 1523 campaign against Northumberland, designed to take pressure off Francis by opening a 'second front', fizzled out and in May 1524 Albany returned to France for good. He died there in June 1536, without heirs, leaving the Hamiltons as the only adult male heirs to the Stewarts.

Anti-French nobles now planned to terminate the 'Governorship' – which Henry and his ministers hoped would be accompanied by the restoration of Margaret (now urging her son against France) to political influence. Arran now moved towards this faction. On 26 July 1524 Arran led the way in the investiture of James V with the symbols of sovereignty, thus marking his technical assumption of authority in Albany's place. An embassy was sent to England to arrange an alliance, with expectations that the young king might acquire a Tudor bride. Beaton was temporarily imprisoned and Angus was restored to the council, but the temporary alliance of Arran, Argyll, Lennox and Angus with Angus's ex-wife Queen Margaret soon broke up. A substantial faction of nobles saw Angus as an English puppet, and the queen turned against her ex-husband and allied to Arran. She was by now involved with a junior guards officer, Lord Avandale's son Henry Stewart, and was seeking a divorce from Angus. The queen wanted Angus exiled, and in retaliation he arrived on 23 November with a picked body of horsemen at Edinburgh, stormed the gates, and tried to drive the queen out of Holyrood Palace. Her use of cannon dissuaded him, and he agreed to withdraw at the king's request. With aristocratic and clerical opinion moving in his favour he was able to summon a 'convention' of the estates to Stirling and request the king to be sent to them, and when this was refused their faction advanced into Edinburgh to call a parliament. An uneasy truce saw the two factions having guardianship of the king in rotation, but when it was Angus's turn to hand James on to the queen's ally Arran he refused (November 1525). Arran rallied Angus's opponents at Linlithgow and the queen joined them, but Angus brought the king with him as he advanced to attack them and could now hold a 'packed' parliament which on 12 June declared the king of age, enabling James to cancel all past grants of office which were now re-awarded to Angus's allies; Angus soon replaced Beaton as chancellor.

Angus now dominated the 'adult' king's government, with

his stepson a powerless puppet, and the opposition resorted to the 1460s tactics of trying to physically seize the king. A first attempt was made on him by Scott of Branxholm in July 1525 during a royal expedition to the Borders to preside at legal sessions, and the would-be kidnappers' backer, the Earl of Lennox, then withdrew from court to join the queen and archbishop and sent a small body of horsemen under the Master of Kilmorris to Edinburgh Castle to 'rescue' the king. They, too, were spotted and driven off by Douglas guards – with James apparently wanting to go with them and being prevented. Lennox was killed in a clash with Arran at the ford of Manuel, the queen's group of plotters were forced to surrender Stirling Castle and Angus ordered his estranged wife to send her favourite, Henry Stewart, packing. She was later able to return to Stirling and with Albany's help secured a divorce (which Angus did not recognise) at Rome in 1528, marrying Stewart and having him made Lord Methven by her son once he was free of Angus's control. Angus lasted as ruler of Scotland until June 1528, when the King was allowed or fled unnoticed to join his mother at Stirling – a miscalculation on Angus's part – and announced that he was proscribing his stepfather and all the Douglases from coming within 7 miles of him. The king was able to summon the nobles to escort him to Edinburgh, and with the nobles' armed backing James held a parliament that outlawed Angus and his allies for treason (September 1528). Angus defied his ex-stepson at Tantallon Castle but eventually had to flee to England and his attempt to persuade Henry VIII to intercede failed as James would not listen. In May 1534 an Anglo-Scots treaty agreed peace for the lifetimes of the two sovereigns plus a year.

From June 1528 James was in charge of his own government and could be expected to be hostile to Angus and the latter's patron, Henry VIII, given his experiences in recent years. Aided by Albany, who never returned to Scotland but acted as his cousin's agent in France, he sought a Continental bride. James backed Albany's idea of his marrying Pope Clement VII's niece

Catherine de Medici; fearing that this would bring about a Franco-Papal-Scots alliance against him, Henry VIII persuaded King Francis to secure Catherine for Francis's son Henri instead. James then wanted Francis's frail daughter Madelaine (born 1520). Francis, claiming – accurately, given the tragic outcome of this marriage – that Madelaine was too fragile to live in Scotland, offered his cousin Mary of Vendôme instead in autumn 1534. Francis agreed terms on 29 March 1536 and the Scots king decided to sail to France himself for the wedding – the first monarch to voluntarily leave his realm since David II's visits to England. He arrived at Dieppe on 10 September; however when he arrived at Francis's court to inspect his fiancée he decided that he did not like her and asked for Madelaine instead. Francis agreed, with the contract providing for a dowry of 100,000 livres plus the annual rents at an additional 120,000 livres. James and Madelaine were married on 1 January 1537 at Notre Dame Cathedral in Paris; they arrived in Scotland on 19 May but the frail teenage queen was probably consumptive and died after a chill on 7 July. Determined to persevere with the French alliance and needing an heir, the widower king coolly opened negotiations for another French bride and settled on Marie de Guise (born 1514), daughter of the Duke of Aumale – from a younger branch of the ruling dynasty of France's ally, Lorraine, but descended in the female line from the younger son of King John II of France, Duke Louis of Anjou. The widow of Louis of Longueville, she already had a son so she was fertile; Henry VIII, widowed that autumn, was also interested so Marie could have been Queen of England instead of mother of Mary, Queen of Scots. But a marriage between James and Marie was agreed on 1 January 1538 with a dowry of 150,000 livres and it took place by proxy on 18 May; Marie arrived in Scotland in June and was married to James at St Andrews on the 12th. This time the bride proved healthy, though their two sons (James and Robert) died as infants. The Guise connection was to prove crucial in linking the Scots monarchy to the 'ultras' of the Catholic Counter-Reformation.

The king planned a new 'college of justice' – a body of trained civil lawyers to operate new civil law courts. Half of the latter were to be churchmen. As a result of this, the current permanent royal civil law court (attendant on the court), which James IV had set up, was replaced by the new 'Court of Session' in 1532. This served to extend the efficient administration of justice and the reach of royal power as the principal guarantor of even-handed and fast legal redress, but most of the bishops were said to be hostile to it (and the tax paying for it). The king's principal ecclesiastical ally was Archbishop Gavin Dunbar of Glasgow, his ex-tutor, not Archbishop Beaton of St Andrews (who was to be tried for treasonable correspondence with England in 1532). Beaton, leading resistance to the king, was replaced as a royal ally by his nephew and ecclesiastical coadjutor David, a French-trained and much more cooperative clerical diplomat who arranged the king's marriage to Marie de Guise in 1537. Beaton junior was also in favour at Rome, and acquired a cardinal's hat in 1538.

Meanwhile the vigorous young king also showed his combination of determination to see justice done and assertion of central governmental control in his fierce treatment of the obstreperous Border 'reivers', whose obedience to royal law was notoriously lax. Ironically, what sporadic control of them had been possible in the 1520s had been due to his stepfather Angus's military efforts. James led armed expeditions to enforce justice on the Borders, most famously in 1530 after he had summoned the principal minor Border lords, who were accused of ill-doings to Edinburgh, and arrested them en masse for failing to keep the peace. Three of them were hanged to impress the rest with his firmness. James and up to 10,000 troops descended on the Borders to round up and execute suspects, principally the notorious Armstrong clan of Liddesdale who had been running extortion rackets and pillaging goods and livestock at will on both sides of the Border. Ballads were subsequently composed about how he lured the leading brigand Johnnie ('Black Jock') Armstrong into his presence for an interview, probably under a safe conduct, and was so infuriated at his arrogance and at his splendidly clad escort of thugs that he had him arrested and strung up on the spot. Similar personal intervention marked James's treatment of the Highlands and Hebrides, though less frequently than James IV had acted.

James's ruthlessness was usual for his family and served to keep order – and indeed his reputation for showing concern for the needs of ordinary folk led to later stories that he went among his people in disguise as the 'Guideman of Ballengeich' to collect evidence of injustice and oppression which he then acted upon (it is not clear how authentic this nickname, first mentioned by Sir Walter Scott, is). His legislation served to deal with issues of concern for the less well-off, including excessive rents, arbitrary evictions and paying mortuary duties to the Church, and he created a special advocate for the poor, though 'social legislation' was not an innovation. But his harshness towards certain noble offenders showed a sign of the arbitrary and/or grudge-driven harshness of James I and III, particularly in his treatment of Douglas connections. This had political logic but was also reminiscent of James I and III. He notoriously executed Janet, Lady Glamis, the sister of his exiled ex-stepfather, by burning in 1537; though this was the legally correct punishment for one of her alleged crimes, killing her husband, her presumed links to Angus and the English were probably equally important. It was the accused rather than the king who received a sympathetic 'press' in later stories. The Master of Forbes, another Douglas relative, was executed days later for allegedly planning regicide. The king aroused suspicions of greed as had James I. He created new non-hereditary 'lords of council' and 'lords of session'; does this represent a generic distrust of the great nobles? His large-scale expenditure on new royal buildings, particularly a French-style palace for his second wife at Linlithgow and extensions at Stirling and Falkland, were in line with his father's pretensions to live as a European prince should do.

Like the better-educated and less paranoid James IV, the fifth

James was brought down by his entanglements with England. This was complicated by his continuing as a devout ally of the Papacy at the time of Henry VIII's breach with Rome, by his links to Francis I (by 1538 a foe of Henry's) and by his role as the king's nephew. Until October 1537 Henry had no legitimate son, and there was the danger of opponents of his breach with Rome and divorce from Catherine of Aragon (the Emperor Charles's aunt) seeking James's aid. In autumn 1541 James agreed to meet Henry when the latter made a rare State visit to York, but was persuaded not to go by his council. This was not unreasonable as the devious English king was rumoured to have considered kidnapping him, but Henry expected his nephew to turn up and was furious at the snub. The English king was easily persuaded into war, and in August 1542 Sir Robert Bowes raided across the Border to be defeated by the Earl of Huntly at Haddon Rig. James mustered his army to invade England and held a muster at Lauder in late October. The magnates agreed to a new campaign within a month with the Earl of Moray in command. The king planned this expedition at Edinburgh with a small group of advisers including Moray (the only noble present); Cardinal Beaton (as of August 1538 his uncle's successor as Archbishop of St Andrews), who intended to broadcast the Pope's interdict against Henry VIII to stir up a revolt against that ruler; and the new favourite, Oliver Sinclair, a junior member of the house of the earls of Orkney and the new keeper of Tantallon Castle. Whether James seriously intended a major attack this late in the year or a smaller raid, the 'command' was unclear, with unpopular Sinclair having a role. James and around 14,000 men advanced to Lochmaben, whence he sent Sinclair ahead with the vanguard to march east round the head of the Solway Firth into England. The king would take a more direct route across the Solway sands when the tide permitted. However, on 24 November Sinclair's force was unexpectedly attacked near the River Esk by Lord Wharton, the English deputy Warden of the West March, and was driven into the bogs of the Solway Moss. The Scots panicked, possibly after a precipitate retreat on horseback by local Lord Maxwell (according to some accounts in dispute with Sinclair over command) and other nobles, and the infantry ended up floundering in the boggy ground by Arthuret mill, being killed or rounded up at leisure. Though not many were killed, around 1,200 were captured, including Sinclair (with the royal banner) and many nobles such as Maxwell. But did this relatively small-scale clash only seem significant in retrospect? The discomfited and humiliated king returned to Edinburgh, and moved on to his heavily pregnant wife at Linlithgow before going to his new palace at Falkland. There he received news that his wife had had a daughter, Mary, on 8 December, took to his bed and died on the 14th aged just thirty. But it is not clear if the battle or the birth of a daughter really drove him into deep depression, as his daughter's foe John Knox later claimed. Whether or not he ever spoke his alleged epitaph for his dynasty, 'It came with a lass [i.e. Marjorie Bruce], it will pass with a lass', is unclear. His death was surprising given that there is no clear indication of any serious illness earlier; but some infectious fever is more likely than a long-term problem. James left his kingdom weakened by an unnecessary (but less serious) defeat, as his father had done. His rule was a contrast between his vigorous concern for justice, the family tendency towards autocratic toughness and a vindictiveness and acquisitiveness reminiscent of James III. Accordingly, he has received a poor 'press' from some modern historians such as Jenny Wormald, a hostile tradition dating from John Knox's indictment of him as a Catholic tyrant, though his biographer Cameron thinks he was consistent and just, if harsh to some, in his policies. He was clearly a less flexible character than his father, though he shared the latter's promiscuity and left a large number of bastards. Is it too harsh to judge him poorly for a rule suddenly cut off at thirty?

6

The Stuarts: 1542–1651

Mary Stuart: Romantic Heroine or Impulsive Failure?

Scotland now had its sixth long regency in a row, with its youngest sovereign yet – testimony to the mixture of bad luck and bad judgement that prematurely killed off sovereign after sovereign. Unlike after Flodden, the recent military disaster was not catastrophic – but the men who assumed power were equally divided, with religion and English overlordship now thrown into the mix. James Hamilton, the 2nd Earl of Arran (born *c.* 1518), was nearest male heir as the grandson of James III's sister. He was proclaimed 'Governor' on 3 January and so headed a regency council comprised of Cardinal Beaton and the earls of Moray, Huntly and Argyll, apparently by James V's nomination. However, the cousins Arran and Beaton were at odds, the latter regarding the former as a heretic for favouring reform of the Church in line with recent events in England – though the English king was as hostile to radical reform as was Beaton. Discontent with Beaton (a Francophile) was used by Henry, who had the nobles taken at Solway Moss brought to his court and induced them to agree that Queen Mary should be betrothed to his son and heir Edward (aged four) – and if Mary died, Henry, rather than Arran, should be the next king. The exiled Angus and his brother George were also at the English court as these plans were finalised. Henry needed them to spearhead a pro-English faction in Edinburgh and secure Queen Mary; they needed him to overcome their enemies at home, by force if necessary. They were to arrange for Arran's and Beaton's arrests and deportations to England.

Angus now returned to Scotland unmolested, followed by Bothwell, to meet Arran; Beaton was arrested and in March 1543 Parliament cancelled Angus's forfeiture. Henry sent Arran a manual of instructions on how to reform his Church and rid himself of monasteries and upstart clerics. Commissioners were appointed to arrange the Edward-Mary marriage, and Lord Maxwell – the first to flee at Solway Moss – introduced a Bill to allow reading of the Bible in the vernacular rather than Latin, another Henrician innovation. Reading the Bible and debating Scripture now became a fashionable pursuit among the elite laity and some monastic houses were soon being attacked by rioters or seized by lay proprietors, but – as in England – 'heretical' reformist literature was banned and the reforms were used to emasculate Church power and enrich lay allies of the government. In retaliation, King Francis sent the exiled Matthew Stewart, Earl of Lennox (son of the earl killed in revolt in 1526), home to assist the French Queen Mother Marie and the cardinal in resisting the Anglophile regency. Arran was not as compliant as Henry had hoped, but the marriage treaty went ahead and was signed on 1 July. Under this Treaty of Greenwich Mary was to marry Edward, by proxy in the next few years, and be sent to England when she was ten; Scotland was to remain a separate country with its own government and institutions, an advance on the previous 'union' plan of Edward I. Henry promised Arran 5,000 men if needed and assured that, if their enemies married off the queen to another candidate, Arran could be king of the lands north of the Forth while Henry annexed the rest of Scotland.

Henry's demands that Scotland break its alliance with France and his continued efforts to get his hands on Queen Mary, plus English naval depredations, caused a backlash against the treaty and the irresolute Arran wisely decided that 5,000 English troops would not be sufficient to deal with opposition. He swung back to the defiant Beaton, who was holding out in his castle at St Andrews, and agreed to admit the Queen Mother and cardinal to an expanded and more powerful regency council. Beaton was restored as chancellor. Henry had failed to confirm the treaty within the two months legally required, and Parliament cancelled it and reaffirmed the alliance with France. This amounted to a declaration of war on Henry, and the French duly sent arms and money to the government while the Papacy made Beaton its legate. However, the ascendancy of the pro-French faction alienated Lennox, who was angling for the hand of Henry's niece Margaret Douglas (daughter of the late Queen Margaret by Angus) via an English alliance, as well as Angus. Lennox – the next heir to Scotland after the Hamiltons – was promised English troops and the governorship of Scotland if his party seized Queen Mary. Arran besieged Lennox in Glasgow in April 1544; he was forced to surrender and fled to England, and Angus was arrested. Henry resorted to force, sending Edward, Earl of Hertford (uncle to Prince Edward), the brother of his late wife Jane Seymour, to ravage Lothian with a large army to remind the Scots of the price of defying him. This 'Rough Wooing', as it was called with grim humour, saw Hertford's army disembarking at Leith in May and sacking Edinburgh, while another army marched up from Berwick destroying all within its path en route.

Lothian was devastated, but no territory was held and Henry was not able to secure his intention of destroying St Andrews too as a personal retort to the Francophile cardinal. In June a convention of the estates at Stirling suspended Arran from the 'Governorship' for failing to stop the invasion and replaced him with the Queen Mother. In reply Lennox now married Margaret Douglas, which gave him and any children a distant chance of the English throne if all Henry's children died, and was promised the 'Governorship' as Henry's nominee. He rose in rebellion to attempt to take Dumbarton, failed and retreated to England. Arran, defying his suspension, summoned a parliament in November, the Queen Mother summoned a rival one to Stirling and mutual denunciations were eventually calmed down by a stalemate. Neither side wanted a civil war, which would only benefit Henry, and a truce was patched up that lasted until 1547; meanwhile another English raid in 1545 was defeated at Ancram Moor.

The most famous of the crop of executions of radical Protestants by Beaton, the burning of the Cambridge-trained preacher George Wishart at St Andrews on 1 March 1546, was carried out in the cardinal's presence. It was followed by the murder of Beaton on 29 May by a band of plotters who broke into his castle at the town, disguised as workmen. Beaton was reportedly seized after a night with his mistress, a 'public relations' bonus for anti-clerical reformists, and was hacked to death and hung from the castle walls for the edification of the populace. The murderers then held St Andrews castle against the regency's forces; they held out against an ineffective siege by Arran (whose son was one of their prisoners). The castle was on the shore, so it could not be attacked from all sides and the rebels could bring in supplies and men. The castle finally fell to French forces only in July 1547. The garrison, including the preacher John Knox who had arrived during a truce to start his militant Calvinist preaching in Fife, were sent to the French galleys as convicts.

By this date Henry VIII was dead (28 January 1547), Edward was on the English throne, aged nine, and his uncle Hertford was in control of the regency as 'Lord Protector' and Duke of Somerset. The English Reformation now became explicitly reformist Protestant and Somerset sought to export it to Scotland and to secure Queen Mary for his nephew, resuming the 'Rough Wooing'. In early September he led around 16,000 men across the Border to advance on Edinburgh while a fleet sailed into the Forth, and on the 10th the English defeated a larger but worse-armed Scots army (led by Angus and Arran) at Pinkie, north-east of Edinburgh, near Musselburgh. The

Scots had around 30,000 men, the English possibly 17,000 according to English Protestant academic John Hooper; however both Hertford and his deputy, the Earl of Warwick, were experienced and ruthless commanders. The two Scots commanders were long-term enemies and do not seem to have cooperated well, as might have been expected, and the Scots abandoned a strong defensive position on Edmondstone Edge to march across the Esk into a new position under fire from the English ships offshore in the Forth. Arran failed to back up Angus's embattled vanguard, the Scots cannon had not been moved up from their previous position to 'cover' the army's new position and both leaders soon fled. Around 16,000 were casualties being hacked down by cavalry, and around 1,600 prisoners were taken. Lack of supplies for a long stay meant that Somerset soon had to evacuate Edinburgh, but in spring 1548 a new land expedition across Lothian seized the town of Haddington.

Bowing to the need for French help, Arran opened negotiations with the new King Henri II although this meant a virtual French 'dictat' – marrying Queen Mary to the latter's son. In June 1548 a French expeditionary force under André de Montalembert, Seigneur d'Esse, landed at Leith and marched to assist with the siege of Haddington. The Treaty of Haddington between the Scots and French delegates on 7 July agreed that Queen Mary would marry the Dauphin Francis and the Scots were promised their full customary freedoms, liberties and laws (in general terms only). The bargain made under duress was worse than that proposed with England, but it saved Scotland from the 'Auld Enemy' and the French troops were to be the vital backbone of Scotland's defence once Haddington had fallen (September 1549). Ironically, the danger soon passed for a decade as England fell into domestic turbulence, the fall of Haddington being followed by that of the Duke of Somerset; once King Edward died in July 1553 England returned briefly to pro-Papal Catholicism under his half-sister Mary.

Henri required Queen Mary to be brought up in France, though there was a danger in 1548 that she would be kidnapped by anti-French nobles and handed over to Somerset. The French ships that had brought the troops to Leith rounded Scotland to pick up the queen and her entourage – including her young female ladies-in-waiting, the 'Four Maries' – at Dumbarton on 29 July, and proceeded to Morlaix, near Brest in Brittany. In October Mary's party arrived at St Germain-en-Laye near Paris, home of the royal nursery for Henri's children. Mary was brought up with the young French royals, which was preferable to her father's grim upbringing but made her more French – and European Catholic – in her outlook than Scottish.

In April 1554 the Queen Mother replaced Arran (now Duke of Chatelherault) as regent, and the slavish Scots adherence to the orientation of French foreign policy – as dictated by Henri – was one major weakness for an otherwise competent and reconciliatory government. Marie of Guise, indeed, was among the more skilful of Stewart regents and was able to balance successfully among the competing interests of the nobility, though she had the unusual advantages of a 'standing army' (the French garrisons) not reliant on the nobles and of a hiatus in English Protestant meddling in rising anti-clericalism when the equally resolute Catholic Mary Tudor was ruling England in 1553–58. The long-delayed negotiations for finalising the arrangements of Queen Mary's marriage to the Dauphin in December 1557, at Henri's request, meant the right to levy a useful new tax to pay for the wedding, though the political fallout was detrimental – and the teenage queen would be living in France indefinitely and Scotland would be tied to France and its expensive wars. The French king proved as determined to bind Scotland into his international schemes as a permanent junior ally as Henry VIII had been. The marriage of queen and Dauphin was duly solemnised on 24 April 1558 at Notre Dame in Paris, with Francis granted the 'Crown Matrimonial' as King of Scotland – in theory.

As well as the resistance to the cost of the French alliance, religious 'reformism' was spreading among the nobility and in 1557 a group of nobles secretly invited the firebrand preacher John Knox, who had made a great impression for his Protestant fervour in 1547, back to Scotland to lead anti-Catholic preaching and implicitly to stir up anti-French rebellion. They changed their minds and asked him to delay coming, and in December 1557 the earls of Argyll, Glencairn and Morton, along with several other lords, signed a first 'Bond' to promote the Reformation but could not attract the support needed for open action. Illegal preaching spread in the South and the regime withdrew a legal summons for assorted miscreants in 1558 due to protests by local gentry and made half-hearted attempts to promote a 'godlier' clergy by tackling abuses, but occasionally even the irresolute Archbishop Hamilton had to burn heretics to satisfy the hard-line Catholics.

The political situation changed drastically as a result of Mary Tudor's death on 17 November 1558. Her half-sister Elizabeth succeeded to the English throne, though Margaret Douglas (staunchly Catholic) had been talked of as an alternative by those worried at Elizabeth's Protestant leanings. As the daughter of Henry VIII and his second wife Anne Boleyn, born in his first wife's lifetime and with the annulment of Henry's first marriage not recognised by the Pope, she was seen as a bastard by Catholics and so ineligible for the throne; and England was still at war with France. Technically the senior legitimate heir to England was Queen Mary of Scotland, as grand-daughter of Margaret, Henry VIII's elder sister, and for those who held Elizabeth to be illegitimate Mary was now rightful Queen of England – if Henry VIII's will, which had banned the Stuarts from the throne, was invalid. Henri II now provocatively proclaimed Mary a Queen of England, and she and Francis assumed the titles and heraldic arms of king and queen as a direct challenge to Elizabeth. But Henri's death followed unexpectedly, as the

Franco-Spanish peace treaty of Cateau-Cambrensis in June 1559 was celebrated by a tournament in Paris where Henri, aged only forty, was fatally injured in a freak tilting accident. On 8 July the Dauphin, aged fifteen, became King Francis I and Mary became Queen of France; according to her legal claims she was now rightful ruler of three realms. In practice, government remained with her mother-in-law, Catherine de Medici, and with Marie de Guise's ultra-Catholic brothers, the Duke and Cardinal de Guise.

Elizabeth returned the English ecclesiastical settlement to Protestantism, though a less militant or Calvinist form than that envisaged by some Edwardian reformists (or Knox), and the new English government sent reformist preachers and money to assist the radicals in Scotland in the task of overthrowing the Francophile regency. The revolutionary mood gathered steam against the well-endowed Catholic clergy, and at New Year 1559 a 'Beggars' Summons' pamphlet was spread around ordering the friars to quit their friaries in favour of the poor by the Whitsun legal term. Knox arrived in Leith on 2 May and, with radical preaching and iconoclastic attacks spreading (especially in Perth and Dundee), Marie de Guise summoned the preachers to appear before her at Stirling to explain themselves. But the townsmen of the two 'rebel' towns and the local countrymen assembled en masse ready to accompany their preachers to Stirling, and the summons was not answered on time; instead, on the 11th Knox preached an inflammatory sermon in St John's church, Perth, against 'idols' and the enthusiastic congregation proceeded to vandalise the local friaries. Looting spread, some congregations abandoned the Mass and the Perth congregation appealed for support from their fellow believers; Glencairn and other nobles rallied to the protesters.

The result was armed challenge to the government, and the reformist 'Lords of the Congregation' assembled at St Andrews to support the mutinous townsmen of Perth and to intervene if the regent broke her promise in a brief truce not to attack the town or introduce French troops there. This promise was broken, and as a result the rebel lords were joined by Argyll and the young James, Earl of Moray (born *c.* 1531), eldest and most politically competent of James V's many bastards and already a potential leader for the Protestant cause. The rebels appealed to England for help. The regime's forces ended up retreating to Dunbar to await French reinforcements and the rebels advanced to Edinburgh at the end of June, sacking religious houses and imposing the 'reformed' Geneva Prayer Book and Calvinist services en route. The apparatus of medieval Catholicism was dismantled and iconoclasts enthusiastically sacked religious houses and purged the churches of 'idolatry', and Knox was installed at St Giles' in Edinburgh as minister. However the undisciplined mass of volunteers who had formed the rebel army mostly drifted home and as a result the Regent and her Frenchmen were able to recapture Leith. Edinburgh was left un-garrisoned by either side and the Protestants' gains so far accepted in a truce; Parliament was to decide on a permanent settlement. But despite the shock caused in France by the death of King Henri the new government there managed to send some 3,000–4,000 troops to back Marie up over the next few months, tipping the military balance in her favour, and in reply the 'Lords of the Congregation' urgently sought English help. Once Chatelherault's son, the Earl of Arran – in France so in danger should his father join the rebels – had escaped with English help the duke joined the insurgent Lords at Stirling on 15 October, and within days they had occupied Edinburgh. Marie de Guise held out at Leith with French troops.

The rebel lords had the worst of the initial clashes with the better-armed and trained French troops, and had to fall back on St Andrews and Glasgow. The situation was radically altered by the belated appearance of an English fleet in the Forth on 23 January, and the French in Fife had to fall back hastily to Leith, which was now besieged by the lords on land

and the English by sea. Rebel negotiations with the English (led by Chatelherault for the lords and the Duke of Norfolk for England) at Berwick led to a treaty on 27 February, guaranteeing English military aid to evict the French and preserve the liberties of the Scots. Mary was guaranteed her subjects' obedience provided that she preserved their liberties. As a result an English army under Lord Grey entered Scotland in March and proceeded to join the siege of Leith, while Marie de Guise retreated into Edinburgh Castle. The French government was now beset by its own religious unrest from Protestants and negotiated a withdrawal. With Elizabeth's agreement the embassy proceeded north to negotiate the evacuation with English envoys. The resulting talks were interrupted by the death of Marie de Guise, aged forty-seven and suffering from dropsy, at Edinburgh Castle on 1 June. The Treaty of Edinburgh/Leith on 5 July provided for the evacuation of Leith and the withdrawal of both English and French armies from Scotland; Mary was guaranteed her throne but had to cease using the heraldic arms of England and to accept a council made up of representatives of both the 'loyalist' and rebel factions. Parliament met and adopted a new, Calvinist 'Confession of Faith', with the Mass and papal authority banned. However, actually implementing the Reformation was left to local initiative rather than central direction. The enforced secularisation of Church property was dependent on lay approval and local initiative. Enthusiasm for Reformation in the towns and in the Lowlands was in marked contrast to the continued Catholic dominance of the remote and rural Highlands, where staunchly Catholic magnates held sway; and the unreliability of the Catholic Mary as a reformist led to Chatelherault meddling with the English to seek their support to remove her and/or to offer his son Arran as a husband for Elizabeth.

The political situation was altered again by the early death of the young King Francis II of France, long ailing, of an ear complaint on 5 December 1560. His widow's scheming Guise uncles planned to marry her off to King Philip of Spain's epileptic and mentally unstable heir Don Carlos to bolster the ultra-Catholic alliance between France and Spain, but Mary chose to return to Scotland and accepted the advice of her visiting half-brother, Moray, not to interfere with the official change of faith. On 19 August 1561 Mary landed at Leith, in a fog which the unwelcoming and distrustful Knox later saw as a metaphor for the sorrows and religious impiety which she brought with her – with a large French entourage. She issued a proclamation that she would not seek to alter the Protestant religion but that she expected her foreign Catholic servants to be allowed to practice their religion unhindered too. But as she celebrated Mass at her palace chapel on her first Sabbath in Scotland a riot broke out, hotheads called for the priest to be lynched and Moray had to guard the door and harangue those zealots who tried to storm it. The queen's seeming 'Papist' godlessness duly aroused the ire of the formidable Knox, whom she invited to Holyrood and who sternly warned her about the iniquity of her religion; he would concede her right to rule if she did not persecute the 'Saints' but he compared their positions to St Paul under the Emperor Nero. An impasse followed, but Mary's tact, good humour and failure to live up to rabid Calvinist expectations as a persecuting 'Papist' helped her to achieve the support of her lords for continuing to practise her religion in private and this rare Reformation-era example of a sovereign worshipping in a different manner from their subjects survived. In these first years, Mary proved a competent and adroit sovereign; she achieved Elizabeth's admission that Mary had the most right to the English succession, and Elizabeth ratified the Treaty of Leith without her original requirement that Mary should abdicate her right to the English crown not only for the lifetime of Elizabeth (and her children if she had any), but permanently.

The leadership of the 'ultra' Catholics in the French religio-civil war by Mary's Guise uncles damaged her standing with

Protestants in England if not in Scotland. Her passion for music and dancing aroused the predictable ire of Knox and the rarefied atmosphere of her culturally Francophile court life was alien to almost all of the nobility. But such matters were of little immediate political import, and for governance the queen wisely relied on the duo of Moray, closely linked to many of the aristocracy via his mother's Erskine relations, and the lesser-born 'new man' Maitland. Luckily the intolerant Knox alienated Moray and others by his rabid attacks on the 'ungodly' life at court, and his views on women rulers made him equally unwelcome to Elizabeth so he was unlikely to be useful as an English agent. In August 1562 Mary's first tour of the north-east was used to demonstrate her even-handedness in taking on high-born Catholic malefactors – namely the 4th Earl of Huntly, chief of the Gordons, and his sons. Huntly's obstreperous son, Sir John Gordon, had been flouting the law and Mary's expedition sought to arrest him but was met with Gordon resistance. Sir John escaped custody and raised an army without his father stopping him.

Later Huntly was accused of planning to kidnap Mary if she had stayed at his castle of Strathbogie as invited. The royal party found themselves denied entry to Inverness Castle, a royal possession, by its castellan on the orders of Huntly's heir; the earl ordered her to be admitted. Huntly refused to come before the queen except with a large armed escort to protect him, and assembled an army; he and his sons failed to intercept the royal party en route back south but then marched on Aberdeen. The queen and Moray marched out to confront him, and the resulting low-key battle at Corrichie saw the royal artillery strafe the ill-armed host of 700–1,000 or so Gordons as Moray's men gradually wore them down. Huntly was captured, brought before Moray and died on the spot of a probable heart attack. The result left the Northern Catholic magnates cowed and Moray's position enhanced.

The decline in Mary's fortunes commenced with her choice of husband, which was made despite Elizabeth's attempt to interest her in her own devoted admirer Robert Dudley (now made Earl of Leicester) in 1563–64. Mary had already made an attempt to interest Philip II in offering his heir Don Carlos to her, and this had frightened her Guise uncles into proposing the Austrian Habsburg Archduke Charles instead. Charles was, however, too poor, and Philip had to drop the Don Carlos plan as his son's insanity became apparent in spring 1564. Elizabeth preferred a 'controllable' Englishman as Mary's husband, and in November Moray and Maitland met her envoys at Berwick to discuss Leicester's candidacy. Elizabeth seems to have been keener on this than Leicester, whose enemies backed the proposal as a way of removing him from the English court – and he also had the problem that his first wife Amy had died in suspicious circumstances amid rumours that she had been pushed downstairs so he could marry Elizabeth.

In February 1565 Elizabeth surprisingly allowed Lady Margaret Douglas's elder son by the Earl of Lennox, Henry, Lord Darnley (born 1545), to visit Scotland and he quickly emerged in Mary's favour. The ambitious Margaret Douglas was clearly behind the move; also Leicester seems to have backed him in order to forestall Elizabeth packing him off to Scotland. On 17 February 1565 Mary met Darnley – young, handsome, charming and well-turned-out – at Wemyss Castle, and despite Elizabeth's furious disapproval of the idea of him – another descendant of Henry VII and claimant to her throne – Mary took no notice. On 29 July Mary and Darnley were married at Holyrood Abbey and Mary, clearly infatuated, proceeded to give her husband the 'Crown Matrimonial'. As Darnley and his mother were Catholic the marriage could be seen as boosting the Catholic faction, and both Moray and the Hamiltons now turned against the queen. In Darnley's favour, he was of royal blood, young and potentially malleable, and marrying him did not open Scotland to foreign influence and control as Mary's marriage to Francis had done. But he soon proved himself to be vain, spoilt, drunken and prone to jealousy – and to suggestions from intriguing nobles.

Moray launched a rebellion in Ayrshire in August 1565 after withdrawing from court and refusing to return as summoned, backed by Chatelherault and Argyll and several other Protestant peers. He claimed that the country was endangered by bad government and Catholic revival, as shown by the queen's marriage, but the lack of support he received shows that he mistimed his appeal. The queen acted with vigour and outlawed him; she called a muster of troops and reassured her subjects that no change of religion was planned. On 26 August she left Edinburgh for Glasgow with a substantial force, and the rebels had to withdraw into Galloway in the hope of English aid. The resulting non-contact campaign was known as the Chaseabout Raid; Mary chased the evasive rebels across the south-west without any clash, and Moray and his men eventually had to withdraw into England. Moray had thrown away his strong position and it left Mary unchallenged – temporarily. With the Hamiltons in disgrace Mary could restore the eldest son of the late Earl of Huntly to his father's title and estates, and another beneficiary was the quarrelsome Border magnate James Hepburn, Earl of Bothwell, a notorious brawler and rake who had been imprisoned in Edinburgh Castle and later exiled after dubious accusations of treason by his personal foe Arran in 1562.

The swift reversal of Mary's fortunes after autumn 1565, however, points to the mutability of elite politics in Scotland and to her own miscalculations, as well as bad luck. Like her predecessors Mary came to rely on a 'middle-class' secretariat of competent and personally loyal careerists for company as well as transacting business, and her use of foreigners was not unprecedented either. The fact that Scotland was now Protestant and most of her protégés were Catholic added to the usual disgruntlement of various nobles about these 'low-born' men; and the fact that the queen was a woman led to allegations of improper conduct by mischief-makers. These allegations came to centre on her Savoyard secretary, a skilled but ugly Italian musician called David Riccio (a.k.a.

Rizzio), and alienated ultra-Protestant nobles seem to have spread the rumours in order to damage the queen's reputation in retaliation for her failure to pardon their ally Moray. They worked on Darnley as a useful ally at court, a cynical move given that as a Catholic he was technically one of their targets, and were joined by Secretary Maitland who was alarmed at the failure of his efforts to tie Mary into a pro-English policy. Once Mary was pregnant it was whispered that Riccio, not Darnley, was the father of her child, and rumour had it that Darnley and his father Lennox planned to depose her (or worse?) with the possibility implicit that Darnley, as Margaret Douglas's son, could then claim the throne. A 'bond' was now drawn up by the plotters, including the Earl of Morton, lords Ruthven and Lindsay and (in England) their allies Glencairn, Rothes and Moray himself. The notorious outcome of this was the incident at Holyrood Palace on the evening of 8 March 1566 – four days before Parliament was due to discuss Mary's proposal to attaint all the refugee 1565 rebels and seize their lands. Darnley, clearly in on the plot, turned up unexpectedly at the queen's supper party in her private apartments, at which Riccio was present with her ladies. Then the supposedly seriously ill Lord Ruthven burst in wearing armour under his gown, reproached the queen for favouring Riccio and demanded that the latter accompany him. The queen tried to protect her secretary and on Ruthven's signal his accomplices burst in to seize Riccio, prised his hands from Mary's skirts, dragged him outside and down the stairs and stabbed him to death. Mary was threatened, too, and the suspicion arises that some of the lords (and even Darnley?) hoped that she would have a fatal miscarriage and they could find a new sovereign. Darnley's dagger was left in Riccio's body to implicate him. The plotters then took over the palace, but if this was another intended royal kidnap it was mishandled. Mary was able to win her husband round and warned him that he was in danger too; she agreed to the plotters' demands to allow Moray to return home, then once he had arrived she escaped through a back door with Darnley. They rode through the night to Dunbar with a few loyalists led by lords Erskine and Bothwell, the young Huntly, and other lords joined them there. The rebels abandoned Edinburgh, most fleeing to England; the royal party returned and on 19 June Mary's son, James, was born at the castle.

The succession seemed assured and the ultra-Protestants were now in exile, but the breach between Mary and Darnley was not repaired whether or not the increasingly erratic and drunken King Consort still had doubts about his son's paternity. The next act in the increasingly violent unravelling of Mary's regime was the assassination of Darnley, now loathed by those nobles who felt he had betrayed their allies in the plot to remove Riccio. In November a 'bond' was drawn up, at Craigmillar Castle outside Edinburgh, by a group of leading figures who were agreed that Darnley must be removed (means unspecified), among them Bothwell, Huntly, Argyll, Maitland and Sir James Balfour; Morton signed later when he returned from abroad (Moray did not sign, and the actual paper later disappeared so its contents were only known by rumour). Darnley retired to the stronghold of his father Lennox at Glasgow where he fell ill with the 'pox' – probably smallpox but his enemies said it was syphilis. According to the Spanish ambassador in London, he was writing around to major Catholic sovereigns and the Pope that Mary was of dubious loyalty to the faith, so it is not impossible that he was planning to depose her with their help and become regent for his son or king. On Mary's subsequent visit to Glasgow she persuaded him to return to Edinburgh and complete his convalescence under her control. Prince James was also moved back to Edinburgh – to prevent kidnap?

It was Darnley's choice, not Mary's, to be lodged at the former provost's house of the dissolved collegiate church of St Mary – the 'Kirk O' Field' – on the outskirts of Edinburgh. The house was owned by the brother of plotter James Balfour, as was the one next door. Darnley was not carefully placed in an isolated location by a cunning wife intent on vengeance for Riccio. Hours before the attack, on 8 February Mary and her courtiers rode from Holyrood to the house so she could spend the evening with Darnley, who was due to leave for the palace next day – and while they were with him the conspirators were piling up gunpowder in a room on the ground floor ready to blow up the house. Mary had intended to stay the night, but was reminded that she had promised to return to Holyrood to attend the wedding masque of her French valet and left. As she did so, she reproached her page Paris, one of the plotters, for his dirty face and clothes – which were due to the gunpowder he had been handling, so she evidently did not know what he was up to. In the early hours of the following morning, the house exploded. Darnley and his attendant were found dead – but in their nightclothes in the garden, apparently caught and strangled while trying to escape. The killers were identified as a party of Douglases from a nearby house, kinsmen of Morton whom Darnley had betrayed over the Riccio murder. Darnley had presumably seen them lurking outside the house and believed they had come to kill him; he had been heard begging for mercy as they caught him.

The whitewash of the resulting official enquiry, which cleared Bothwell to the fury of Lennox, the murder victim's father, and the subsequent blackening of Bothwell's name once he was safely exiled have muddied the waters concerning the facts, and it is far from clear that Bothwell was the only or the principal murderer. The anti-Bothwell evidence that his lackeys brought the gunpowder publicly through the streets from Holyrood is unlikely, as the Balfours could more easily have moved it from their house next door. That Bothwell was involved seems almost certain, and those minor figures who were indicted for the explosion were his kinsmen and lackeys. Ironically, as Sheriff of Edinburgh he had the judicial duty of dealing with the bodies and instigating the first enquiry. A cover-up of the part played by figures prominent in the post-1567 regency (e.g. Morton) and their ally James

Balfour (who had been purchasing gunpowder recently) is very probable. Mary mishandled the scandal; Elizabeth had wisely advised her to take concern for her honour as well as for revenge but this was ignored. Bothwell was allowed to swagger around the streets of Edinburgh with a large body of armed retainers threatening violence on anyone who accused him, and no attempt was made to require him to disarm his men. Nor was Lennox allowed to bring the armed escort to Edinburgh for the prosecution of Bothwell, which he launched before Parliament on 12 April – this was needed for his safety, so when it was refused he did not turn up. The putting up of placards in Edinburgh denouncing Bothwell as the murderer included 'The Mermaid and the Hare', showing the queen in company with the Hepburns' family symbol in the form of a mermaid, which in contemporary terminology meant a prostitute. The 'trial' of Bothwell for murder quickly cleared him, and within a week a group of prominent noblemen, among them Morton, Argyll and Huntly, was signing a 'bond' at Ainslie's Tavern in Edinburgh with their host Bothwell, agreeing to his plan to promote his candidacy as Mary's next husband. One visitor heard that Moray and Morton wanted Bothwell to marry Mary because it would incense the populace and they could then dispose of them both. Bothwell may well have felt aggrieved that he alone of the plotters was being blamed for the murder. Bothwell could provide strong and Protestant leadership and was a capable soldier – but in terms of international politics it would be disastrous for Mary to be seen to marry the reputed murderer of her previous husband.

The dilemma over whether Mary should marry Bothwell was resolved by him in typical impatient and brutal Borders fashion. As she was returning from a visit to her son at Stirling, Bothwell and a large escort intercepted her party at the Bridge of Almond on 24 April and the earl required her to accompany him to Dunbar Castle. The latest royal kidnapping was probably accompanied by sexual relations;

whether it was rape or consensual has been hotly disputed and some historians believe that Mary knew about the abduction beforehand. Marriage was now necessary to save her honour, and after Bothwell had brought her back to Edinburgh she duly married him at Holyrood on 15 May – once he had hastily been divorced from his previous wife. This was followed by the queen having a nervous breakdown and probably threatening suicide. Maitland fled Edinburgh claiming Bothwell had tried to murder him, and the queen called a muster for 15 June at Melrose to deal with a rising in the south-west but was overtaken by events. The rebel lords, led by Morton, had taken control of Prince James at Stirling and were advancing, and on 6 June Bothwell took Mary from Edinburgh to Borthwick Castle to rally his supporters but they ended up besieged by a rebel force. Bothwell managed to escape unnoticed and later Mary slipped out, too, disguised as a man. They proceeded to Dunbar and back towards Edinburgh, lured by promises of aid from the supposedly still-loyal Balfour, commander of the castle, who had in fact joined the rebels. The armies met outside the capital at Carberry Hill on 15 June, and hours of failed negotiations saw Bothwell vainly inviting any of his opponents who were brave enough to accept single combat. Eventually, the queen's army started to desert, Bothwell slipped away and Mary surrendered herself in return for a promise of fair treatment. This was shamelessly violated, as she was escorted in disgrace through the streets of Edinburgh, with the populace jeering at her as a whore, and was lodged overnight in the provost's house surrounded by a hostile mob. Bothwell escaped from Dunbar to the Orkneys and ended up in Denmark but was thrown into prison for life where he went mad.

Mary was deported to the isolated island castle of Lochleven in Fife, where she was kept in strict captivity by Sir William Douglas, half-brother of the Earl of Moray, and was plausibly reported to have miscarried of a child or twins fathered by Bothwell. She refused to divorce Bothwell, which would have strengthened her hand politically. The lords' representatives (Sir Robert Melville and Lord Lindsay) brought her papers to sign, in which she agreed to her deposition. She was deposed in her son's favour on 24 July and on the 29th the thirteen-month-old James VI was crowned at the nearest church to his secure lodgings in Stirling Castle.

James VI: 'Cradle King' to 'Wisest Fool'

The seventh regency in as many reigns saw Scotland once more at the mercy of a clique of senior peers who were to be expected to fall out among themselves and to use the young king as their pawn. Moray, more competent a statesman than some past regents and at least of close royal blood, was sworn in as regent on 22 August when he arrived back from England. Morton was in effect his deputy, and the third-in-command was the Earl of Mar, keeper of Stirling Castle and guardian of the king. But the new regime faced hostility both from Elizabeth, who had not wanted her sister-queen deposed, and from the marginalised Catholic peers, and the Hamiltons were unhappy at their being sidelined and at Moray's semi-royal pretensions so boycotted the December 1567 parliament. The regency resorted to a crude attempt to smear the ex-queen with the charge of murdering Darnley so that she could not benefit from any resentment against them, producing the so-called 'Casket Letters', which appeared to have been discovered. By Morton's account in 1568, they had been 'found' when Bothwell's henchman, the tailor George Dalgleish, was spotted visiting Edinburgh Castle and seized in June 1567 and took his interrogators to his lodgings in the city where he kept the 'casket' under his bed. Parliament was assured that they proved that Mary was an accomplice in Darnley's murder and therefore her deposition had been justified. Moray made sure that the parliament ratified the 1560 religious settlement to legally approve the transfer

of religious authority from Catholicism to Protestantism
– something which Mary had neglected to do throughout
her reign, adding to fears that she intended to reverse the
Reformation at the first opportunity.

But the situation was dramatically altered on 2 May 1568
by the escape of Mary from Lochleven Castle in a suitably
dramatic incident that added to her romantic image then and
in legend. A smitten young member of the Douglas family,
junior attendant Willy Douglas, holed all but one of the
boats while a roistering May Day pageant gave the ex-queen
the excuse to retire to her room afterwards, and while host
William Douglas was at dinner his namesake Willy stole his
keys from the table. Those who were 'in' on the plan escorted
her to the one useable boat, and then Mary was rowed to
shore where another Douglas was waiting with horses stolen
from his brother's stables. Mary set up her standard, issued
proclamations denouncing her deposition as invalid and
was joined by nine earls, nine bishops, eighteen lairds and
numerous lesser supporters. Lords Herries and Maxwell were
holding out for her in Galloway and Archbishop Hamilton
led his family to defect to her; within weeks she had around
6,000 men and outnumbered the regent's forces substantially.
They headed for loyal Dumbarton. Moray was offered pardon
but refused it. As Mary's forces passed through Langside near
Glasgow, the regent and his army advanced from Glasgow
to attack them in the rear on 13 May. They had experienced
commanders in Morton and Kirkcaldy of Grange, and the
regent's pikemen managed to hold back the Marian Galloway
cavalry under Herries; for some reason Argyll failed to come
to Herries' rescue and soon fled – he later claimed he had
suffered an epileptic attack. The queen's forces were routed,
losing around 100 men with another 300 captured, and the
Hamiltons suffered worse casualties. Mary fled into Galloway,
and at Terregles Castle she was later reported as making the
fateful decision to head for England and ask Queen Elizabeth
for help, rather than taking a ship for France where her

ex-mother-in-law Catherine de Medici was likely to have refused aid. At the time, the English queen seemed a politically more useful choice as she had shown Mary no hostility since the latter had abandoned her 1558 claim to be the rightful Queen of England and she had opposed the deposition in 1567. But when Mary arrived at Workington, Cumbria, by boat asking for help the English monarch showed her usual caution by putting the issue on hold and refusing her an interview or immediate aid. She was lodged in Carlisle Castle rather than being invited to court. The Scots regency was Protestant and well disposed, and Mary was a Catholic, the close relative of the anti-English Guises and accused by her supplanters of murdering her last-but-one husband. Elizabeth seems to have preferred to send Mary home, hopefully as queen, rather than to keep her in England or let her go on to hostile France (which might revive her claim to the English throne), but that must be with her subjects' consent. So Elizabeth required that Mary be cleared of murder before she would let her into her presence or help her, as a matter of 'honour', and the ex-queen was moved to Bolton Castle while an enquiry was set up at York to look into the question of Darnley's murder.

Moray was assuring Elizabeth that he had the documentary proof that Mary was guilty and secured her unofficial assurances that if the case was proved she would not be aided by England; though Elizabeth was theoretically opposed to the idea of anyone being able to judge a sovereign, the enquiry could be used as an excuse for preventing Mary from returning to Scotland. The depth of hostility to the ex-queen by her opponents should show if it was too risky to restore Mary. An English board, headed by the Duke of Norfolk (a noble of royal blood, an eligible widower soon to be shown to be interested in marrying Mary), was to preside, and the letters' authenticity would be argued by the regency's representatives (including Moray and Maitland) and denied by Mary's (including Bishop Leslie of Ross and Lord Herries).

Moray was determined to ruin his half-sister's reputation and keep her out of Scotland, but Maitland was open to a compromise that restored her in name but not complete power. The possibility that some of the letters had been forged to incriminate Mary was recognised by the English, particularly the Earl of Sussex who admitted frankly that their authenticity mattered less than the political usefulness of keeping Mary out of power. Elizabeth transferred the initial enquiry at York to London in November and added her most loyal councillors, led by Cecil and Leicester, to the commissioners. The 'originals' of the letters were apparently shown by Moray to the English commissioners, but not to Mary's representatives – and Mary was refused permission to come to London to speak (though the snow would have delayed her anyway). The English commission acted as judge and jury; the final result was announced by Cecil on 10 January 1569. But even so it was not decided that the letters were definitely genuine, merely that nothing could be proved to the dishonour of either Mary or the nobles who had deposed her. The status quo was upheld with Moray returning home as regent (with a loan of £5,000) and Mary being kept in England. Modern examination of the copies made at the time, which still survive, have suggested that genuine love-letters by Bothwell to another woman and extracts from letters by Mary on unrelated matters (quoted out of context) were tampered with to make it appear that Mary and Bothwell were committing adultery and planning murder in Darnley's lifetime, and that her handwriting was forged by someone familiar with it.

Mary's hopes of Scottish support were not finished, and several earls still backed her in arms with her followers holding Dumbarton. In July 1569 she was able to send a proposal that she should divorce Bothwell and marry Norfolk to a Scots convention at Perth, backed by Maitland, Argyll and Huntly. Norfolk was not himself a Catholic and Mary had flirted with Anglicanism since she arrived in England and only turned to the Continental Catholics for aid later in the 1570s. Could this solution have worked but for Moray's determination to stop it? It was defeated by forty votes to nine, and then the 'Northern Rising' of English Catholic nobles opposed to Elizabeth in autumn 1569 damaged Elizabeth's perception of Catholics' loyalty and was to add to her suspicion of Mary's intentions on her throne. The rebels sent men to Tutbury to rescue Mary as their candidate for the throne – she had already been taken south to Coventry. As the English queen's troops restored order with the usual massacres, the refugee rebel leaders fled to Scotland and were interned to reassure Elizabeth, but then Moray was assassinated at Linlithgow on 23 January 1570 – shot through the stomach while riding by one of the Hamiltons of Bothwellhaugh with the apparent foreknowledge of Archbishop Hamilton. He was the lynchpin of the new politico-religious settlement and had been unwavering in his Protestantism, as well as being hailed as the best ruler Scotland had had since James V. However, his combination of deviousness and miscalculation (e.g. over his revolt in 1565) must stand against his reputation, and arguably he played a fatal role in isolating his half-sister from the 'moderate' Protestant leadership in 1564–65 and halting her rehabilitation in 1568–69. If anyone apart from Mary herself destroyed her chances after 1564 it was Moray.

Moray had left the guardianship of King James to his ally and relative, the Earl of Mar, but by Scots tradition the nearest adult male of the royal house should hold the regency. Chatelherault was under arrest, his son Arran was insane and under restraint, the Hamiltons were Marians implicated in rebellion and Mar and Morton held the government together until English troops arrived to assist the siege of Marian-held Dumbarton. Kirkcaldy of Grange had changed sides and was holding out in Edinburgh Castle too. In April 1570 the Marian earls of Argyll, Atholl and Huntly arrived in the city to temporarily join him; their force withdrew as the English approached. The anti-Marian nobles allowed Elizabeth to mediate in choosing a regent, and she came down in favour of the Earl of Lennox, King James's grandfather and the head of the line of Lennox Stewarts who were genealogically next in line after the Hamiltons. But the new regime was shaky without English military aid, and once the king's party was on its own the Marians in Edinburgh revived. The regime held a sparsely-attended parliament in the Canongate in May 1571, under fire from Kirkcaldy's cannons in the castle, and in June the ex-queen's noble supporters retaliated with their own parliament in the more usual meeting place, the Tollbooth. But they could not press their advantage and, later in the summer, Argyll, Cassilis and others deserted to the regency; the latter now held a better-attended parliament at Stirling although Kirkcaldy then daringly attacked the lords' lodgings there at night and staged a mass kidnap. But their supporters came to the rescue, and in the resulting fight Lennox was fatally wounded (3 September). Mar now became regent as Moray had wished, and in April 1572 the French government of Mary's brother-in-law Charles IX came to an agreement with England to abandon Mary.

With France in chaos there was no hope of French help to the Marians in Edinburgh Castle, and Elizabeth now recognised James VI as lawful king. Mar died at dinner in October 1572 amid claims of poison, and the forceful and ruthless Morton took over as regent. The Hamiltons left Edinburgh, and under the mediation of the English envoy, Killigrew, they surrendered and recognised James as king in the Pacification of Perth. In May 1573 Elizabeth sent 500 cannoneers from Berwick to assist the siege of Edinburgh Castle. This tipped the balance, and after a ferocious week-long bombardment Kirkcaldy and Maitland had to surrender unconditionally as Morton demanded. Both were promptly sentenced to death for treason; Maitland took poison but Kirkcaldy was hanged. The elimination of these two removed almost all the senior figures of Mary's reign, barring Morton whose regency now provided some much-needed stability; Argyll died in 1574 and

Chatelherault in 1575. Morton set up a small standing army to keep order and combined judicial firmness and occasional ferocity with clemency in restoring central authority, with the lords cooperating in keeping the peace. The regime survived until March 1578 when, as the king approached his twelfth birthday, Morton's enemies Argyll and Atholl, annoyed at the regent interfering in their private disputes, used the opportunity of the birthday to suggest that James should formally assume power at twelve as James V had done. Morton met the king and indignantly offered to resign if he was not given the king's full confidence to punish mischief-makers who had been challenging his authority, and James was persuaded to accept it. The ex-regent swiftly staged a comeback using his alliance with the king's schoolfellow, the young Earl of Mar, who asserted his hereditary right to be the king's new guardian over the existing holder of this role, his uncle Alexander Erskine. Morton, in possession of the king, and his opponents at Edinburgh had a stand-off, but neither risked war and English ambassador, Robert Bowes, negotiated terms whereby some of the latter were admitted to the council. Thereafter Morton's power was limited.

The young king's growing self-assertion was reflected in his partiality for his cousin, Esme Stuart d'Aubigny (born 1541), handsome cadet of the line of the earls of Lennox, who had been living in France and was a gentleman of the bedchamber to King Henri III. The death of Lennox's younger son, Darnley's equally sickly brother Charles Stuart, in 1576 (leaving an infant daughter, Arbella) left Esme's uncle, Robert Stuart, sexagenarian Bishop of Caithness, as heir to the Earldom of Lennox and James gave him the title in 1578, and Esme returned from France to challenge for the Lennox estates. He was accused by indignant Protestant hard-liners of being a Catholic and the agent of ex-Queen Mary's 'ultra' cousin, the ferocious Duke of Guise, but James showed him strong physical affection and he became the first of the king's so-called male 'favourites'. A homosexual element to this relationship was hinted at later, but it is more likely that James was showing enthusiastic affection for the dashing and sophisticated international courtier who had showed him more regard than his ruthless guardians or his stern tutor, the ageing ultra-Protestant historian George Buchanan. In March 1580 James induced Earl Robert to surrender the Lennox title and transferred it to Esme, and a dukedom followed. Lennox duly became the lynchpin of those councillors opposed to Morton, who was arrested on 31 December 1580 on a charge of involvement in Darnley's murder and was attainted as a traitor and executed (by the prototype for the guillotine, which he had introduced to Scotland) in June 1581.

One ultra-Protestant faction now consisted of Morton's nephew the Earl of Angus, the Earl of Glencairn and Lord Ruthven (Earl of Gowrie from 1581), and was backed by the militant Presbyterian clergy. Against the radicals stood the Catholic leadership of the northern nobility, political and religious conservatives such as the younger Earl of Huntly; the Catholic cause was backed by the Guises in France and their ally King Philip of Spain. The Spanish embassy in London now proceeded to use the Jesuit mission to reconvert England to send Jesuit priests to Scotland too, to stir up the northern nobles and to rally support for a scheme of 'Association' of Mary with James on the throne. Hopefully Mary, allied to the ultra-Catholics in France and Spain as a source of troops (she despaired of any aid from Elizabeth to restore her), could then persuade her son to convert to Catholicism.

Lennox's domestic foes were more determined to remove him than Elizabeth was, and though he managed to survive a plot by the Earl of Angus (who fled to England) his open profession of Protestantism failed to convince the Presbyterian clergy. A group of nobles led by Ruthven and Mar took direct action and on 22 August 1582 intercepted the king's party en route to Perth on a northern tour. Ruthven seized the king's horse's bridle and forcefully 'invited' him to Ruthven Castle, and next day James was prevented from leaving and held prisoner (the 'Ruthven Raid'). He was taken to Perth and forced to issue a proclamation that he was not being held against his will – this fooled nobody and Lennox fled to Dumbarton. The rebel lords moved the king to Stirling Castle and an English embassy arrived to show him written proof that Lennox was in league with the French, and despite James's delaying tactics the council ordered Lennox out of the country in December. The duke fled back to France, dying there in 1583; his son Ludovick Stuart soon returned to Scotland from France, in company with Mary's representative Patrick Gray, and stayed out of politics as the king's trusted cousin and lieutenant (he died in 1624).

James, meanwhile, remained effectively prisoner of Ruthven's faction as their puppet ruler, another naked assertion of Scots magnate 'realpolitik' as had humiliated James II, III and V, but like the other kidnappers Ruthven soon faced dissent from excluded nobles. Huntly, Atholl, the new Earl of Bothwell, the Earl of Montrose and Lord Seton formed a conspiracy against him, and James's custodian Sir James Melville reluctantly agreed to his sovereign's insistence that he help an escape. In June 1583 James was allowed to accept an invitation from the Earl of March to come to St Andrews for some hunting, and en route March and the town's provost met him and escorted him to safety. Ruthven and his allies were given a proclamation banning them from the royal presence and obeyed, and they were soon pardoned. The council was remodelled and Huntly, Argyll, Maitland of Thirlestane and Crawford now emerged as leading figures. With them, presumably to reassure radical Protestants, was the buccaneering figure of Captain James Stewart of Bothwellmuir, new (1581) Earl of Arran and ex-protégé of Morton, who had led the ex-regent's arrest in December 1581. Arran and Mar struggled for influence and the latter lost and ended in exile; after a revolt at Stirling Castle Arran proceeded to have Ruthven rounded up and executed.

Arran (Knox's brother-in-law) now became chancellor

and Maitland treasurer, and radical Presbyterian preachers who had backed the 'Ruthven Raiders' were prosecuted; the Edinburgh firebrand Andrew Melville, who had been insolently hectoring the king, fled to England with around forty others. The authority of the king and his bishops over the Church was now asserted in the 'Black Acts', restoring discipline and ending the threat of political defiance of the monarchy. But Arran was not able to exert the grip on power that Morton had done, as the king was now semi-adult, and struggles for influence on the impulsive, secretive and justifiably nervy young king continued, based around the intrigues of the Catholic nobles and their foreign backers for the restoration of Mary as co-ruler in the 'Association'. Now Elizabeth chose to send a new embassy headed by her cousin Lord Hunsdon to negotiate with the Scots regime (August 1584), and this accepted James's desire for a new treaty. Mary's personal envoy Patrick, Master of Gray – a Machiavellian expert at intrigue who had been living in Paris and had become a Guise protégé – had been sent to Edinburgh to encourage James to back his mother's restoration and demand this of Elizabeth; the king had duly promised his support for the 'Association' in July 1584. Gray abandoned a hard-line position on insisting on the ex-queen's release, as James refused to support it, and proceeded to London that autumn as the king's envoy to negotiate a treaty leaving Mary's status alone. Elizabeth agreed to a treaty and in May 1585 sent Sir Edward Wotton to Scotland with an offer of £4,000 down payment plus an annual subsidy of another £4,000, and this was accepted. But when Elizabeth agreed to let the refugee 'Ruthven Raiders' go home and attempt to overthrow Arran by force, apparently persuaded by Patrick Gray that the king would abandon him to a determined assault, on 2 November 1585 Mar, Angus, Glamis, lords Claude and John Hamilton and their allies appeared at Stirling Castle with a large armed escort to demand that James dismiss Arran. The king had to receive them as Arran fled, and agreed to sack and demote

Arran and restore them and their exiled clergy allies to their positions and estates.

This ended the somersaults of political fortune in Scotland, and the English treaty was duly signed on 5 July 1586; it assured James that Elizabeth would not directly or indirectly prejudice his claim to the English throne provided that he remained friendly towards her. That claim, it would turn out, was James's principal ambition in his English policy – and Mary's claims to both crowns were abandoned again. But his requests for an English earldom and attempts to secure 'naturalisation' of each country's nationals in the other – two moves for closer association in anticipation of James's succession to England – were blocked by Elizabeth. The king made no move to save Mary and risk endangering the treaty when she was arrested for her part in the Babington Plot to murder Elizabeth and put Mary on the English throne, and Mary's trial and her execution at Fotheringhay Castle (8 February 1587) proceeded without James threatening to break off the treaty. The fact that Mary had been fooled in a 'honey trap' into writing incriminating instructions to have Elizabeth killed so this could be used against her was glossed over. As Walsingham pointed out in answer to James's envoys' threats to break relations, James could not invade England successfully on his own and Spain or France would only do so for their own agendas. Nor could James blackmail Elizabeth into recognising his right to succeed her in return for his acquiescence. In any case James had been brought up by his regents and tutors to hate his mother as a Catholic adulteress who had murdered his father, and had not seen her since he was under a year old.

But despite James's own Protestant alignment there were still powerful ex-Marian Catholic nobles ruling unmolested over their tenants in the North and these had the manpower to intervene in national affairs if interested – with the Spanish and the Jesuits keeping in touch to plot a Catholic revival in Scotland. The most dangerous of these was young Huntly, due to his court connections – he had married the late Esme Stuart's daughter and become Captain of the Guard. James balanced ministers and courtiers from the two religions, keeping his international links on both sides, and the most senior figure in the administration, as chancellor (July 1587), was Maitland of Thirlestane, the first holder of that office to be neither noble nor cleric. Maitland, a classic new man bureaucrat and not linked to any faction, favoured efficient government and financial administration rather than international involvement or religious extremism and his caution suited the canny, devious king. James sought to reconcile his nobility, recalling exiles such as the Hamilton brothers and including men from all factions in his government.

James had been negotiating with both King Henri of Navarre, Protestant leader in the French civil war and heir to the French throne, and King Christian IV of Denmark (descendant of James IV's maternal uncle) for the hands of their sisters – Catherine of Navarre, eight years older than James, and Anne of Denmark, eight years younger. The Danish match was chosen in autumn 1588, probably due to the bride's age and a more certain dowry, but Princess Anne and her entourage, escorted by the Earl Marishal, failed to arrive from Copenhagen on time due to storms. With unusual daring James decided to emulate his grandfather James V and sail to his bride's homeland for the wedding. He and his party arrived in Oslo by sea and the marriage took place on 23 November; James was twenty-two (old for marriage by contemporary practice) and the bride fourteen. They then went on to Elsinore in Denmark to spend the winter with Anne's teenage brother Christian IV, his mother and regents and the Danish court. They landed at Leith on 1 May 1589. Anne was to give James a large family, commencing with Prince Henry in 1594, but never matched her husband's erudition; she became a secret Catholic and by the late 1590s was largely living apart from her husband. The latter was already being accused of undue partiality for handsome young men and homosexual tendencies. He also fell victim to one of the age's leading superstitions, the fear of witchcraft, and sought to examine and understand the phenomenon in learned detail; he came to believe that the storms that had delayed him and his queen had been due to witches and that a coven of devil worshippers at North Berwick had tried to sink his ships as he returned. In 1590–91 over a hundred alleged witches were investigated and many were burned, James taking part in interrogations, and he subsequently published a book, *Daemonologie*, asserting the seriousness of the threat against a scornful recent English writer, Reginald Scot.

A similar obsession to use his knowledge and literary skills on a personal 'hobby-horse' can be seen in his *Counter-Blast to Tobacco* of 1604, where he turned his pen against what he regarded as a particularly obnoxious and dangerous modern fashion. His most politically important work was his *Basilikon Doron* of 1598 – a collection of statesmanlike advice to his eldest son on the art of learning to rule wisely. The latter particularly showed his distaste for the lack of respect that the more radical Presbyterian clergy showed to the monarchy. James was keen to stress the importance of the clergy accepting discipline under the leadership of the bishops, much to the fury of Andrew Melville and other heirs of Knox. His learning and cultural interests were the most accomplished of his dynasty, if paraded with something of the obsessive pedantry of his tutor George Buchanan. Unfortunately his self-acclaimed role as the nation's supreme scholar was not to the taste of many of his contemporaries. His wearing thick clothing to prevent stabbing and his slovenly habits attracted ridicule, especially after 1603, in England; a speech impairment from an over-large tongue added to this. Even the flattery that he was a 'new Solomon' was turned against him, with wits saying that this was appropriate as he was the 'son of David' (i.e. Riccio).

The international and domestic situations gradually became more stable in the late 1590s, the French civil war having ended in 1594 with Henri IV (Henri of Navarre) triumphant but turning Catholic to appease his Catholic subjects and the Anglo-Spanish war winding down after naval expeditions in 1596–98. The threat of the Spanish using the Northern Catholic nobles, e.g. Huntly, against James never materialised though it led to tension over the affair of the 'Spanish Blanks' and Huntly was temporarily disgraced after a half-hearted revolt. A more serious personal threat to James was the unruly, Protestant-allied Bothwell, a favourite of the radical clerics, who at one point attacked Holyrood Palace and was eventually exiled, too. Philip II died in 1598 and his son's near-bankrupt government had less interest in reclaiming England for the Faith, so a Catholic-run Scotland ceased to be a side-door into England for them. Elizabeth still refused to openly name James as her successor, but the likelihood of this eventuality was recognised by rival factions at her court who kept a channel of communications open to James for their mutual benefit. The only realistic alternative to James as the next king was the English-born Arbella Stuart, son of Darnley's consumptive brother Charles (died April 1576) by the Countess of Shrewsbury's daughter Elizabeth (died 1582). As the grand-daughter of James V's half-sister Margaret Douglas, this isolated Stuart relative lived with her other grandmother the Countess of Shrewsbury ('Bess of Hardwick'), Queen Mary's ex-captor, and was a negligible factor in Scottish dynastic matters.

The questions of violent aristocratic threats to royal power and serious distrust of James's intentions marked the bizarre incident of the so-called 'Gowrie Conspiracy' on 5 August 1600. The king was hunting near Falkland Palace when Alexander, Master of Ruthven (heir to the Earl of Gowrie), approached him and said his brother the earl had found a treasure in his nearby house at St Johnstone. He invited the king to go over for dinner and take a look at it, and James did so and dismissed his companions, the earls of Lennox and Mar (which would suggest that he had no idea of danger).

They however followed and joined the party at dinner. Alexander lured James away from dinner upstairs to look at the treasure but, according to the king, locked various doors behind them and in the final room they entered drew his dagger and threatened to kill him. Struggling to the window, James shouted for help and his followers outside ran inside and despatched Alexander on the spot. The Earl of Gowrie had told Lennox and Mar that the king had left and gone upstairs. When they realised what was going on, the pair ran upstairs to join in the fray and killed Gowrie too. This was the official version that James put out, but many people – led by a group of Presbyterian ministers in Edinburgh – refused to believe it and the details of the story were claimed to be unlikely. The forfeiting of the Gowrie estates that followed made an example of a notorious dynasty which had been involved in royal coercion in 1566 and the early 1580s, but it is unlikely that the king set them up for summary execution using himself as bait given his timidity.

The death of Queen Elizabeth at Richmond Palace on 24 March 1603 finally brought James to the English throne, though reportedly the obstinate and wary queen would only say to her ministers' desperate promptings as she was dying that a king should succeed her without naming him. Her cousin Sir Robert Carey rode through the night northwards on a relay of horses to present James with her signet ring as proof (and secure rich rewards for himself), and on 4 April he left Edinburgh for his new realm. He would return only once, in 1617.

Absentee Monarchs and 'Government by Pen': James VI and Charles I, 1603–37

From spring 1603 James was resident in England, with his queen and children soon following him. The respect and obedience given to a monarch in England, plus the revenue available and the greater royal control of a bishop-dominated Church, were much to the new King James I's liking after his turbulent reign in Scotland. He was also attended by a large group of raucous, hard-drinking Scots nobles, who dominated his bedchamber appointments and were supposed by their indignant, excluded English rivals to be sucking up royal patronage. Resentment at the influx of Scotsmen in London was quoted by Guy Fawkes as a reason for his attempt to blow up the king and the entire Protestant elite in Parliament in November 1605. Politically, the only major Scots player in James's English court and government was to be Robert 'Carr' (Kerr), a handsome young Borders nobleman who had followed him south and was to become his acknowledged 'favourite' by the late 1600s, later becoming Secretary of State after Robert Cecil. A boon companion rather than a politician, the vain and greedy Carr, who became Earl of Somerset, ended up at the centre of the reign's greatest scandal, as the king helped his lover Lady Frances Howard to have her marriage (to the Earl of Essex) annulled so she could marry Carr; and she apparently poisoned an ex-ally, Sir Thomas Overbury, in the Tower of London for threatening to blackmail her.

James's imaginative and centralising attempts to formalise the new 'union of crowns' with legal links between the two countries – extending the post-1603 personal monarchical link between two independent states – ran into the sand, largely due to hostility in England. His efforts to interest the English Parliament in creating a formal union under the name of Great Britain were also blocked, though he assumed the title of King of Great Britain on his own authority in 1604 and devised a new flag and coinage. In October 1604 a commission of forty-eight English and thirty-one Scots delegates met to negotiate on the form and mechanism of a union – without James attending the opening sessions as he was too busy hunting. He desired free trade between the two countries, the abolition of laws that were hostile to the other's nationals, a mechanism to deal with Border region disputes and granting automatic rights of 'naturalisation' to Scotsmen born after 24 March 1603 in England. The latter, the so-called 'post-nati' (Scots born before this date were the 'anti-nati'.), were technically subjects of the King of England (James I) as well as of the King of Scots (James VI), so why not formalise the arrangement? But the English delegates blocked this, and only the abolition of hostile laws was agreed and was duly decided by Parliament; the ending of disputes and petty pillaging by raiders on the Borders was dealt with by a gradual legal process of extending English-style county administration to the Scots side of the Border to remove the powers of local lairds who connived at, or took part in, disorder. In 1605 a joint commission of five English and five Scots was set up to regulate and enforce impartial Borders justice. The Borders were to become the 'middle counties' of one realm, not a dividing line.

Judicial centralisation also featured in post-1603 Scotland against the more obstreperous and defiant Highland clans, with special legal rights and 'enforcement' duties given in Argyll to Clan Campbell against local troublemakers. In 1597 all landholders in the Highlands and Islands were ordered to submit their legal titles to their property to the government for approval and to pay up their due rents – which the king was convinced they had been evading – to the Exchequer. As an example, the Island of Lewis was confiscated from its defiant Macleod lords and handed over to royal – Lowland – nominees for settlement. The Mackenzies (whose chief now became Earl of Seaforth in 1624) were raised up in the Northern Hebrides as royal 'enforcers' as the Campbells had been in the south. But reliance on particular dynasties to control their less loyal rivals opened the danger of raising up a new group of men to commit misrule, as Bishop Andrew Knox of the Isles recognised. Knox preferred to entice the clan chiefs to enter the royal systems of justice and administration willingly, and to sign up to guarantee their followers' good behaviour, which they policed; he achieved this in an important meeting of the senior chiefs of the old 'Lordship of the Isles' at Iona in 1609. James was more ruthless, at least against those within his reach. In 1603–04 a special campaign was launched by cooperating local clans under royal order to punish the Macgregors of Glengyle, east of Loch Lomond, for a massacre of the Colquhouns, and in 1610 James took the drastic step of ordering the entire 'Clan Gregor' to be killed or expelled from their lands and banning their surname. James also took steps to bring the nobility under royal control, having the traditional recourse to 'blood-feud'-style personal vengeance banned, and executing offenders. Centralism extended even to the Orkney Islands, where the king's uncle, James V's illegitimate son Robert Stewart (Earl of Orkney from 1581), had been appointed to control the Crown estates there by Queen Mary in 1564 and had added the Church estates of its bishopric in 1568. Robert and his son Earl Patrick had ruled unchallenged as viceroys of the remote islands ever since, using its unclear legal status to avoid Scottish conciliar interference. In 1608 Patrick was summoned to Edinburgh to answer charges of abuse of power and underhand dealings with Denmark, and was executed in 1615 after his son rebelled.

After the 1590s James came to rely almost entirely on 'new men' for his administration as the power of the old nobility waned, not a new policy for his dynasty but one thrown into sharper focus by the end of open and violent magnate defiance. Such figures were often junior members of noble dynasties, such as Sir George Home (treasurer 1601–11) who became Earl of Dunbar and increasingly resided in England. Other royal administrators raised up to new peerages included Walter Stewart of Blantyre (treasurer from 1596 and Lord Blantyre 1604); Alexander Seton, Chancellor 1605–22 and Earl of Dunfermline 1605; and James Elphinstone, royal secretary from 1598, Lord President of the Council 1605 and Lord Balmerino 1603. From a lesser, urban burgess family came Sir Thomas Hamilton, popularly known as 'Tam o' the Cowgate', secretary from 1612–26 and Lord President 1616–26 (then later Earl of Melrose/Haddington). These men, mostly from the fringes of the nobility or minor gentry plus successful urban men of business, dominated a new burst of peerage creations after 1600, and these 'lords of erection' eclipsed the existing nobility in royal service. Centralism also applied to religion. When a group of defiant Presbyterian ministers insisted on holding an assembly at Aberdeen in 1605, despite James's cancelling it, they were rounded up and imprisoned. Andrew Melville and eight of his leading followers were 'invited' to London and were refused leave to go home when they stood up for the detainees; Melville was deported to the Continent and others were either kept in England or placed in detention in Scotland. The crucial role of permanent 'moderators', i.e. overseers, of the grass-roots local presbyteries had so far been vetoed by the Church's synods despite James's loaded hints, but was now imposed by a carefully selected assembly at Linlithgow (December 1606). It is generally agreed that James's initially Calvinist religious views altered under Anglican influence, aided by the anti-monarchic tone of the Presbyterian radicals, and in 1614 he required the celebration of Communion at Easter. The restoration of other ceremonies of the Christian year – regarded as Catholic by their opponents – and a new liturgy were examined by a Church Assembly at Aberdeen in 1616 and proposals were drawn up, and the royal visit to Edinburgh in May–August 1617 saw James consulting the leading clergy. His resulting 'Five Articles' required the restoration of the Christian calendar's old ceremonies, kneeling at Communion, private administration of the Sacraments of Communion and baptism, and Confirmation. They were rejected by a first assembly at St Andrews that November, but accepted (by a two-to-one majority) at Perth in 1618. The king had become less flexible or concerned about resistance, aided by his physical distance from his homeland, but his new draft liturgy of 1618 was never imposed. Parliament finally approved the

'Five Articles' in 1621, but only after assurances that there would be no more innovations.

When James died on 25 March 1625, aged fifty-eight, he had reigned over Scotland for fifty-seven years – the longest reign to that date and only surpassed three times since. Despite his unheroic character and frequent descent from wisdom and cunning into farce, he had been the most successful of his dynasty to date, though it was only when he had the resources of England behind him that the political situation had stabilised. His political aims had been at odds with much of the 'old' nobility; his desire for central control in religious matters had also seen him finally defeat the Melville faction in the Church (democrats or disrupters?) but he had grown distant from the majority opinion of the religious elite. The problem of physical distance was to be greater for his less approachable or canny son Charles – who to make matters worse was married soon after his accession to a Catholic (Henrietta Maria of France). The monarchy continued to be based in London, with a crucial problem now being that James's elder son Henry had died aged eighteen in 1612. Matters of temperament, education (in England) and preference for formality apart, Charles was to show a naïve belief that he only had to issue orders and they would be obeyed, and that to question them was insolence and probably treason. This would prove dangerous when dealing with the often informal and confrontational world of Scottish politics, while in religious matters he had abandoned early contacts with Calvinism and was showing support for the most Popish elements of the Anglican Church's ceremonial and liturgy – plus the concept of discipline imposed by bishops. He continued to rely on the bureaucrats who had served his father, and the only Scots peers influential at his hierarchical court were expatriates such as the Duke of Lennox (Ludovick Stuart's son) and James, Marquis of Hamilton (Chatelherault's great-grandson), who were out of touch with 'home'. His ceremonious court put off visiting Scots nobles such as the future rebel leader Montrose, whose manners were regarded as uncouth. Charles also sought to use the new reign's initial Act for 'revocation' of all past royal grants of Crown lands – this time since 1540 – to ecclesiastical property too, in order to reassert control over the vast amounts of Church lands that had been alienated during the Reformation. This had impoverished the bishops, whom Charles wished to restore to authority and prestige as a bulwark of royal power, and although in practice the purchasers' descendants were allowed to keep their acquired lands – now as royal tenants – the measure caused temporary panic and longer hostility. An impression was given of arbitrary royal threats to long-established rights and a devotion to rebuilding the pre-1560 power of the Church, which was bolstered by granting the Chancellorship to Archbishop Spottiswoode of St Andrews (1635). Charles's most useful noble adviser, Menteith, was disgraced in 1633 for boasting of his more legally secure Stuart descent to the king's.

The king's belated visit to Edinburgh for his Scots Coronation in 1633 was marked by the tactless use of the English Prayer Book of 1559, which was regarded by the majority of Presbyterians as too close to pre-Reformation Catholic words and practices, and the wearing of Anglican-style surplices rather than the plain gowns of the Reformed Church. The 'High Church' Anglican-style Coronation ceremony on 15 June caused much offence as being 'Popish', but Charles combined a passion for uniformity across his realms with ignorance of Scots sensitivities and a haughty objection to compromise as demeaning to his majesty. In 1634 the bishops were asked to draw up a new set of canons and Book of Common Prayer. The canons imposed, but not acted upon, in 1618 were now incorporated into this and a new liturgy introduced, revising that of 1618 to introduce inflammatory practices such as using the Sign of the Cross. Charles's aggressively 'High Church' new Archbishop of Canterbury, William Laud – erroneously believed to be pro-Catholic in his theology – required uniformity of liturgy with the Anglican Church, though it appears that it was a group of Scots bishops rather than he who insisted on issuing a new Scots Prayer Book. Possibly the post-1603 royal policy of selecting bishops from lower down the social scale than before meant that these men were consciously royal protégés lacking social or political status and so unwilling to stand up to either the king or Laud – or had any social links to the increasingly alarmed and angry Lowlands nobility. The new prayer book in fact avoided inflammatory pro-Catholic language, was Calvinist in theology and was authored by the Calvinist Bishop Wedderburn – but it was the perception of it as Catholic that mattered.

Revolution and Civil Wars: 1637–48

The storm broke on 23 July 1637, with the scheduled first use of the new prayer book at St Giles's Cathedral in Edinburgh. The congregation rioted and a housewife called Jenny Gordon famously threw a stool at the officiating cleric – before he had started to read the book, so the protesters seem to have been organised rather than acting with spontaneous outrage. Suspiciously, although the Privy Council was supposed to be in attendance to demonstrate its support for the book, some members with strong Presbyterian beliefs, such as the Earl of Rothes and Lord Lorne (Archibald Campbell, heir of the Earl of Argyll), failed to turn up. There were other riots at services and most clergy were intimidated into abandoning the book. Nobles such as Rothes and Lorne and the local gentry coordinated resistance, and the suspicion arises that the presence of bishops on Charles's Scots Privy Council in the 1630s was their target as much as the liturgy. Most of the protests' organisers were Lowland landowners, so able to bring armed and angry tenants to Edinburgh to intimidate the Privy Council. The latter was led by Archbishop Spottiswoode and by the Lord Treasurer, Lord Traquair, who was not a forceful figure and was no match for the ruthless Rothes and Lorne.

Spottiswoode duly suspended the book's implementation pending an appeal to the king, and in October twenty-four nobles and 2,000–3,000 lairds signed a 'supplication' for the suspension of the bishops from Parliament. The 'loyalist' councillors and their supporters failed to oppose the spread of armed militancy in favour of the 'threatened' Presbyterian Church, and the spectre of private armies reappeared for the first time since the 1590s, as militant lairds and nobles drilled their men in defence of the Church. The most powerful Lowlands landed magnate in favour of the king's policies, Hamilton, tried to assemble his own tenants in 1638 but this was not implemented locally, probably following intimidation. The Church provided a vital national network for grass-roots coordinated armed activity in favour of the resistance, and this was used ruthlessly. But even Hamilton may have been opposed to the bishops' new political power and unwilling to risk too much obloquy in defending them – and if Charles was to be suspended or deposed by his subjects Hamilton was the next adult male Protestant in line for the Stuart throne. The king lacked a standing army, in England as well as Scotland, and his finances were in a precarious position due to his ruling without an English Parliament since 1629. The alternative was to bring in troops and pro-royal clansmen from Ireland via Dumbarton, as offered by its hard-headed and fiercely loyal Lord Lieutenant, Thomas Wentworth (soon to be Earl of Strafford), but this would take time.

In spring 1638 Charles sent Hamilton as his Commissioner to Edinburgh to negotiate. But this was only to play for time, as troops were being raised and hired in England. He could not afford to hire many expatriate Scots who had been fighting in the Thirty Years' War; instead it was the Scots 'rebels' who were able to entice back such men as Alexander Leslie to lead and train their expanding army. The protesters now regularised their alliance into an official organisation with the creation of the 'Tables', committees representing the various social classes of the resistance. On 23 February 1638 a mass rally at the Greyfriars Kirk, where the leading opposition cleric Alexander Henderson preached, was followed by the signing of a 'National Covenant' by the attendees in the churchyard. This document had been drawn up by Henderson and the extremist Calvinist lawyer Archibald Johnston of Warriston, men who were passionate about the imminence of the threat to their faith that the Papist innovations presented, advised by Rothes and lords Loudoun and Balmerino. It pledged resistance to all ecclesiastical innovations, in the language and following the precedents of the Old Testament – and if the Presbyterian Scots were to be seen as the 'new Israel', the people of Moses, then Charles was cast in the role of Pharaoh and he was accused of breaching his Coronation oath. The notion of a 'chosen people' had echoes of the Declaration of Arbroath.

Charles conceded the summoning of a parliament and Church Assembly, and on Hamilton's advice reissued James VI's unequivocally Calvinist 'Confession' of 1580. The radicals now took over and effectively rigged elections for the Church Assembly, though opinion in the Lowlands was probably heavily in their favour anyway. Supporters of the Prayer Book were banned from standing. The assembly, meeting at Glasgow in November 1638 with Hamilton acting as royal commissioner but unable to bring his armed tenants there, voted themselves the right to decide on episcopacy and banned the bishops from sitting, and Hamilton walked out to legally invalidate their actions but they proceeded anyway. The bishops, prayer book, canons and liturgy were all abolished. Having lost control of events in Scotland, Charles planned an ambitious triple invasion – one by land across the Borders, another by sea from Ireland led by Wentworth and the MacDonnells and a third by sea to Aberdeen to link up with the Marquis of Huntly's Catholic tenantry. But even if men, supplies, ships and the weather were adequate it would be difficult to coordinate this. Indeed, there was considerable support for the Covenanters in left-wing Protestant circles in England, among the so-called Puritans who opposed Laud's authoritarian revival of Church powers and 'Catholicising' ceremonial; these men included a section of the English nobility led by the Earl of Warwick. The Covenanters were in contact with them from an early stage, arguing that the Reformation in both countries was in danger. They surprised Dumbarton and Edinburgh castles in March, seizing the king's artillery. Huntly was caught unprepared by a quick advance on his lands by Montrose, who captured Aberdeen and routed his followers at the 'Brig O' Dee' on 17–18 June. Wentworth failed to arrive with his troops from Ireland, and Hamilton's English fleet blockaded the Firth of Forth ineffectively and could not stop men and munitions arriving from the Continent. Charles belatedly arrived in the North of England in May with under his planned 6,000 cavalry and 24,000 infantry, many of his men inexperienced and untrained, and with the inexperienced Earl of Arundel in command. In early June the royal cavalry commander, the Earl of Holland, was told to lead around 300 cavalry and 3,000 infantry over the Border in a 'probe' against the larger Scots army, led by Leslie, at Kelso. There was a resultant clash at Duns Law, where the English cavalry outpaced their infantry and ran into a larger Scots force (about 800?); the latter's 'half-moon' crescent formation threatened to envelop Holland's men so he lost his nerve and as the Scots charged the English galloped out of danger.

Duns Law was only a minor clash, but the English leadership lost their nerve and the king agreed to a truce and to resume negotiations. A new Church Assembly and Scots parliament were called. This was more a matter of playing for time than sincerely seeking a permanent agreement, and Henderson for one did not trust him. The 'Pacification of Berwick' signed on 18 June thus ended the so-called First Bishops' War and Huntly was released, but Covenanter ministers did not stop their aggressive preaching. The assembly met in Edinburgh on 12 August. Presided over by Traquair, it repeated the previous assembly's resolutions and declared episcopacy incompatible with the national religion. Parliament backed this up, and Argyll led the 'Lords of the Articles', the committee which sat while it was not in session. A 'one-party' state thus emerged in Scots politics, and Charles prepared for a second military campaign in 1640.

In August 1640 Leslie's army of around 30,000 infantry and 3,000 cavalry crossed the Border and headed for the royal army's headquarters at Newcastle, bypassing Berwick. Charles's commander Lord Conway had around 14,000 infantry and 2,000 cavalry, nowhere near as well-prepared and trained (or armed) as the Scots, and Charles was not ready to march his reinforcements to add to this force. The main army was still at York and Conway had to fight on his own. Leslie's army duly crossed the Tyne at Newburn on 28 August, in a pitched battle against Conway and about a third of the Newcastle army; the Scots stormed the hastily erected English earthworks and Conway retired to Newcastle, which he then evacuated. Charles, marching to Northallerton to find the enemy advancing, lost his nerve and avoided a further clash, resulting in stalemate, and at this juncture the pro-Covenanter English Calvinist opposition peers (led by Warwick) made their objections to the war and the king's policies known with a virtual mutiny. The threat of an armed stand by the opposition peers in London to coerce the king, now at York, commenced the open political struggle between Charles and his critics, which was eventually to lead to the Civil War and which now caused the calling of a new parliament in November 1640. The Scots army was left in control of Northumberland and Durham with no danger of attack, and the Covenanters became a powerful factor in the struggle for control of the English executive and Church as they backed the king's critics and their delegates in London allied to hard-liners in Parliament in favour of abolition of episcopacy and a purge of 'Popery' in England as in Scotland. Leaders of both nations' anti-royal noble factions favoured reducing the powers of the untrustworthy king to make him their virtual puppet.

But Charles had his own strategy for political survival, and by mid-1641 was prepared to concede political and religious defeat in Scotland to win over its leadership to support him and turn them (and their army) against his enemies in England. His key potential ally was Montrose, who was deeply suspicious of Argyll's growing power and was now at the centre of pro-royal intrigue to overthrow the so-called 'King Campbell'. As a firm Calvinist, Montrose required the king's guarantees of confirmation of all the religious revolution's achievements of 1637–39, but Charles was prepared to concede this. Secret royal contacts with Montrose's allies were however leaked to Argyll, and in June the latter had Montrose arrested and put in Edinburgh Castle. Charles arrived in Edinburgh in mid-August 1641, and on 25 August Charles signed the Treaty of Edinburgh, conceding all the Covenanter government's requirements – the demolition of his prerogative powers by the Scots Parliament, control of the executive by the Covenanter-run Privy Council and Parliament, and all the religious reforms enacted since 1637. Parliament now secured the right to veto all royal appointments of officials, councillors and judges. In effect he became a nominal, constitutional monarch and the Church was restored to its 1560s position under its militant grass-roots clergy. However Charles quickly showed his real intentions with a murky plot for a coup against Argyll and his allies while he was in Edinburgh, the so-called 'Incident'. In this obscure episode his influential bedchamber official Will Murray liaised with the Earl of Roxburgh, a moderate Covenanter peer at odds, to have Argyll, Hamilton (his current ally) and Hamilton's brother, the Earl of Lanark, summoned to a royal audience at Holyrood, arrested and removed by loyalist officers. This may have involved murder and would enable the king to release and rehabilitate Montrose as his new strongman. The plot was discovered and Charles denied all knowledge, but it was a hint at his deviousness and readiness to promise one thing to one party while plotting with their rivals.

The outbreak of the English Civil War in October 1642 saw the Scots regime having to choose which side to support. If Charles defeated the Covenanters' fellow-Calvinists in England, would he then use his army to turn on Scotland more decisively than in 1639–40? The Covenanters were not convinced of the goodwill of the Parliamentarians towards their religious experiment or their political autonomy, and when military reverses forced Parliament to seek their alliance in summer 1643 they insisted that the latter agree to impose the Covenant and a fully non-episcopal Presbyterian Church in England. The resulting Anglo-Scots alliance against Charles agreed in November 1643 was a matter of mutual necessity rather than conviction on the part of many of its backers. The Convention of Estates required the English to pay £30,000 a month for the hire of their army – £100,000 in advance of any action. 18,000 Scots infantry and 2,000 cavalry were to assist the English Parliament, commanded by Alexander Leslie (now Earl of Leven). The English envoys had no choice but to agree, and early in 1644 the Earl of Loudoun, Johnston and Lord Maitland went to London as the resident Scots commissioners. A 'Committee of Both Kingdoms', an executive of peers and MPs from both countries, was set up in February to direct the war effort and coordinate the campaigns.

Alexander Leslie's army now crossed the Tweed in January 1644, with his kinsman David Leslie in charge of the cavalry. He had 18,000 infantry, 3,000 cavalry, 500 dragoons and 120 cannon. He pressed back the outnumbered Northern Royalist army under William Cavendish, Marquis of Newcastle; as the Marquis's southern flank was threatened by the West Riding Parliamentarians he had to retreat towards York and was besieged in the city. The king's nephew Prince Rupert brought an army north while the Parliamentarian army in the East Midlands and East Anglia under the Earl of Manchester (with Cromwell in charge of his cavalry) moved up to aid the Scots. The Parliamentarians and Scots duly won the resulting battle at Marston Moor near York on 2 July, destroying the king's cause in the North. Meanwhile the king had given up hope of Hamilton succeeding in swinging those still nominally pro-royal Covenanter peers to overthrow Argyll, and was preparing a rebellion against the Covenanter regime, which was to be led by the defecting Montrose, Argyll's bitter enemy. The Covenanters held the Lowlands in an iron grip. But it was assumed that Catholic clansmen in the Highlands would rise once they had the king's general and commission among them and Huntly and his more militarily competent sons were at odds with Argyll's rule. Also, a force of around 1,600 Catholic Ulstermen raised by the MacDonnells of Antrim, led by the Earl of Antrim's kinsman Alistair Macdonald ('Mac Colkitto', i.e. son of the 'left-handed' laird Macdonald of Colonsay), were shipped to the western Highlands in spring–summer 1644 to attack their hereditary foes, the Campbells. They moved on to Atholl en route to help Huntly attack Aberdeen, but he was driven out by Argyll before they arrived while the Earl of Seaforth, head of the Mackenzies, refused to join them. In mid-August Montrose joined them near Blair Atholl after travelling secretly north with a few companions, dressed as a groom with the king's commission and standard hidden in his luggage. He persuaded the local Royalists to join up with the Irishmen and the combined force then marched on Perth. On 1 September the Royalists (around 5,000 men) confronted around 7,000 well-drilled but inexperienced Lowlander Covenant troops under Lord Elcho at Tippermuir outside Perth. The attendant Presbyterian clerics urged on their men with a watchword of 'Jesus and no quarter', and the Royalists were so short of ammunition that Montrose had to tell those who had bullets to fire one volley then charge and the rest to throw stones. But the Covenanters were routed by a ferocious Highland charge in which their greater firepower was of less importance than their hesitation; the majority were townsmen used to formal drill not hand-to-hand combat. Around 2,000 were killed.

The Covenanters put a price on Montrose's head for

bringing in a horde of Irishmen and priests, and the swift-moving though small Royalist force, commanded by one of the best guerrilla leaders since Robert Bruce, embarked on a hectic campaign across eastern Scotland, out-marching and outsmarting the well-equipped but lumbering Covenanter armies. Montrose marched on Aberdeen and defeated around 2,500 defenders under the inexperienced Lord Balfour of Burleigh outside the walls on 12 September. The city was devastatingly sacked, the first major atrocity of the civil wars on the British mainland, which was afterwards used for Covenanter propaganda but was not entirely Montrose's fault as his untrained men were out of control and an envoy had been shot despite a flag of truce. Alistair Macdonald's Western Highlanders then returned home to deposit their loot and collect reinforcements, and Montrose and his Ulster lieutenant Magnus O'Cahan were chased across the north-east by Argyll and his Campbell levies but fought them off in a skilful defensive action at Fyvie Castle in October.

Montrose escaped into the mountains, eluding Argyll, and when his new troops arrived, launched an attack on the Campbells' home territory in Argyll in midwinter. The Earl of Argyll suffered the humiliation of having his home, Inveraray Castle, sacked. Another Covenanter army, Lord Seaforth's Mackenzies from Ross, hurried down the Great Glen from Inverness to try to trap Montrose near what is now Fort Augustus, but he eluded them in a thirty-six-hour march round the flanks of Ben Nevis and attacked the Earl of Argyll's Campbell army at Inverlochy by surprise on 2 February 1645. The veteran Sir Duncan Campbell of Auchinbreck was commanding Argyll's well-armed infantry, and around 2,000 Campbells and 1,500 troops from Robert Baillie's Lowland army, with a few cannon, faced a smaller and tired army of Highlanders. A charge by the latter, however, carried the day; the Campbells panicked and fled and their chief left his men to die and Inverlochy to burn as he prudently sailed off down the loch on his private galley. Montrose now seemed invincible and moved on into Moray to try to win over local support and to sack the homes of those who resisted. Huntly, not known for his decisiveness, hung back, but his eldest son Lord Gordon and Seaforth defected and Montrose marched via Buchan to Forfarshire in late March where Baillie (with troops from Leven's army in England) and Colonel Hurry arrived to outnumber him. He stormed Dundee (4 April) and within hours had to abandon the town as Baillie and Hurry arrived with superior numbers to retake it and try to trap him. The Covenanter generals narrowly missed a chance to defeat the Royalists as they fled. Hurry went north to deal with the Gordons, rather than assisting Baillie, Montrose pursued him and the resultant battle at Auldearn near Elgin on 9 May saw a smaller Royalist army short of ammunition winning by tactical skill and bravery in combat. In practical terms the showy Royalist victories did not do much to aid the hard-pressed king in England apart from drawing Leven's main army north to block a Royalist march to Carlisle.

On 14 June the king was heavily defeated in person by the Parliamentarian 'New Model Army' at Naseby in Northamptonshire, and from then on his cause steadily declined as region after region was overrun. Montrose's success came too late. In the long term however, the success of a confident, new Parliamentarian army, mostly led and manned by religious 'Independents' who opposed a Presbyterian State Church in England, threatened the alliance of Covenanters and Parliament.

Montrose now destroyed Baillie's army at Alford by the River Don on 2 July, and headed south to confront the virtually defenceless Covenanter leadership. They could not recall Leven in time and had to raise an army of volunteers to add to their few remaining trained troops, but they still insisted on having a committee of Scots Parliament representatives to assist – and control – the more experienced Baillie on the battlefield. Around 6,000 Covenanter infantry and 800 cavalry confronted Montrose and his 5,000 or so men at Kilsyth on 15 July, and due to the usual Covenanter tactical blunders and Royalist ferocity the latter won with another massacre taking place. The Lowlands were left helpless until Leven returned and on 16 August Montrose entered Glasgow; Edinburgh had to surrender and he was able to summon a new parliament. But he had to attempt to conciliate the locals and win over the crucial moderate Covenanter peers. He could not extort money to pay his men, and many of the latter assumed the campaign was over and went home to celebrate and rest. Until they returned Montrose was left with around 1,000 Ulstermen plus some Royalist Lowlanders, and his army's success meant that the casualties they had inflicted increased Lowlander resentment. Montrose let his usual strategic brilliance and alertness lapse as he tried to coax the magnates of the Southern Uplands into backing his army, and his small force of around 1,700 men faced the vastly larger and better-armed Scots army that had been campaigning in England. David Leslie and around 4,000 Covenanter cavalry arrived in Scotland and on 13 September Leslie used a tip-off that Montrose was encamped near Selkirk, unawares of his proximity, to launch a surprise attack on his camp at Philiphaugh and cut the Royalists to pieces.

Montrose and a few cavalry managed to escape to the Highlands, but all that he had achieved in his year-long campaign was lost and the resulting bloodbath of his supporters terrorised potential allies into refusing to help him. He finally left for exile in 1646, after Charles had failed to have his pardon included in the complex royal negotiations with the Covenanters. The Covenanter clergy jubilantly encouraged a vindictive round of executions of Montrose's officers, especially the Catholics. Meanwhile the naive king was opening negotiations with the Scots Commissioners in London, assuming that Montrose could be pardoned by the Covenanters and that the latter would accept an Anglo-Scots religious assembly to sort out the form of Church government. Charles's efforts were assisted by the new French ambassador in London, Montreuil, representing the regency of his wife's sister-in-law, Anne of Austria, who was endeavouring to patch up a settlement and was negotiating with the Scots commissioners for their terms to be modified. Montreuil was over-optimistic of the Scots government and Church accepting Charles's caveat that he must not be forced to sign anything that was against his conscience. But the king's cause was now lost in England so he could not resist militarily, and Charles was finally forced to flee from his 'capital' at Oxford in April 1646. He chose to hand himself over to Leven's army, who were besieging Newark in Nottinghamshire, in order to seek to interest this powerful military force in restoring him to power in England, on 5 May – and was placed under guard and urged to sign the covenant.

As Charles saw it, hopefully the Scots would now put pressure on their allies to come to an early agreement with him involving not too onerous terms – though this was bound to include a Presbyterian Church in England, which he opposed. He was taken north to Newcastle (13 May), much to the annoyance of the English Parliament who had to negotiate – and pay – for him to be handed over. Complicated talks ensued with Covenanter leaders, lay and clerical. Charles would guarantee the Scots politico-religious settlement of 1641, but refused to sign up to the covenant and become a Presbyterian himself as his (Catholic) queen and her French backers urged. The chances of an alliance between Charles, the Covenanter leadership and the embattled Presbyterian majority in the English Parliament against the disgruntled New Model Army collapsed. But the Scots reached agreement with the English Parliament on the financial terms for handing Charles over to them – £400,000 to cover their expenses while campaigning in England. The first instalment having been paid, their army left Newcastle on 30 January 1647 and Charles was left in the hands of Parliament's troops. The evacuation of the north-east of England followed.

In England there now occurred a power struggle between Presbyterians and Independents. The New Model Army refused to be neutered by a mixture of partial disbandment and despatch to Ireland and mutinied, and as the Presbyterian MPs and peers could not rely on their own army there was talk of them calling on the Scots army for help. Charles was kidnapped by pro-Independent soldiers from Holdenby House and brought to the army headquarters, and the army marched on London and evicted the hard-line Presbyterian leadership from Parliament. This meant that the army leaders, the 'Grandees', and their religiously pluralist soldiers were likely to veto any parliamentary attempt to impose a Presbyterian Church on England as the Covenanters desired. New Scots commissioners, Loudoun and the Earl of Lanark (Hamilton's brother), joined Lauderdale in London to negotiate with Charles. But, abandoning his negotiations with the 'Grandees' as militant soldiers and their civilian allies threatened his safety and crown, Charles fled from detention at Hampton Court in October 1647, failed to reach the Continent with a typical mixture of bad luck and incompetence and ended up in a loose form of custody at Carisbrooke Castle on the Isle of Wight. This gave him more room for political manoeuvre, and Hamilton now won round crucial opinion among moderate Covenanter peers to conclude an agreement with him to help him retain his crown in England. The 'Engager' faction, which Hamilton had been organising in 1646–47, wanted Charles to promise to accept a three-year Presbyterian experiment for the English Church and to open England to Scots commerce, in return for which the Scots would assist him militarily to be restored to power. The Scots commissioners reached a secret agreement with Charles to this effect at Carisbrooke on 26–27 December 1647, without either Argyll or the English leadership knowing. Charles secured a promise of Scots military intervention if the English authorities refused a treaty with him. In the resulting debates in the Scots Parliament a majority supported this 'Engagement', but most of the clergy resisted it strongly in their assembly. They duly assisted Argyll in hampering the raising of an army to invade England on Charles's behalf and Leven and David Leslie refused to serve in it, while the king's own machinations and allied Royalist plots led to a second outbreak of civil war in England.

Hamilton could move ahead to arrange an invasion for July 1648 as the English failed to respond – but the timing was out of synchronisation with the English Royalist plans as the latter's scattered risings broke out before the Scots crossed the frontier. By the time Hamilton was on the march, the main Southern rebel grouping was cornered at Colchester. As Hamilton's army invaded, the Parliamentarian commander General Lambert fell back from Carlisle. There were Royalist risings in Yorkshire. Hamilton halted at Carlisle to await the arrival of experienced Ulster troops under General Munro, who joined them later at Kendal but refused to take orders from Hamilton's deputy Lord Callendar. Munro was left behind to guard the rear, and Lanark failed to arrive with the artillery train until mid-August; during the delay the Parliamentarians had had time to defeat rebels in Wales. Oliver Cromwell, who had been besieging Pembroke, arrived to join Lambert; though their army of around 8,000 was still outnumbered two-to-one it was far more coordinated, disciplined and used to combat. They then crossed the Pennines to intercept the Royalists at Preston on 16 August, with the latter minus their cavalry vanguard, which was ahead of them at Wigan. Around 2,000 of 18,000–20,000 Scots were killed in the battle, and the rest were left demoralised but holding the town. Hamilton bolted to join the vanguard rather than trying to hold out with Baillie's infantry, and the latter had to straggle on southwards in a desperate attempt to find Royalist help. Instead they were cornered at Warrington and had to surrender, and Hamilton was caught and was later executed for treason on dubious grounds.

With the 'Engager' army destroyed, the political field was left clear for the Covenanter hard-liners, and Munro's surviving troops at Edinburgh had to give in as an angry host of lower-class Strathclyde and Galloway Covenanters marched on Edinburgh. Leven took over Edinburgh Castle as the Earl of Lanark fled, Argyll returned from Inveraray to take political command and, with Cromwell's victorious army on the Border threatening invasion, Argyll was able to assume full control of the government to coordinate resistance. The 'Engagers' holding out at Stirling had to flee. The situation in England now turned against the disgraced king, and the parliamentary Presbyterian leadership managed to induce Charles to sign a political agreement at Newport, Isle of Wight, to find it invalidated by an army coup. Charles was seized by the army, Parliament was purged of all those MPs prepared to keep the king on the throne and set up a State Presbyterian Church and the unprecedented trial of Charles for waging war on his people followed. On 30 January 1649 Charles was executed at Whitehall – the same fate as his grandmother Mary, but this time tried as a reigning sovereign for crimes against his own (English) people.

Charles II (Part One): 1649–51

The majority reaction in Scotland was one of horror, not least at the English regime presuming to kill their sovereign without any reference to them. It rallied opinion to the disgraced 'Engagers' – now led by Hamilton's brother Lanark who succeeded to his dukedom – and the removal of Charles I, a man prepared to call in Catholic aid from Ireland and the Continent against his Protestant subjects, opened the possibility of a far easier agreement with his 'untainted' eighteen-year-old heir. Ideally, Prince Charles should sign up to the role of figurehead of a Covenanter regime – the role envisaged for his father in 1641. The new king was duly proclaimed in Edinburgh on 5 February as his father's death automatically made him sovereign, but Argyll and his hard-liners insisted that to acquire their recognition as head of the government he must accept the Covenant personally, enact the terms of their 1643 alliance with Parliament and agree to act as they directed in their 'godly' cause – which included a Presbyterian Church in England and Ireland too. Charles II refused the terms required, as he still had a large body of support – much of it Catholic – in Ireland and preferred to rely on this to build up his forces for an attack on England.

Cromwell's invasion of Ireland duly neutralised Charles's Irish support later in 1649, forcing Charles back into negotiations – though many of his advisers opposed any link to the Covenanters, who had been the first to rebel against his father in 1637. There was an 'Auld Alliance' element to the schemes as the new king's French mother, Henrietta Maria, and her countrymen sought hard-headedly to revive the old Scots-French alliance to counter the threat to France of Cromwell's menacing army and the regicide republican regime in London. The Argyll faction would not pardon the 'Engager' leaders as Charles wished, and Charles duly gave cautious backing to the exiled Montrose's actions as the late king's most brilliant general raised men and money in Sweden. Montrose was unable to collect as many men as he wished or much weaponry and had to rely on Scots expatriates plus a few mercenaries, but on 12 January 1650 Charles sent him his unequivocal backing. Montrose sailed to the Orkneys with around 1,200 men in March and a month later landed in Caithness. But by this time Charles had opened negotiations with Argyll's faction's second embassy to him – which the hard-line Johnston of Warriston joined to ensure that there was no compromise. The terms required him to sign the covenant, have a Presbyterian household, ban all those proscribed by the regime from his presence, accept all post-1641 Scots legislation to which his father had not agreed (including the proscription of assorted Catholics and Royalists) and submit all political decisions to Parliament and all religious decisions to the Church. In effect, he was to be reduced to a cipher.

The devious new king was following two contradictory lines of policy, one backing Montrose's invasion and the second signing up to whatever the hard-line Covenanters required. The Royalist invasion was a fiasco; Montrose had the advantages of many Covenanter troops being in Ulster, David Leslie being far to his south which gave him time and the multiple defector Colonel Hurry having joined him at the Ord of Caithness, but he had too few troops. The main local landowner, the Earl of Seaforth, was in exile and his brother and their Mackenzie clan failed to turn up, the Earl of Sutherland stayed loyal to the regime and Leslie's troops held out in local castles. Marching south towards the Gordons' lands beyond the Great Glen, Montrose was caught by surprise by Leslie's deputy Colonel Strachan at Carbisdale in Strath Oykel on 27 April and routed – a repeat of his disaster at Philiphaugh. Taking to the hills, he was captured hiding at Ardvreck Castle due to the treachery of Neil Macleod of Assynt and handed over to the Covenanter leadership for the implementation of his 1644 death sentence. Charles II was too desperate for their aid to make difficulties about Montrose being executed. The Royalist commander was duly hanged at the Mercat Cross in Edinburgh as a common criminal, a gratuitous piece of spite to an earl who could have expected a 'proper' execution. His body was still on display as Charles, the man who had asked him to invade, arrived in Scotland. Montrose duly entered Royalist legend as a martyr, and his subsequent admirers have been legion – with Argyll cast as the villain. In defence of the Covenanters' vitriolic attitude to him it should be noted that his campaigns had been marked by atrocities, and thousands of troops and civilians had been butchered by his Highlanders.

Sending orders to Montrose to give up his campaign, unaware of the disaster at Carbisdale, Charles signed up to the Covenanters' demands at Breda on 1 May. He appears to have intended to sail to Scotland without taking the covenant or banning his 'Engager' allies from his court in order to rely on a pro-Royalist backlash on his arrival to save him from full implementation of the Breda terms. But the Scots envoys' compromises on accepting these matters were denounced by both Parliament and Church Assembly, and the objectors refused to allow Charles's 'Engager' courtiers into Scotland.

Charles, already at sea, had to sign up to their requirements before he was allowed to land. His agreement horrified many of his supporters, and arguably commenced the long-term criticism of him as a political cynic with no principles, who would sign up to anything but could not be trusted. Charles was forced to act as a puppet king for the Covenanters and was lectured by their clergy about doing his duty as a 'godly' king with virtues that were incompatible with his character – not least his already notorious womanising. He was not allowed to take part in military operations lest he seduce senior military officers from their allegiance to the hard-line faction. English 'Lord General' Fairfax had refused to fight an aggressive war against his fellow Presbyterians, so Cromwell was now in full command. The New Model's 16,000 or so troops were outnumbered by David Leslie's army of around 27,000 and Leslie had served with the parliamentary army in England and so knew its weaknesses, but the Church insisted on purging all unreliable and 'ungodly' officers and men, which undermined its effectiveness. The Church even required Charles to sign up to a declaration denouncing his father's tyranny and his mother's Catholicism and tried to open negotiations with Cromwell. A committee of clergy and representatives of the estates accompanied Leslie on campaign with the power to veto his decisions – a form of political control like that of commissars in the Soviet army. They had no military experience, and after Leslie outmanoeuvred Cromwell's attempt to march round Edinburgh and forced him back to Dunbar they intervened disastrously. The New Model troops were penned in by the sea without an easy line of retreat, but the committeemen insisted that Leslie abandon his waiting game and march down onto the coastal plain to attack them. The resulting Battle of Dunbar on 3 September 1650 was a total victory for the better-organised, experienced and disciplined New Model, with around 3,000 Scots killed and 10,000 captured for a loss of around 20–30 Englishmen. Leslie had to retreat beyond the Forth and Cromwell occupied Edinburgh.

The disaster at Dunbar was not the end of the Covenanters' cause as they held Scotland north of the Forth, and indeed it benefited the king by humiliating his hard-line foes. The clergy blamed their defeat on their sins rather than any military failings. An enthusiastic but incompetent army of hard-line Galloway volunteers was recruited, and Leslie was blamed for the defeat. Argyll, who was rumoured to be endeavouring to marry off his daughter to the king, endeavoured to help Charles to secure permission to recruit 'Engager' help, but in the meantime the king was boosted by a Royalist revolt in Atholl and endeavoured to slip away from his Covenanter supervisors to join them on 4 October. The resulting fiasco of 'The Start' saw Charles captured by Covenanter pursuers in Glen Clova and taken back to Perth protesting that he had been tricked and had never really intended to take part in a revolt. This was surely the low point of his humiliating rule as the puppet of the Covenanters, but at least their dire shortage of officers meant that they now had to allow some of his noble 'Engager' nominees to join the army. Strachan and his ally Colonel Kerr in Galloway refused to have anything to do with the 'ungodly' alliance of Presbyterians and 'Engagers' now assembling at Perth and opened talks with Cromwell at Edinburgh, but were attacked and defeated by the latter. Charles was able to have Hamilton, Lauderdale and other allies of his restored to his court and army. On 1 January 1651 he was crowned King of Scots in a Presbyterian ceremony at Scone – the final coronation of a Scottish monarch. Fittingly, it was Argyll the 'kingmaker' who crowned him.

The military stalemate ended in summer as Leslie succeeded in manoeuvring to keep Cromwell back from Stirling only to face him using the English navy to land troops in Fife at North Queensferry (17 July). Lambert brought more than 4,000 men across the Forth in time to fall upon and rout General Browne's attempt to drive the English back at Inverkeithing. Cromwell took a substantial force over the Forth to join Lambert's men and take Perth on 2 August. But Charles and Leslie took the opportunity to slip past the remaining English troops south of the Forth; around 15,000 Scots now headed for Carlisle and opened the possibility of a repeat of the 1648 attempt to link up with the Northern English Royalists. This was wildly optimistic, as there had been a coordinated Royalist rising underway in England in 1648 and there was no such aid likely this time. Charles gambled on the magic of his name and the appeal to opponents of the new Commonwealth. In addition he hoped to call on the help of English Presbyterians. He marched swiftly southwards into the West Midlands, heading for the Royalist areas of the Welsh Marches, while Cromwell and Lambert followed. No major rising occurred, and the Royalist army of around 16,000 were trapped at Worcester by around 28,000 New Model troops and were decisively crushed as they attempted to assault Cromwell's lines outside the city on 3 September, the anniversary of Dunbar. Cromwell's 'crowning mercy' ended with around 3,000 Royalists dead and 10,000 captured, including Hamilton who was executed. The king famously escaped to France via a network of devoted Royalist partisans – and never returned to Scotland after his restoration in 1660, a sign of his alienation from the humiliating existence he had had as its king.

Meanwhile those of Cromwell's troops who had been left behind in Fife, commanded by General George Monck, proceeded to take Stirling on 14 August. The Committee of Estates were rounded up by Commonwealth soldiers and on 1 September Monck stormed Dundee where his men carried out atrocities on the civilians who were caught up in the savagery of the assault. Aberdeen fell on 17 November and the final mainland stronghold, isolated Dunottar Castle, surrendered in May 1652. The Scots regalia or 'Honours', which had been in the castle, had been smuggled out by a woman in a sack of flax and were hidden in the nearby churchyard of Kineff until the Restoration. For the second time in its history the Scots administration ceased to exist under English military occupation.

7

From One Union to a Second: 1651–1707

Commonwealth and Protectorate, 1651–60

Scotland and England had had one sovereign and two separate administrations since March 1603, with a personal union of crowns. This was now redundant in England by a unilateral decision of the ruling clique of army and allied civilian hard-liners led by Cromwell, and was imposed on Scotland. The English 'Rump' Parliament set up its own body of nominees to govern Scotland in October and announced that the two nations were to be one Commonwealth. The commissioners (five of them English military officers, led by Monck) set up a new parliament which rubber-stamped a union as required by the 'Rump', and the union was proclaimed on 21 April 1652, as soon as English Parliament had passed the necessary Bill. The Scots delegates then proceeded down to London that October but were not consulted there except on details, and were required to approve what the 'Rump' and its Council of State had decided. A Bill of Union setting out the details of administration was then drawn up, but had not yet been passed when Cromwell dissolved the 'Rump' in April 1653; the measure was formally enacted in Parliament in April 1657. Scotland was now represented by thirty MPs in the English Parliament that met under the constitution of the Protectorate drawn up in December 1653 (as was Ireland), but was clearly a junior and very minor partner (as was Ireland). In effect government remained with the commissioners, who were replaced in September 1655 by a Council of State of nine members. The administration was headed by Monck as commander-in-chief, and had a distinctly military tone with local elections of councils and magistrates suspended. Office holders were required to take an oath to recognise the Commonwealth and later the Protector and a number of prominent Royalists remained in custody throughout the regime, but this was the norm for England too.

Indeed, order was kept and justice administered with more speed, efficiency and impartiality than under the monarchy, and favouritism by landlords and clergy in justice and administration were cracked down on – with the Highland clan chiefs now forced to keep down disorder by local English military commanders scattered around castles and new forts. The role of the latter in many ways anticipated that of the similar but harsher English military occupation after 1745, while large-scale confiscations of lands from those nobles who had fought for the king in 1650–51 added to their political marginalisation. The Presbyterian Church found its powerful position of 1637–51 completely reversed; those ministers who were prepared to recognise the new regime were not evicted, but religious toleration (of Protestants not Catholics) was enforced by government 'fiat' and the initial success of the anti-monarchic 'Remonstrants' in securing appointments was reversed as the State commissioners found them too assertive. The pro-monarchic 'Resolutioner' clergy faced initial suspicion and widespread dismissals from office but, once the hope of rebellion succeeding had faded, 'Resolutioners' proved more tractable than 'Remonstrants', as they were more used to accepting de facto authority and most could pledge to live peaceably under the present regime. Some form of accommodation and partial reinstatement was reached, backed by moderate Cromwellian civilian leaders on the governing council such as the Protestant Irish peer

Lord Broghill. The Church Assembly was not allowed to meet.

The Earl of Glencairn, head of the Cunninghams in the southern Highlands and a former 'Engager' from Hamilton's party in 1648, had now taken over Montrose's role as leader of the disaffected Royalists. Widespread confiscations of Royalist nobles' estates by the new regime (twenty-four leaders were exempted from pardon) and a harsh tax assessment to pay for the army of occupation had stirred up discontent in the aristocratic elite, to add to the clans' firm Royalism. Glencairn attempted to raise the clans with a commission from Charles II, and was backed by the Earl of Argyll's son, Lord Lorne, along with Lord Kenmure and others; they had soon taken over much of the central Highlands and were raiding south. At this juncture the new regime, headed by temporary commander-in-chief General Lilburne while Monck was serving at sea against the Dutch, could not count on the Presbyterian Church's support either. The Church Assembly had attempted to meet at Glasgow and rejected the requirement for toleration of the other non-Anglican Protestant sects; they ignored an order from Lilburne to disperse, so his officers closed the assembly by force. Months of unrest and sporadic Royalist attacks followed until Monck returned in spring 1654 with more men. The Earl of Middleton, a more experienced Royalist commander, arrived from Holland to replace Glencairn that February, and proceeded to the western Highlands. Despite having around 5,000 men Middleton lacked the ability or daring of Montrose and frittered away his campaign in the central-western Highlands, targeting the Campbells, while Monck marched across the mountains to the Great Glen to spread fire and the sword through Glenmoriston. As Monck returned east, Middleton made a bolt for the north, but was cornered en route by Monck's lieutenant, Thomas Morgan, at Dalnaspidal and routed in a cavalry clash on 19 July 1654. After this defeat the risings subsided. Large new fortresses at Leith, Ayr, Perth, Inverlochy and Inverness served to cement a ruthless military occupation of the country, though the size of the army of occupation was reduced after the 1653–54 crisis due to financial problems. Unlike in Ireland the country retained a military supreme official – Monck – throughout 1654–60. He was duly able to use his army in Scotland as the springboard for his move south to restore order in January 1660, after Cromwell's death and his son Richard's deposition had led to the government in London collapsing into vicious and unstable factional disputes and successive coups.

Charles II (Part Two): 1660–85

The restoration of the monarchy to all three kingdoms of the British Isles followed Monck's overthrow of the post-Cromwellian military junta ruling in London early in 1660, and on 25 May Charles II was proclaimed king. But the return of the monarchy to Scotland was no more of a restoration of the exact status quo before the revolutions and civil wars than it was in England. The old machinery of government – king, Privy Council, Parliament and judiciary – was returned to its pre-1637 situation with a few changes and in early 1661 the king's new councillors in Edinburgh, headed by the Earl of Middleton, agreed that the committee of 'Lords of the Articles' should take over the crucial role of preparing legislation for Parliament. The latter would end up as a rubber stamp for what the lords, a clique of Royal loyalists, decided. The council now decided that it was politically safe to restore the king's right to appoint all officials, judges and military officers and to require all of these to swear an oath recognising his supremacy over the Church – a measure which led to those with crises of conscience over this blow to the covenanting form of Church government having to resign. But there was one significant change in that the covenanting aristocratic clique that had triggered the revolt achieved one major goal – ending the autocratic administration of policy in

State and Church from London; it would now be organised by the king's men in Edinburgh. Office and power were concentrated in the Protestant nobility – some ex-Covenanters and anti-bishops. Lauderdale, the new royal Secretary, had been one of the leading Covenanters in the 1640s and one of the regime's commissioners in London after 1646. Glencairn, Chancellor from 1661–64, was the Royalist commander of 1653–54 but also a firm Presbyterian and an 'Engager' rather than an 'ultra'-Royalist; the Earl of Rothes, president of the council from 1661 and Chancellor from 1667, was the equally Presbyterian son of the rebel leader of 1637–38. The only 'new man' in high office was the king's commissioner to the Scots Parliament, Middleton – a self-made Royalist general, hard-drinking and ruthless.

Nor did the end of the Commonwealth and restoration of an Anglican State Church in England lead to a revival of Charles I's ecclesiastical plans for Scotland. The Church Assembly had been crushed by military power and 'police' supervision of dissidents under the Cromwellian occupation, and this triumph of secular power was continued. As of the Restoration the majority of office holders in the Church were of the moderate 'Resolutioner' faction which had backed Charles in 1650–51 and their hopes were that their past conduct would secure his approval of a Church run by presbyters not bishops, keeping the 1638–41 settlement. Lauderdale supported them and Charles seemed initially favourable, provided that the radical 'Remonstrants' who had defied him in 1651 were excluded. Advised by the 'Resolutioner' cleric James Sharp to accept the situation that had existed in 1650–51, he wrote to the Scottish Church that he would accept the Church as it now stood. There would however be no mercy for the hard-liners whose leaders were arrested. Keeping a Covenanter but moderate Church would have been in line with plans in England to include moderate Presbyterians in the Church there – and the failure of the latter in 1661 assisted failure in Scotland. Middleton inveigled an increasingly Royalist Scots Parliament to ban the covenant and reverse the post-1637 legislation, restoring bishops – which the king approved. Then despite the efforts of Sharp, most of the 'Resolutioner' leaders turned down the chance to become bishops and left those offices to Royalist hard-liners; he however did enter the new Church himself. Middleton played on the king's fear of subversion to target those who might revolt; potential rebels and/or republicans were rounded up and persecuted as subversives and old scores were settled, although only a few high-profile examples were made. Argyll and Johnston of Warriston were the two main victims, being executed for past treason in 1661 and 1663. Both pro-Caroleans of 1650–51 and men who had accepted office under Cromwell from 1652 were treated as collaborators by the aggrieved hard-liner Presbyterian 'Remonstrants' after 1660, preventing a unified stand – and they lacked aristocratic backing.

The legislation of all parliaments since 1633 was cancelled in the Act Recissory of 1661, lay patronage of clerical appointments was restored and conventicles and the covenant were declared unlawful. But it was the moderate, episcopally supervised but theologically Calvinist settlement of the Church under James VI which was restored, without Charles I's plans of 1633–37. The nobility jealously watched the senior clergy for any signs of a return to their old pretensions. When the inevitable purge of those clerics who refused to recognise the legality of the Episcopal Church led to ousted ministers holding illegal services, government action followed, with heavy fines – collected by the army, who billeted themselves on the delinquents until they paid up. This led to an armed rising in Galloway in September 1666, on a small scale and hampered by bad weather and local indifference as the protesters attempted to march on Edinburgh. They were defeated by Sir Thomas Dalzell of the Binns at Mullion Green. Around thirty men were hanged and hundreds more sent as indentured servants to Barbados. Among other casualties of the episode was Rothes, who had been in London assuring

Charles that Scotland was quiescent as the revolt broke out, so his reputation suffered. Some pardons and reinstatements of those ex-clergy who would swear to recognise the king's authority – without accepting bishops – followed under a generous Church policy of 'comprehension' in the early 1670s, and hard-line anti-Presbyterian leader Archbishop Alexander Burnet of Glasgow was replaced in 1671 by the moderate Robert Leighton, Bishop of Dunblane. Leighton believed in 'comprehension' of as many Presbyterians as possible within the Church. But those ex-Covenanters who accepted readmission into the national Church via these individual Royal 'indulgences' were treated as collaborators by the hard-liners, who ran a banned underground Church.

Parliament sat for longer than pre-1637 with more serious involvement in framing legislation, and its importance as a centre of national political debate was illustrated by the emergence of what it is no longer anachronistic to call opposition MPs. Politics from 1660 was more a matter of who was 'in' and who was 'out of' royal favour in London and a struggle for monopoly of office holding by individuals and aristocratic factions – and Charles II was content to include more disloyal figures from the 1640s, particularly the astute Lauderdale, than he was in England. The political struggles for influence in London saw the gradual eclipse of Glencairn and Middleton by Lauderdale, a master of intrigue who was aided by his equally ambitious wife Elizabeth (*née* Murray), Countess of Dysart and mistress of Ham House near London. Charles resisted Middleton's attempts to have Lauderdale sacked and replaced him as commissioner with the more reliable Rothes (1663). Glencairn died suddenly in 1664 and thereafter a triumvirate of Lauderdale, Rothes and Archbishop Sharp led the Scots government until the 1666 rebellion led to the removal of Rothes as treasurer and his transfer to honorary rather than real power as chancellor. Sharp, who had fallen out with Lauderdale, was sidelined too, as Lauderdale passed around documents he had written in the

1650s praising Cromwell to stir up court resentment of him. John Hay, Earl of Tweeddale, now emerged as Lauderdale's chief associate; he and the less important Earl of Kinnoull were vital in encouraging more toleration of the moderate Covenanters.

The English Parliament had excluded Scotland from the benefits of the Navigation Act in 1660 by treating Scottish shipping as foreign and so banning it from carrying English commercial goods, and the resulting problems were worsened by the 1665–67 Dutch war, which cut off trade to a major ally. As a result an economic slump coincided with royal demands for money to pay for the war. Charles agreed to a plan for a customs union presided over by a joint Parliament, and backed a plan which the Privy Councils formulated. This fell apart through lack of agreement on detail. Late in 1669 a second royal initiative saw a joint Anglo-Scots parliamentary committee investigating the mechanics of creating a union. But the English Parliament blocked the proposals due to objections over the nature of the unified Parliament, and Charles abandoned the scheme.

Lauderdale remained secure as viceroy until the next crisis in both realms in 1678–79, and shamelessly abandoned his policy of religious 'comprehension' of the majority of Covenanters to line up with the 'High Anglicans' for persecution. The restored Burnet had his way on the suppression of conventicles and mass arrests, but his coercion of Galloway only led to wiser local lairds refusing to implement his proclamations, against which they petitioned the government as counterproductive. Lauderdale presented this as subversion and a threat of revolt, and in early 1678 a 'Highland Host' of loyal militiamen (some in fact Lowlanders) was quartered on Ayrshire as the opening shot in a plan to disarm, supervise and intimidate the entire region. The outbreak of a new political crisis in London in autumn 1678 distracted the King from strong action as the extremist Covenanters now began collecting defiantly in larger assemblies, and the panic in the English political nation over alleged Catholic plots meant that Charles's ultra-Anglican minister Danby was driven from office under suspicion of Catholic collaboration. The new English Parliament of 1679 was dominated by Protestant zealots, and the resultant 'Exclusion Crisis' threatened the right of Charles's Catholic brother James, Duke of York, to succeed to the throne. This could have implications for the succession in Scotland too – would Parliament's choice of heir be James's Protestant daughter Mary, married to her Calvinist Dutch cousin 'Stadtholder' William of Orange (who had given sanctuary to Presbyterian exiles and was the son of Charles I's daughter) or Charles's eldest illegitimate son James, Duke of Monmouth? Monmouth was married to the heiress of the ancient Borders dynasty of Scott of Buccleuch.

With London distracted, and no money available for repression, a new Covenanter uprising broke out, triggered by the coincidental encounter with and murder of the unpopular Archbishop Sharp at Magus Muir near St Andrews on 3 May 1679 by a group of radicals. The brutal nature of the killing – Sharp was dragged out of his coach in front of his daughter and hacked to death – reflected their anger at Sharp's 'betrayal' of their cause in deserting the Covenanters. The murderers then fled to the south-west to link up with the increasingly militant conventicles and persuade the latter that they must strike to ward off the government backlash, and their rally duly agreed the Rutherglen Convention of 29 May, which denounced all violations of the Covenant from the 1648 'Engagement' onwards. Colonel John Graham of Claverhouse, commander of one of the three troops of cavalry currently occupying the region, was defeated at Drumclog on 1 June and the rebels marched on and occupied Glasgow. The government in Edinburgh had to appeal to London for military aid, and Lauderdale's enemies in London told the king that if the duke and repression were abandoned the rebels would come to terms without need for an expensive campaign. However, the Covenanters in Glasgow then wasted a chance of Presbyterian unity (which might have given Charles pause for thought on invasion) in arguing over whether they merely wanted a free Parliament and Church Assembly or a complete condemnation of all those co-religionist clergy who had accepted the 'indulgences' plus a return to the 1640s religious regime. They had support from the nobility as in 1637–38, and the king decided on military action, with Monmouth in command and Dalzell as his deputy. The rebels had around 7,000 men, armed from the seized arsenals at Glasgow, but were routed by the disciplined English regiments under Monmouth at Bothwell Bridge near Hamilton on 22 June. Monmouth was both personally tolerant and a political sympathiser of the Presbyterian cause, having linked his cause in England to the opposition to Danby's Anglican-orientated 1670s government. Thus he soon secured an amnesty for most of the arrested rebels, provided that they swore never to rise against the government again, and a new 'indulgence' for conventicles to meet privately. Some hard-line rebels remained unconvinced and revolted again in 1680 after Monmouth was recalled; they were defeated at Airds Moss on 22 July, and the survivors – known as the 'Cameronians' – were reduced to a desperate but undaunted guerrilla campaign in the wilds of Galloway.

The 'Exclusion Crisis' had led to the Duke of York having to leave London due to the hostile political climate, and from December 1679 to January 1680 he was briefly resident in Edinburgh at Holyrood House with his Italian Catholic second wife, Mary of Modena. The presence of a resident court for the first time since 1651 was appreciated, with James proving much more gracious and less domineering than the much-disliked and now ageing Lauderdale. The hard-line anti-Covenanters in London persuaded the king to launch a new round of repression of the conventicles in the south-west, and in September 1680 Lauderdale was finally persuaded to resign. Moray replaced him as Secretary, but the return of James to Edinburgh that autumn with full authority as the king's commissioner showed who had the real power.

James's rule in Scotland lasted until his recall to London in March 1682, by which time Charles had seen off the Exclusionists, Monmouth was in disgrace and soon to be forced into exile and James's succession was secure. His commissionership saw renewed harsh repression of the Covenanters by military occupation and intimidation, and he saw to it that the politically 'packed' Scots Parliament, which met in July 1681, voted to uphold the right of the lawful heir to the succession whatever his religion and imposed an oath on all office-holders to be loyal to the established religion and the royal family's legal line of succession. The most notorious agent of repression was the army officer Graham of Claverhouse, the future 'Bonnie Dundee' but known to the Covenanters as 'Bluidy Clavers'. Judicial severity was imposed by the Lord Advocate, Sir George Mackenzie ('Bluidy Mackenzie'). Archibald, ninth Earl of Argyll, son of the Covenanter leader executed in 1661, was the most prominent noble to express concern at the legal demands now made on all office-holders. He declared that he would take the oath (the 'Test') in so far as it was compatible with the Protestant religion, and was charged with treason and perjury. He was tried in Edinburgh on 10–11 December 1681 and sentenced to death – almost certainly to hold it over him for the future rather than with the intent to carry it out. Instead he escaped from Edinburgh Castle after changing clothes with his wife's page, and fled to Holland as did many leading radicals. Meanwhile the early 1680s saw the proponents of royal autocracy, led by the Drummonds, consolidate their grip on Scotland.

James VII, 1685–89

The accession of James VII, aged fifty-three, as the first Catholic monarch of Scotland since Mary Stuart would have caused more serious political problems but for the recent repression of potential opposition. He had a dogged determination to impose religious toleration of his co-religionists on his subjects – and to improve the Catholics' numbers as well as their legal position. The element of approvable religious pluralism in this has led to many modern historians regarding him as a proponent of toleration, and he did encompass the 'Dissenters' – eventually including the Presbyterians – in his challenge to the Anglican domination of the governing elite. But recent revision has suggested that his ultimate aim was the reconversion of his lands to Catholicism in the long term, as alleged by those who overthrew him – and his harsh rule in Scotland in 1679–81 was a warning of his ruthlessness. Also, he was less flexible though more principled and hard-working than Charles II.

The only open challenge to his accession came from the exiled Earl of Argyll, who coordinated his attack with his fellow exile Monmouth's plans and sailed from Holland via the Orkneys to his former lands in May. He raised his flag in Monmouth's name against 'usurper' James VII in Kintyre and attempted to lead a Protestant rebellion against the 'Papist' king, but had little clan support and no aid from the extreme Cameronians. He could not take his own confiscated Inveraray and, after a royal naval force arrived to bombard his garrisons, many of his men deserted. He marched on to Dumbarton with around 1,500 men, but his lieutenants funked a chance to fight the local royal forces and as more men deserted he rode off for Galloway to try to win Covenanter support. Instead he was quickly rounded up by the militia near the Clyde and executed (June 1685). He timed his challenge badly as James had not given serious indications of his private hopes to reconvert as many of his subjects as possible to Catholicism.

James attempted to lure the Scots Parliament of 1686 into granting relief to Catholics from the current penal laws in return for free trade with England, but both the 'committee of articles' and the main assembly objected. It was decided to write to James promising to go as far as their consciences allowed while bearing in mind the legal establishment of the Protestant religion; this amounted to a threat of refusal and Parliament was adjourned and then dissolved. James resorted to encouraging high-status conversions to Catholicism with promises of rewards for those who did so; both the Duke of Perth and his brother Lord Melfort, a Secretary of State, converted quickly, followed in 1687 by the other Secretary, Moray. The Duke of Queensberry refused and was replaced as commissioner to Parliament and later as treasurer. However, the list of prominent supporters of the king's aggressive proselytisation were few, and the open celebration of Masses in Edinburgh again led to riots. Meanwhile Holyrood Abbey was partly turned into a Catholic Chapel Royal, a Catholic printing press was set up and the Jesuits were allowed to open a free school. James granted freedom of worship in private to both Catholics and his other potential religious allies, the Quakers, in February 1687 provided that they did not hold public processions or worship in the fields or Protestant churches. So far the Presbyterian conventicles were still banned as subversives, but all the king's subjects were guaranteed free worship in their homes or churches by a royal proclamation – avoiding the need for parliamentary approval – in June 1687. This ironically gave more stimulus to Presbyterian revival and confidence than it did to the extremely limited number of Catholics in the Lowlands; more congregations were set up independently of the official clergy in parishes, and the exiles returned from Holland. The birth of a Catholic male heir to James on 10 June 1688 did not lead to the fevered political activity against the king in Scotland that occurred in England. Scotland was largely quiescent during the resulting Dutch invasion and the 'Glorious Revolution', with its army called south to London by James as his own forces crumbled. The revolts across England and the Anglo-Dutch march on London were followed by James's flight to France, and only then did the council in Edinburgh have to contemplate what to do about the political vacuum. There was an outbreak of anti-Catholic rioting in Edinburgh and, after Chancellor Perth fled, law and order collapsed and the mob went on the rampage; the Jesuit chapel at Holyrood was sacked and the Stuart dynastic tombs in the abbey were broken into. But the attacks on Catholic personnel and property in the Lowlands were less important than the organised evictions of around 160–200 ministers of the Episcopalian Church by gangs of militant Presbyterians in a coordinated action taken on Christmas Day. This and the subsequent systematic hunting down of more ministers, known as 'rabbling', decapitated the post-Restoration Church and served to show that the resistance of a major element of the Presbyterian laity to the bishops had not been crushed. The lack of a response from the army-less council dispirited the bishops and their defenders. Crucially, the Calvinist Church in Holland did not have bishops and was closer to the model of the Covenanters' Church, the Presbyterians in England had backed William and assorted exiled radical victims of James were in the invader's entourage. William, in effective control in London from mid-December and elected as co-ruler with his wife by the 'Convention' in February 1689, was not sympathetic to the bishops' plight. Once a vacuum was created by events in England the Presbyterian radicals were able to use the advantages they possessed by virtue of numbers and determination.

William II (III of England) and Mary II, Anne, and Union: 1689–1707

James's flight from London left the throne of England declared vacant, but the authorities in Scotland did not follow their counterparts' deposition of him immediately. Technically James was still King of Scots as well as of Ireland, and a Convention of Estates did not meet in Edinburgh to decide on the new government until William sent orders to summon one in March 1689. The Duke of Hamilton served as commissioner. By this time the extremist 'Cameronians', as well as more moderate Covenant loyalists, had poured into Edinburgh, and with their armed militants roaming the streets in alliance with the city's crowds it was no surprise that many elected Episcopalian representatives to the Convention failed to take their seats. Those extremists who were elected demanded the abolition of episcopacy and a return to the pristine Covenanter Church of the 1640s, and other attacks were made on the political 'model' of the 1680s with demands to secure free parliaments by abolishing the controlling committee of 'Lords of the Articles'. William's appointee, General Hugh Mackay, and his 600 troops were outnumbered by the militia of Presbyterian militants who had stolen weapons from the State arsenals and, in the case of 'Cameronians', brought their own from hiding. Mackay shrewdly incorporated some of them into his army and so used their fervour for William's cause – but their goodwill was dependent on a Presbyterian religious settlement. William also sent a conciliatory letter to the Convention, promising to redress grievances, and disastrously James (in France) would only demand their support without any guarantees for the Protestant religion.

The ex-king's supporters, soon to be known as Jacobites, were a minority in the Convention, and in a few weeks they withdrew to plan a military solution. Their best general, Graham of Claverhouse (now Viscount Dundee), retired to his home at Dudhope after failing to persuade his allies to gather a rival Convention for King James at Stirling, but was threatened with arrest and raised the ex-king's standard at Dundee. He had to flee as the new regime's forces advanced, going to the Western Highlands to gather a clan host as Montrose had done in 1644–45. His small but well-armed force around 2,000 men, mostly Macdonalds (of Keppoch and Clanranald) and MacIans, were also motivated by their traditional hatred of the Campbells as the new, tenth Earl of Argyll was backing William and seeking the recovery of his family's extensive pre-1681 lands. They advanced on the fortified home of the 'Williamite' Marquis of Atholl at Blair Castle in the middle Tay valley, and Graham ordered a Jacobite kinsman to garrison the castle, which the 'Williamites' then besieged. Graham defeated Mackay's larger army of around 4,000 in a bloody clash at the pass of Killiecrankie on 27 July, but was killed by a stray bullet in his hour of triumph and the victorious army was left without an effective leader. Clan chief, Sir Ewan Cameron of Lochiel, had most men but was denied the command and left. The ex-king's army was halted at Dunkeld by an inferior but determined garrison of 'Cameronians' on 21 August. They could not take the town and retreated, but were not finally cornered and broken up until General Buchan won the battle of Cromdale near Grantown-on-Spey on 1 May 1690.

The radicals had the ability to carry the Convention by real or threatened intimidation, but in any case many of the 'political nation' had been excluded from decision-making since the mid-1660s and were keen to prevent such rigging in future. As in 1638, the bishops were banned from participating as the Convention's committee drew up a plan for reformed governance. When William and Mary were offered the crown this came with a 'Claim of Rights' and a 'Declaration of Grievances'. These required the abolition of the 'Lords of the Articles', thus preventing the king from using a committee of loyal 'place-men' to arrange the nature of legislation in Parliament, and cut down on assorted abuses of power by the judiciary. The abolition of episcopacy was voted, and all clergy were required to pray publicly for the new sovereigns and read out their proclamation. Around 400 clergy were deprived. William resisted signing up to the abolition of the 'Lords of the Articles', and in retaliation the supporters of this measure in the Convention – known as 'the Club' – coordinated refusal to grant the king financial supply.

In March, William sent a new commissioner, Lord Melville,

to win over the opposition by giving way on the 'Lords of the Articles' and to submit to the re-establishment of a fully Presbyterian form of Church government with an Assembly and local self-run presbyteries. The first Assembly was to be formed of proven Presbyterian loyalists, i.e. men who had been purged from their clerical offices by Charles II as unacceptable in 1661 and their nominees, and it had the role of purging the Church of all incapable, negligent or scandalous ministers – which would include their enemies. William had no choice, but urged restraint and moderation and the Assembly duly voted to allow godly, orthodox, competent and peaceable clergy who posed no threat or scandal to remain in office. The zealous local commissioners showed less goodwill; by 1695 it was said that only around sixteen Episcopalian clergy remained in office south of the Tay. William's supporters (led by Secretary of State James Johnston) secured an Act in the Estates in 1693 to offer security to those Episcopalian clergy who swore allegiance to the king and queen and recognised the Presbyterian system of Church government and who were then to apply to enter the Church's administrative system of presbyteries. In 1695 another Act gave those Episcopalians who swore allegiance and recognised the new form of Church the options of either joining the presbyteries or not; this secured a *modus vivendi* between two parallel organisations of clergy for the moment.

William had other priorities than Scotland, principally regaining Ireland from his Royal rival in 1690–91 and the long and expensive Continental 'War of the League of Augsburg' against Louis XIV (1689–97). He was campaigning in Flanders for much of the time and never visited Scotland, which once again became an absentee monarchy, governed by the king's ministers – now led by John Dalrymple, Master of Stair – but with substantial political activity centred on an assertive parliament. Dalrymple was son and political partner of the leading constitutional lawyer James Dalrymple (1690), Viscount Stair, who had been forced into exile in

1684 for opposing Duke James's pro-Catholic autocracy and had returned with William in 1688. He and John were now the regime's strongmen, with John joining James Johnston as Secretary of State in 1692. John Dalrymple was the 'villain' of the most notorious incident of these years, the Massacre of Glencoe, which resulted from King William's order of 27 August 1691 offering pardon to all of the Highlands chiefs who had fought for James if they came to swear allegiance to him by 1 January 1692. The participation of the two senior Campbell peers, Argyll and Breadalbane, in the plan to punish the Macdonalds of Glencoe and of Campbell troops of Argyll's own regiment in the massacre has exaggerated the subsequent romantic interpretation of it as another episode in the Campbell *versus* Macdonald feuds. William did not choose to see it as a crime worth punishing, and Dalrymple was too useful to be removed.

The post-1689 sovereigns resident in England had even less interest in Scotland than their predecessors, and viewed it mostly as a security concern. This was linked to the ongoing international problems between England and France, as Louis XIV continued to recognise James VII (now living at the childhood home of his ancestress, Mary Stuart, at St Germain-en-Laye near Paris) as rightful king until the 1697 Treaty of Ryswick. When James died, long sunk into melancholy and ultra-Catholic piety, at the age of sixty-seven in September 1701, Louis provocatively recognised his thirteen-year-old son as 'James III and VIII', and the new Anglo-French war after 1702 saw plans to restore him to his thrones. Meanwhile the post-1689 constitution of Scotland saw rival factions of politicians rather than the sovereign take the political lead – and the royal ministers now had to be able to get his measures through (and funds from) an assertive Parliament. William was content not to meddle as long as Scotland remained safe from Franco-Jacobite invasion, but was unable to secure a stable regime, unlike Charles II had done. After the Dalrymples' eclipse a complex battle ensued between rival factions led by the Earl of Marchmont, the Earl of Tweeddale and the Marquis/Duke of Queensberry. When William died in March 1702 his successor was his late wife's younger sister Anne, a thirty-seven-year-old semi-invalid who was even less involved with Scots politics. But the political crises which led to the move for union after 1701 did have a major dynastic element to them, impelling the English Parliament to seek union more urgently than it had done in the 1660s despite Scots anger at the lack of English support, which had helped in the 'crash' of their new American/Indies trading company in the Darien colonial project in 1697. The economic depression caused by Continental war had been exacerbated by the ruin of the company's investors. The death of Anne's last child, the sickly Duke William of Gloucester, aged eleven, in 1700 left the succession to all three kingdoms in doubt – and the French nationality or alliance and Catholic religion of Anne's closest cousins led to the English Parliament banning their accession. The Act of Settlement of 1701 fixed the succession on the nearest Protestant heir – the Electress Sophia of Hanover, youngest daughter of Charles I's elder sister Elizabeth of the Palatinate (the 'Winter Queen'). But the Scots Parliament provocatively insisted that they would only accept Sophia and her heirs if all future English political influence in Scotland was banned by law. There was a risk that the two crowns would be separated again – and if 'James VIII' was recalled he was Catholic and a French client, a disaster to England while it was at war with Louis. Accordingly the English political elite moved to force the pace of union, with bribery, threats, and goodwill gestures to secure Scots compliance. The Stuart dynasty, which had long preserved Scots independence and then tied the country in a personal union to England, thus served as the crucial impetus to full union – by the extinction of one line and the rigid Francophile Catholicism of the others.

Bibliography

1 The Constituent Kingdoms

Sources: very sketchy in detail and later in date. Mainly the 'Pictish Chronicle', a list of legendary and historical (post-fifth-century) kings of Picts and post-843 Scots; dated to the reign of the last ruler mentioned, Kenneth II (d. 995), but only survives in a fourteenth-century copy in the 'Popplewell Manuscript'. There are also sporadic dates in two Irish chronicles – the 'Annals of Ulster' (covering 431–1489), compiled in the later fifteenth century at Lough Erne in Ulster using earlier data, and the 'Annals of Tigernach' (only data for 489–766 survives), compiled in the eleventh century at Clonmacnois, central Ireland. Some post-766 details may survive within the later 'Chronicon Scottorum' (extant copy dating to *c*. 1640).

Amours, F. J., *The Original Chronicle of Andrew of Wyntoun*, 6 vols (Edinburgh, 1902–9)

Anderson, A. O., *Early Sources of Scottish History, AD 500–1286*, 2 vols (Edinburgh, 1920)

Anderson, M. O., *Kings and Kingship in Early Scotland* (Edinburgh, 1973)

Anderson, M. O., 'The Lists of the Kings' in *Scottish Historical Review*, vol. xxviii, (1949), pp. 108–18 (Scots) and vol. xxix (1949), pp. 13–22 (Picts)

Bannerman, J., *Studies in the History of Dalriada* (Edinburgh, 1974)

Byrne, F. J., *Irish Kings and High-Kings* (London, 1973)

Chadwick, H. M., *Early Scotland: the Picts, the Welsh and the Scots of Southern Scotland* (Cambridge, 1949)

Cowan, E. J., 'The Scottish Chronicle in the Poppleton Manuscript' in *Innes Review*, vol. xxxii (1981), pp. 3–21

Duncan, A. A. M., *Scotland: the Making of the Kingdom* (Edinburgh, 1993)

Hennessy, W. and B. MacCarthy, *Annals of Ulster*, 4 vols (Dublin, 1893)

Hudson, B. T., *The Kings of Celtic Scotland* (Westport, Conn., 1994)

Mackay, A. G., *Robert Lindsay, The Historie and Chronicles of Scotland*, 3 vols (Bannatyne Club, Edinburgh, 1830)

Maxwell, H., *Sir Thomas Grey, Scalachronica* (Glasgow, 1907)

Miller, M., 'The Disputed Historical Horizon of the Pictish King-Lists', in *Scottish Historical Review*, vol. lviii (1979), pp. 7–34

Morris, John, *The Age of Arthur* (London, 1973)

Skene, W. F., *Celtic Scotland: a History of Ancient Alban*, 3 vols (Edinburgh, 1886–90)

Skene, W. F., *John of Fordoun's Chronicle of the Scottish Nation*, 2 vols (Edinburgh, 1872)

Smyth, Alfred, *Warlords and Holy Men: Scotland AD 80–1000* (London, 1984)

Wainwright, F. T., *The Problem of the Picts* (Edinburgh, 1955)

Watt, D. R. *et al.*, *Walter Bower, Scotichronicon*, 9 vols, 1989–97

2 Kings of Scots from AD 843 to 1057

Aitchison, N., *Macbeth* (Stroud, 1999)

Amours, F. J., *The Original Chronicle of Andrew of Wyntoun*, 6 vols (Edinburgh, 1902–9)

Anderson, A. O., *Early Sources of Scottish History, AD 500–1286*, 2 vols (Edinburgh, 1920)

Anderson, M. O. 'The Lists of the Kings' in *Scottish Historical Review*, vol. xxviii, (1949), pp. 108–18 (Scots) and vol. xxix (1949), pp. 13–22 (Picts)

Constable, Archibald, *John Major, A History of Greater Britain* (Scottish History Society vol. x, Edinburgh, 1892)

Duncan, A. A. M., *Scotland: the Making of the Kingdom* (Edinburgh, 1993)

Duncan, A. A. M., *The Kingship of the Scots 842–1292: Succession and Independence* (Edinburgh, 2007)

Hudson, B. T., *The Kings of Celtic Scotland* (Westport, Conn., 1994)

Mackay, A. G., *Robert Lindsay, The Historie and Chronicles of Scotland*, 3 vols (Bannatyne Club, Edinburgh, 1830)

Maxwell, H., *Sir Thomas Grey, Scalachronica* (Glasgow, 1907)

Palsson H. and P. Edwards, *Orkneyinga Saga: The History of the Earls of Orkney* (London, 1978)

Skene, W. F., *Celtic Scotland: a History of Ancient Alban*, 3 vols (Edinburgh, 1886–90)

Skene, W. F., *John of Fordoun's Chronicle of the Scottish Nation*, 2 vols (Edinburgh, 1872)

Smyth, Alfred, *Scandinavian Kings in the British Isles AD 850–80* (London, 1977)

Smyth, Alfred, *Warlords and Holy Men: Scotland AD 80–1000* (London, 1984)

3 The House of Dunkeld: 1057-1286

Amours, F. J., *The Original Chronicle of Andrew of Wyntoun*, 6 vols (Edinburgh, 1902–9)

Barrow, G. S., *David I of Scotland (1124–53): the Balance of Old and New* (Reading, 1984)

Constable, Archibald, *John Major, A History of Greater Britain* (Scottish History Society vol. x, Edinburgh, 1892)

Duncan, A. A. M., *Scotland: the Making of the Kingdom* (Edinburgh, 1993)

Mackay, A. G., *Robert Lindsay, The Historie and Chronicles of Scotland*, 3 vols (Bannatyne Club, Edinburgh, 1830)

Maxwell, H., *Sir Thomas Grey, Scalachronica* (Glasgow, 1907)

Maxwell, H., *The Chronicle of Lanercost* (Glasgow, 1913)

Oram, R., *David I: The King Who Made Scotland* (Stroud, 2005)

Oram, R. (ed.), *Scotland in the Reign of Alexander II* (Leiden, 2005)

Owen, D. D., *William the Lion: Kingship and Culture 1165–1214* (East Linton, 1997)

Reid, N., *Scotland in the Age of Alexander III* (Edinburgh, 1990)

Skene, F. J., *The Book of Pluscarden*, 2 vols (Edinburgh, 1887–80)

Skene, W. F., *John of Fordoun's Chronicle of the Scottish Nation*, 2 vols (Edinburgh, 1872)

Stone, E. G., *Anglo-Scottish Relations 1174–1328* (London, 1965)

Stringer, K. J., *Earl David of Huntingdon 1152–1219: A Study in Anglo-Scottish History* (Edinburgh, 1985)

Watt, D. R. *et al.*, *Walter Bower, Scotichonicon*, 9 vols, 1989–97

Wilson, A. J., *St Margaret, Queen of Scotland* (Edinburgh, 1993)

4 The Wars of Independence and the Bruces: 1286–1371

Amours, F. J., *The Original Chronicle of Andrew of Wyntoun*, 6 vols (Edinburgh, 1902–9)

Balfour-Melville, E. W., *Edward III and David II* (Edinburgh, 1954)

Barron, E., *The Scottish Wars of Independence* (London, 1934)

Barrow, G. W. S., 'A Kingdom in Crisis: Scotland and the Maid of Norway', *Scottish Historical Review* vol lxix (1990)

Barrow, G. W. S., *Robert the Bruce and the Community of the Realm of Scotland* (London, 1965)

Brotherstone, T. and D. D. Ditchburn, '1320 and A' That: the Declaration of Arbroath and the Remaking of Scottish History' in *Freedom and Authority: Historical and Historiographical Essays* (Presented to Grant E. Simpson, East Linton, 2000)

Brown, C., *The Second Scottish Wars of Independence, 1332–1363* (Stroud, 2006)

Brown, M. *The Black Douglases: War and Lordship in Late Medieval Scotland* (Edinburgh, 1988)

Constable, Archibald, *John Major, A History of Greater Britain* (Scottish History Society vol. x, Edinburgh, 1892)

Duffy, S., *Robert Bruce's Irish Wars: the Invasion of Ireland 1306–29* (Stroud, 2002)

Duncan, A. A. M., "O Honi Soit qui Mal y Pense": David II and Edward III, 1346–52', *Scottish Historical Review*, vol lvii (1988)

Duncan, A. A. M., 'The Community of the Realm and Robert Bruce' in *Scottish Historical Review*, vol. xlv (1966)

Duncan, A. A. M., *The Nation of Scots and the Declaration of Arbroath* (Edinburgh, 1970)

Fisher, A., *William Wallace* (Edinburgh, 2002)

Kaufman, M. and W. MacLennan, 'Robert the Bruce and Leprosy' in *Proceedings of the Royal College of Physicians* (Edinburgh, vol. xxx, 2000)

MacDiarmaid, M. and J. Stevenson, *Barbour's Bruce* vols 1–3 (Edinburgh, 1985)

Mackay, A. G., *Robert Lindsay, The Historie and Chronicles of Scotland*, 3 vols (Bannatyne Club, Edinburgh, 1830)

Macnamee, C., *Robert Bruce: Our Most Valiant Prince and Lord* (Edinburgh, 2006)

Macnamee, C., *The Wars of the Bruces: England, Scotland and Ireland, 1306–28* (London, 1997)

Maxwell, H., *Sir Thomas Grey, Scalachronica* (Glasgow, 1907)

Nicholson, R., 'David II, the historians and the chroniclers', in *Scottish Historical Review*, vol lxv (1966)

Nicholson, R., *Edward III and the Scots* (Oxford, 1965)

Nicholson, R., 'The Last Campaign of Robert Bruce' in *English Historical Review*, vol. lxvii (1962)

Penman, M., *The Bruce Dynasty in Scotland: David II, 1329–71* (East Linton, 2004)

Prestwich, M., *Edward I* (London, 1988)

Reid, R. C., 'Edward de Balliol' in *Transactions of the Dumfriesshire and Galloway Antiquarian and Natural History Society* (1956–7)

Sadler, J., *Bannockburn: Battle for Liberty* (Barnsley, 2008)

Simpson, G. G., 'The Heart of Robert I: Pious Crusade or Marketing Gambit' in *B. Crawford, Church, Chronicles and Learning: Essays in Medieval and Early Renaissance Scotland* (2000)

Skene, W. F., *John of Fordoun's Chronicle of the Scottish Nation*, 2 vols (Edinburgh, 1872)

Stone, E. G., *Anglo-Scottish Relations 1174–1328* (London, 1965)

The Book of Pluscarden

The Chronicle of Lanercost

Watson, F., *Under the Hammer: Edward I and Scotland, 1286–1307* (1998)

Watt, D. R. *et al.*, *Walter Bower, Scotichonicon*, 9 vols, 1989–97

Young, A., *Robert Bruce's Rivals: the Comyns, 1212–1314* (East Linton, 1997)

5 The Stewarts: 1371–1542

Amours, F. J., *The Original Chronicle of Andrew of Wyntoun*, 6 vols (Edinburgh, 1902–9)

Boardman, Steven, *The Early Stewart Kings: Robert II and Robert III* (East Linton, 1997)

Brown, M., *James I* (East Linton, 1994)

Brown, M., 'Regional Lordship in North-East Scotland: the Badenoch Stewarts 1. Alexander Stewart, Earl of Buchan, lord of Badenoch. 2. Alexander Stewart, Earl of Mar' in *Northern Scotland*, vol xvi (1996)

Brown, M., *The Black Douglases: War and Lordship in Late Medieval Scotland* (Edinburgh, 1988)

Cameron, J., *James V: the Personal Rule, 1528–1542* (East Linton, 1998)

Constable, Archibald, *John Major, A History of Greater Britain* (Scottish History Society vol. x, Edinburgh, 1892)

Conway, Agnes, *Henry VII's Relations with Scotland and Ireland, 1485–98* (Cambridge, 1932)

Grant, A., 'Scotland's "Celtic fringes" in the later Middle Ages: the Macdonald Lordship of the Isles and the Kingdom of Scotland' in R. R. Davies, *The British Isles, 1100–1500* (Edinburgh, 1988)

Mackay, A. G., *Robert Lindsay, The Historie and Chronicles of Scotland*, 3 vols (Bannatyne Club, Edinburgh, 1830)

Macdonald, A., *Border Bloodshed: Scotland, England and France at War, 1369–1406* (Edinburgh, 2006)

Macdougall, Norman, *James IV* (East Linton, 1997)

Macdougall, Norman, *James III: A Political Study* (Edinburgh, 1992)

MacGladdery, C., *James II* (East Linton, 1990)

Maxwell, H., *Sir Thomas Grey, Scalachronica* (Glasgow, 1907)

Munro, Jean, 'The Lordship of the Isles' in *The Middle Ages in the Highlands* (Inverness, 1981)

Nicholson, R., *Scotland in the Later Middle Ages* (London, 1974)

Watt, D. R. *et al.*, *Walter Bower, Scotichonicon*, 9 vols, 1989–97

6 The Stuarts: 1542–1651

Bevan, Bryan, *King James VI of Scotland and I of England* (1996)

Bingham, Caroline, *James VI: the Making of a King* (1968)

Burnet, Gilbert, *The Memoires of the Lives and Actions of James and William, Dukes of Hamilton* (London, 1677)

Cowan, E. J., *Montrose: For Covenant and King* (London, 1977)

Donaldson, Gordon, *All the Queen's Men: Power and Politics in Mary Stuart's Scotland* (London, 1983)

Donaldson, Gordon, *Scotland: James V to James VII* (Edinburgh, 1965)

Donaldson, Gordon, *The Scottish Reformation* (London, 1960)

Fraser, Antonia, *Mary Queen of Scots* (London, 1970)

Gardiner, S. R., *History of the Great Civil War*, 4 vols (reprint London, 1987)

Goodare, Julian and Michael Lynch, *The Reign of James VI* (East Linton, 2000)

Henderson, T. F., *Mary Queen of Scots*, 2 vols (1905)

Hutton, Ronald, *Charles II* (London, 1989)

Knox, John, *History of the Reformation in Scotland*, ed. W. Croft Dickinson (Edinburgh, 1949)

Lang, Andrew, *James VI and the Gowrie Mystery* (London, 1902)

Lee, Maurice, *Government by Pen: Scotland under James VI and I* (Urbana, Illinois, 1980)

Lee, Maurice, *Great Britain's Soloman: James VI and I in his Three Kingdoms* (Urbana, 1990)

Lee, Maurice, *James Stewart, Earl of Moray* (Columbia University, US, 1953)

Lee, Maurice, *The Road to Revolution: Scotland under Charles I, 1625–37* (Chicago 1985)

Lockyer, Roger, *James VI and I* (Harlow, 1998)

MacInnes, Alan, *Charles I and the Making of the Covenanting Movement, 1625–1641* (Edinburgh, 1991)

Sharpe, Kevin, *The Personal Rule of Charles I, 1629–40* (London, 1992)

Smith, Alan G. R., *The Reign of James VI and I* (New York, 1973)

Stevenson, David, *Revolution and Counter-Revolution in Scotland, 1644–1651* (London, 1977)

Stevenson, David, *The Scottish Revolution 1637–41: the Triumph of the Covenanters* (Newton Abbott, 1973)

Stewart, Alan, *The Cradle King: A Life of James VI and I* (London, 2003)

Wormauld, Jenny, *Mary Queen of Scots: A Study in Failure* (London, 1988)

Wormauld, Jenny, 'James VI and I: Two Kings or One?' in *History*, vol. lxviii (1983)

7 From One Union to a Second: 1651–1707

Ashley, Maurice, *James II* (London, 1977)

Buckroyd, Julia, *Church and State in Scotland 1660–1681* (Edinburgh, 1980)

Pincus, Steve, *1688: The First Modern Revolution* (New Haven, Mass., 2009)

Watson, J. N. P., *Captain-General and Rebel Chief: the Life of James Scott, Duke of Monmouth* (London, 1979)

Wodrow, Robert, *The History of the Sufferings of the Church of Scotland*, 4 vols (1828–30 edition)

Donaldson, *Scotland: James V to James VII*, *ibid.*

Hutton, *ibid.*

Laing, *ibid.*

Table of Sovereigns

Name	Birth	Accession	Death	Age	Years ruled
Kenneth Mc Alpin		843?	858		15?
Donald		858	862		4
Constantine I		862	877		15
Aed		877	878		1
Giric		878	889		11
Donald II		889	900		11
Constantine II	c. 874?	900	942 (abd.)A	c. 78 (952)	42
Malcolm I	c. 890?	942	954	c. 64?	12
Indulf	<910?	954	962	50s?	8
Dubh	920s?	962	966	c. 40?	4
Cuilean		966	971		5
Kenneth II	930s?	971	995	c. 60?	24
Constantine III 'the Bald'		995	997		2
Kenneth III	940s?	997	1005	<60?	8
Giric II (co-ruler)	970s?	997	1005	c. 30?	8
Malcolm III	c. 955?	1005	25 Nov. 1034	c. 80?	29
Duncan	c. 1006?	25 Nov. 1034	15 Aug. 1040	c. 34?	5.8
Macbeth	c. 1002?	15 Aug. 1040	15 Aug. 1057	c. 55?	17
Lulach (Moray only)	c. 1032?	15 Aug. 1057	15 Mar. 1058	c. 26?	0.7
Malcolm III 'Canmore' ('Great Head')	1031? (Lothian)	1054	13 Nov. 1093	62?	39
		15 Aug. 1057 (central)		36.3	

301

		15 Mar. 1058 (Moray)		35.8	
Donald III 'Ban'	c. 1035?	13 Nov. 1093	May 1094 (dep.)		0.6
Duncan II	c. 1059	May 1094	Nov. 1094	c. 35	0.6
Donald III (ii)		Nov. 1094	Oct. 1097	c. 64?	2.9
Edgar	c. 1074	Oct 1097	8 Aug 1107	c. 32	9.3
Alexander	c. 1076	8 Aug. 1107	23 Apr. 1124?	48?	17.3
David	c. 1084	?23 Apr. 1124	24 May 1153	69?	29.1
Malcolm IV 'the Maiden'	20 Mar 1141	24 May 1153	9 Dec 1165	24.8	12.6
William 'The Lion'	c. 1143	9 Dec. 1165	4 Dec. 1214	c. 71	48.11
Alexander II	24 Aug. 1198	4 Dec. 1214	6 Jul. 1249	50	34.7
Alexander III	4 Dec. 1241	6 Jul. 1249	19 Mar. 1286	44.3	36.8
Margaret 'the Maid of Norway'	1283	19 Mar. 1286	26 Sep 1290	6/7	6.6

(Interregnum – Edward I asked by council of 'Guardians' to adjudicate on next ruler)

John Balliol	1250?	17 Nov. 1292	11 Jul. 1296 (dep.)	63? (d. 1313)	3.7

(English conquest 1296–1306)

Robert I Bruce	11 Jul. 1274	25 Mar. 1306	7 Jun. 1329	54.10?	33.2
David II	5 Mar. 1324	7 Jun. 1329	22 Feb. 1371 (exile 1334–41, captive 1346–57)	48.11	41.8
Edward Balliol (ii)	1280s?	Aug. 1332	16 Dec. 1332 (dep.)	0.4	
		Mar. 1333	1341 (dep.)	c. 75? (d. 1364?)	8

Robert II	2 Mar. 1316	22 Feb. 1371	19 Apr. 1390	74.1	19.1
Robert III	*c.* 1337	19 Apr. 1390	4 Apr. 1406	69?	15.11
James I	25 Jul. 1394	4 Apr. 1406	21 Feb. 1437 (exile to 1424)	42.6	30.10
James II	16 Oct. 1430	21 Feb. 1437	3 Aug. 1460	29.9	23.5
James III	May 1452	3 Aug. 1460	11 Jun. 1488	36.1	27.10
James IV	17 Mar. 1473	11 Jun. 1488	9 Sep. 1513	40.5	25.2
James V	10 Apr. 1512	9 Sep. 1513	14 Dec. 1542	30.8	29.3
Mary	8 Dec. 1542	14 Dec. 1542	24 Jul. 1567 (abd., ex. 8 Feb. 1587)	44.2	24.7
James VI	19 Jun. 1566	24 Jul. 1567	27 Mar. 1625	58.9	57.8

Queens and Kings Consort of Scotland to 1603

Name	Marriage/Acc.	Consort of ...	Length in title	Date of death
Gruoch	Aug. 1040	Macbeth	?	<1057
Finnguala (Moray only)	Aug. 1057	Lulach	7 months	Mar 1058 (dep.)
Ingebiorg of Orkney	1058/9?	Malcolm III	<10 years	<1069 (div.?)
(St) Margaret	aut. 1069?	Malcolm III	24 years?	Nov. 1093
Etheldreda	May 1094	Duncan II	6 months	Nov. 1094 (dep.)
Sibylla	c. 1108	Alexander I	?	?
Maud de Senlis (daughter of Waltheof)	Apr. 1124	David	6 years?	1130?
Ermengarde De Beaumont	5 Sep. 1186	William	47/48 years	1234
Joan I of England	18 Jun. 1221	Alexander II	16/17 years	1238
Marie de Coucy	15 May 1239	Alexander II	?	?
Margaret of England	26 Dec. 1251	Alexander III	23 years	1275
Yolande de Dreux	1 Nov. 1285	Alexander III	37/38 years	1323
Isabella de Warenne	17 Nov. 1292	John Balliol	3 years 7 months	11 Jul. 1296
Elizabeth De Burgh	25 Mar. 1306	Robert I	21 years	1327
Joan II of England	17 Jul. 1328	David II	33/34 years	1362

Margaret Drummond	Feb. 1364	David II	11 years?	?1375
Euphemia of Ross	22 Feb. 1371	Robert II	15/16 years	1387
Annabella Drummond	13 Apr. 1390	Robert III	10/11 years	1401
Joan Beaufort	2 Feb. 1424	James I	20/21 years	1445
Mary of Guelders	3 Jul. 1449	James II	13/14 years	1463
Margaret of Denmark	10 Jul. 1469	James III	16/17 years	1486
Margaret Tudor	8 Aug. 1503	James IV	37/38 years	1541
Madeleine of Valois	1 Jan. 1537	James V	6 months	1537
Marie de Guise	12 Jun. 1538	James V	21/22 years	1560
François II King of France	24 Apr. 1558	Mary	2 years 7 months	5 Dec. 1560
Henry Stuart, Lord Darnley	29 Jul. 1565	Mary	1 year 6 months	10 Feb. 1567
James Hepburn, Earl of Bothwell	15 May 1567	Mary	2 months	24 Jul. 1567 (dep); d. 1578
Anne of Denmark	23 Nov. 1589	James VI	29 years 4 months	Mar. 1619

1. Genealogical table of the kings of the Picts

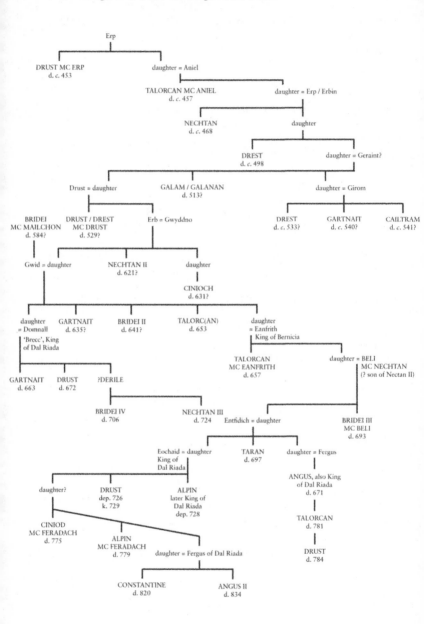

2. Genealogical table of the kings of Dal Riada

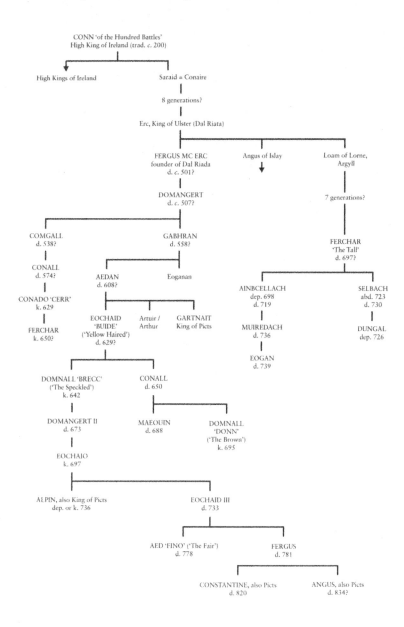

3. Genealogical table of the kings of Strathclyde (or 'Alclud')

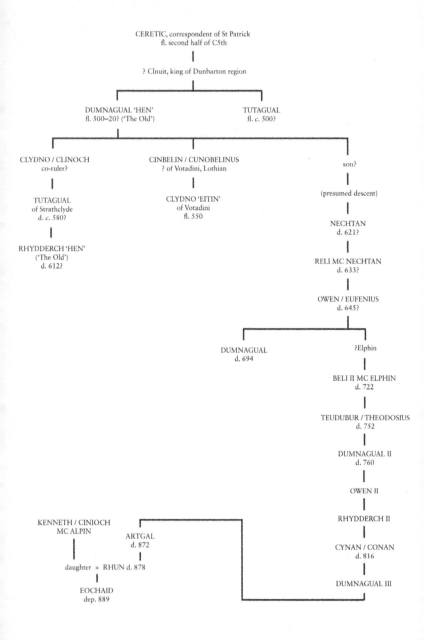

CERETIC, correspondent of St Patrick
fl. second half of C5th
|
? Clnuit, king of Dunbarton region

DUMNAGUAL 'HEN'
fl. 500–20? ('The Old')

TUTAGUAL
fl. c. 500?

CLYDNO / CLINOCH
co-ruler?
|
TUTAGUAL
of Strathclyde
d. c. 580?
|
RHYDDERCH 'HEN'
('The Old')
d. 612?

CINBELIN / CUNOBELINUS
? of Votadini, Lothian
|
CLYDNO 'EITIN'
of Votadini
fl. 550

son?
|
(presumed descent)
|
NECHTAN
d. 621?
|
RELI MC NECHTAN
d. 633?
|
OWEN / EUFENIUS
d. 645?

DUMNAGUAL
d. 694

?Elphin
|
BELI II MC ELPHIN
d. 722
|
TEUDUBUR / THEODOSIUS
d. 752
|
DUMNAGUAL II
d. 760
|
OWEN II
|
RHYDDERCH II
|
CYNAN / CONAN
d. 816
|
DUMNAGUAL III

KENNETH / CINIOCH
MC ALPIN
|
daughter ≈ RHUN d. 878
|
EOCHAID
dep. 889

ARTGAL
d. 872

4. Genealogical table of the kings of Scots after union with the Picts

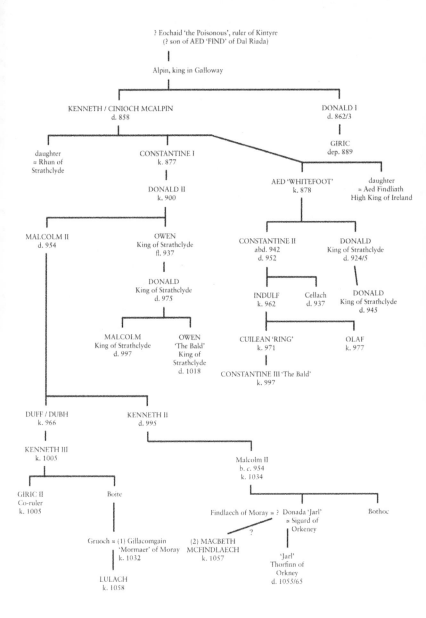

5. Genealogical table of the kings of Scots after union with the Picts, continued

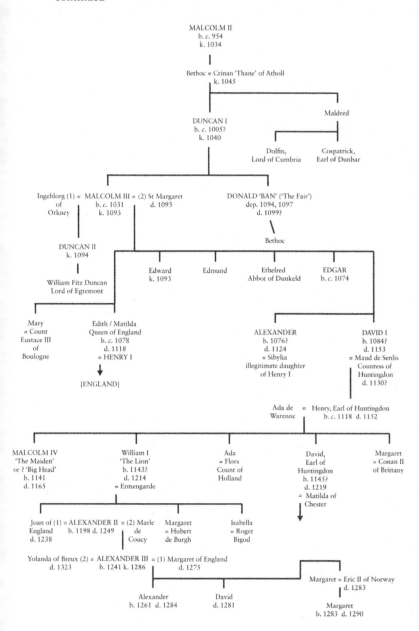

6. The Scottish succession, 1290: Balliol, Bruce and others

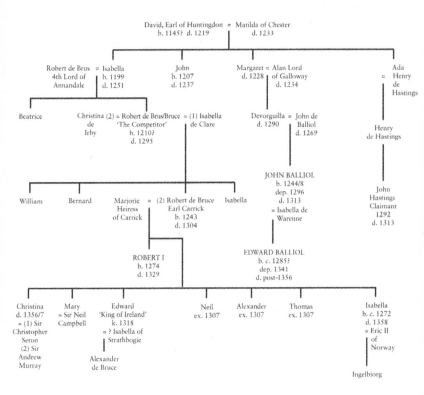

7. Genealogical table of the Bruce and Stewart lines

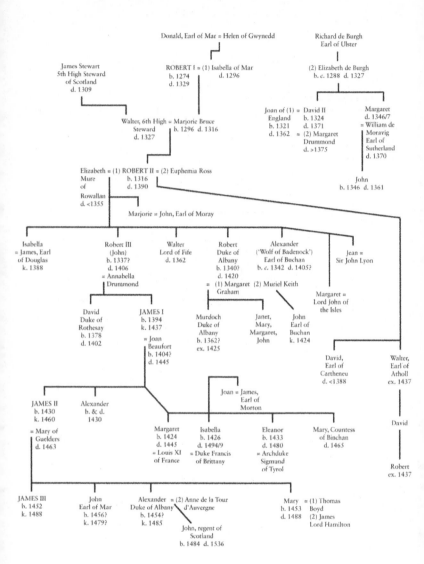

8. Genealogical table of the Stuart line

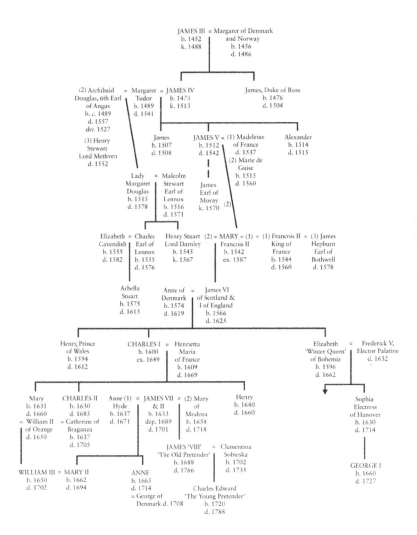

Index

Index

Index